# CAKES AND CAKE DECORATING

# CAKES AND CAKE DECORATING

## ROSEMARY WADEY

octopus

Ovens should be preheated to the specified temperature.

All spoon measures are level.

Metric spoon measures in sizes 1.25 ml ($\frac{1}{4}$ teaspoon), 2.5 ml ($\frac{1}{2}$ teaspoon), 5 ml (1 teaspoon) and 15 ml (1 tablespoon) are available and should be used for accurate measurement of small quantities.

The recipes in this book have been carefully tested using metric measures and you will find that the metric/imperial equivalents vary considerably – this is because it is the proportions rather than the quantities which are important for successful results.

Follow one column of measures – they are not interchangeable.

First published 1979 by
Octopus Books Limited
59 Grosvenor Street
London W.1.

© 1979 Octopus Books Limited
Reprinted 1982

ISBN 0 7064 0964 7

Produced by Mandarin Publishers Limited
22A Westlands Road, Quarry Bay, Hong Kong

Printed in Hong Kong

Sobha chathampally

# CONTENTS

SPONGE AND SANDWICH CAKES — 6

LITTLE CAKES — 20

FAMILY CAKES — 36

SCONES AND TEA BREADS — 52

YEASTED FARE — 64

BISCUITS AND COOKIES — 76

GÂTEAUX AND CHEESECAKES — 88

CELEBRATION CAKES — 96

ICINGS AND FILLINGS — 104

BASIC PASTRIES — 108

THE ART OF CAKE DECORATION — 112

SUCCESSFUL CAKE-MAKING — 148

INDEX — 156

# SPONGE AND SANDWICH CAKES

## VICTORIA SANDWICH (LAYER) CAKE

This is probably the best known sponge sandwich (layer) cake of all. The basic recipe can be varied in many ways to give all sorts of flavours.

| Metric/Imperial | American |
|---|---|
| 100 g/4 oz butter or margarine | $\frac{1}{2}$ cup butter or margarine |
| 100 g/4 oz caster sugar | $\frac{1}{2}$ cup sugar |
| 2 eggs, beaten | 2 eggs, beaten |
| 100 g/4 oz self-raising flour | 1 cup self-rising flour |
| 1 tablespoon water (optional) | 1 tablespoon water (optional) |
| 3–4 tablespoons raspberry jam | 3–4 tablespoons raspberry jam |
| little icing or caster sugar for dredging | little confectioners' or fine sugar for dredging |

Grease two 18 cm/7 inch sandwich tins (layer cake pans) and line the bottoms with greased greaseproof (waxed) paper. Cream the fat and sugar together until very light and fluffy and pale in colour. Beat in the eggs, one at a time, following each with a spoonful of flour. Sift the remaining flour and fold into the mixture with the water, if used. Turn into the tins, level the tops and bake in the centre of a moderately hot oven (190°C/375°F, Gas Mark 5) for about 20 minutes or until well risen, golden brown and firm to the touch. Turn out onto a wire rack to cool. When cold, sandwich the cakes together with jam and dredge the top with sugar.

# ONE-STAGE SPONGE CAKE

This traditional 'all-in-one' mixture for a sponge sandwich (layer) cake is success guaranteed if you use a special soft (luxury) tub margarine.

**Metric/Imperial**
100 g/4 oz self-raising flour
1 teaspoon baking powder
pinch of salt
2 large eggs, beaten
100 g/4 oz soft (luxury)
  margarine
100 g/4 oz caster sugar
little caster sugar for
  dredging
FILLING:
3–4 tablespoons apricot or
  other jam
50 g/2 oz soft margarine
100 g/4 oz icing sugar,
  sifted
few drops of vanilla essence
1–2 teaspoons warm water
  or milk

**American**
1 cup self-rising flour
1 teaspoon baking powder
pinch of salt
2 eggs, beaten
½ cup soft margarine
½ cup sugar
little sugar for dredging
FILLING:
3–4 tablespoons apricot or
  other jam
¼ cup soft margarine
1 cup confectioners' sugar,
  sifted
few drops of vanilla extract
1–2 teaspoons warm water
  or milk

Grease two 18 cm/7 inch sandwich tins (layer cake pans) and line the bottoms with greased greaseproof (waxed) paper. Sift the flour, baking powder and salt into a bowl. Add the other ingredients, mix well and beat thoroughly for 3 minutes using an electric mixer, or about 4 minutes if using a wooden spoon. Divide between the tins and level the tops. Bake in a moderate oven (160°C/325°F, Gas Mark 3) for about 35 minutes or until well risen and firm to the touch. Turn out onto a wire rack and leave to cool.

Spread the jam over one cake layer. Beat the margarine until creamy, then beat in the icing (confectioners') sugar, vanilla essence (extract) and sufficient water or milk to give the consistency of thick whipped cream. Spread over the jam and cover with the other cake layer. Dredge the top with sugar.

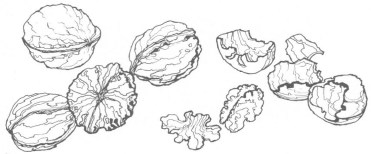

## GINGER CREAM SANDWICH (LAYER) CAKE

A Victoria sandwich (layer) cake mixture, but with pieces of chopped stem (preserved) ginger baked into the cake and a ginger-flavoured butter cream decoration.

| Metric/Imperial | American |
|---|---|
| 100 g/4 oz self-raising flour | 1 cup self-rising flour |
| ½ teaspoon ground ginger | ½ teaspoon ground ginger |
| 100 g/4 oz butter or margarine | ½ cup butter or margarine |
| 100 g/4 oz caster sugar | ½ cup sugar |
| 2 large eggs | 2 eggs |
| 2–3 pieces stem ginger, very finely chopped | 2–3 pieces preserved ginger, very finely chopped |
| BUTTER CREAM: | BUTTER CREAM: |
| 75 g/3 oz butter | 6 tablespoons butter |
| 150 g/6 oz icing sugar, sifted | 1½ cups confectioners' sugar, sifted |
| ½ teaspoon ground ginger | ½ teaspoon ground ginger |
| 1 teaspoon ginger syrup (from the jar) | 1 teaspoon ginger syrup (from the jar) |
| DECORATION: | DECORATION: |
| 2–3 pieces stem ginger | 2–3 pieces preserved ginger |
| few thin strips of candied angelica | few thin strips of candied angelica |

## COFFEE WALNUT SPONGE CAKE

A traditional coffee-flavoured sponge sandwich (layer) cake, this is full of chopped walnuts with a soft coffee butter cream.

| Metric/Imperial | American |
|---|---|
| 150 g/6 oz caster sugar | ¾ cup sugar |
| 150 g/6 oz butter or margarine | ¾ cup butter or margarine |
| 3 large eggs, beaten | 3 eggs, beaten |
| 150 g/6 oz self-raising flour | 1½ cups self-rising flour |
| 1 tablespoon coffee essence | 1 tablespoon strong black coffee |
| 40 g/1½ oz walnuts, chopped | ⅓ cup chopped walnuts |
| few walnut halves or pieces for decoration | few walnut halves or pieces for decoration |
| BUTTER CREAM: | BUTTER CREAM: |
| 75 g/3 oz butter | 6 tablespoons butter |
| 125 g/5 oz icing sugar, sifted | 1¼ cups confectioners' sugar, sifted |
| 1 tablespoon coffee essence | 1 tablespoon strong black coffee |

Grease two 23 cm/9 inch sandwich tins (layer cake pans) and line the bottoms with greased greaseproof (waxed) paper. Cream the sugar and butter or margarine together until very light and fluffy. Beat in the eggs one at a time, following each one with a spoonful of flour. Sift in the remaining flour and fold in with the coffee essence (strong black coffee) and chopped walnuts. Divide between the tins and level the tops. Bake in a moderately hot oven (190°C/375°F, Gas Mark 5) for 20 to 25 minutes or until well risen, golden brown and just firm to the touch. Turn out onto wire racks and leave to cool.

For the butter cream, beat the butter until soft, then gradually beat in the icing (confectioners') sugar alternating with the coffee essence (strong black coffee) to give a spreading consistency. Use half of the butter cream to sandwich the cakes together and the rest to spread over the top using a round-bladed knife to make a pattern. Decorate with walnuts.

Grease two 18–19 cm/7–7½ inch round sandwich tins (layer cake pans) and line the bottoms with greased greaseproof (waxed) paper. Sift the flour and ground ginger together. Cream the butter or margarine and sugar together until light and fluffy and very pale in colour. Beat in the eggs one at a time, following each with a spoonful of flour. Sift in the remaining flour and fold in, followed by the chopped ginger. Divide between the tins and level the tops. Bake in a moderately hot oven (190°C/375°F, Gas Mark 5) for about 20 minutes or until well risen, golden brown and firm to the touch. Turn out onto a wire rack and leave to cool.

For the butter cream, cream the butter until soft, then beat in the icing (confectioners') sugar, ground ginger and sufficient ginger syrup to give a smooth spreading consistency. Use a little butter cream to sandwich the cakes together, then cover the top and sides of the cake, reserving a little for decoration. Decorate with piped stars of butter cream in a star design, with pieces of ginger and strips of angelica.

# MOCHA SANDWICH (LAYER) CAKE

Chocolate and coffee flavours combine to make a moist sponge sandwich (layer) cake, filled with a rich butter cream and topped with icing (confectioners') sugar.

| Metric/Imperial | American |
|---|---|
| *125 g/5 oz self-raising flour* | *1¼ cups self-rising flour* |
| *25 g/1 oz cocoa powder* | *¼ cup unsweetened cocoa* |
| *150 g/6 oz butter or margarine* | *¾ cup butter or margarine* |
| *150 g/6 oz caster sugar* | *¾ cup sugar* |
| *3 large eggs* | *3 eggs* |
| *1 tablespoon coffee essence* | *1 tablespoon strong black coffee* |
| *icing sugar for dredging* | *confectioners' sugar for dredging* |
| FILLING: | FILLING: |
| *50 g/2 oz butter* | *¼ cup butter* |
| *1 tablespoon coffee essence* | *1 tablespoon strong black coffee* |
| *100 g/4 oz icing sugar* | *1 cup confectioners' sugar* |
| *25 g/1 oz cocoa powder* | *¼ cup unsweetened cocoa* |

Grease two 20 cm/8 inch deep sandwich tins (layer cake pans) and line the bottoms with greased greaseproof (waxed) paper. Sift the flour and cocoa together. Cream the butter or margarine and sugar together until light and fluffy and very pale in colour. Beat in the eggs one at a time, following each with a spoonful of the flour mixture. Fold in the remaining flour mixture with the coffee essence (strong black coffee) and divide between the tins. Level the tops and bake in a moderately hot oven (190°C/375°F, Gas Mark 5) for 30 minutes or until well risen and just firm to the touch. Turn out onto a wire rack and leave to cool.

For the filling, cream the butter until soft, then beat in the coffee essence (strong black coffee). Gradually beat in the icing (confectioners') sugar sifted with the cocoa and use to sandwich the cakes together. Lay a widely patterned paper doily over the top of the cake and dredge thickly with sifted icing (confectioners') sugar. Remove the doily very carefully to leave the pattern intact on the top.

*bake under 30 min or dry*

*Note:* To make this cake by the one-stage method (see recipe page 7), use a soft (luxury) margarine, sift 1½ teaspoons baking powder with the flour and cocoa and bake in a moderate oven (180°C/350°F, Gas Mark 4) for 35 to 45 minutes.

# GENOESE SPONGE CAKE

A rich whisked sponge cake, this can be iced and filled with any type of icing, butter cream or jam or served as a dessert filled with whipped cream and fruit.

| Metric/Imperial | American |
|---|---|
| *40 g/1½ oz butter* | *3 tablespoons butter* |
| *65 g/2½ oz plain flour* | *½ cup plus 2 tablespoons all-purpose flour* |
| *15 g/½ oz cornflour* | *2 tablespoons cornstarch* |
| *3 large eggs* | *3 eggs* |
| *75 g/3 oz caster sugar* | *6 tablespoons sugar* |
| FUDGE FROSTING: | FUDGE FROSTING: |
| *225 g/8 oz icing sugar* | *2 cups confectioners' sugar* |
| *2 tablespoons cocoa powder* | *2 tablespoons unsweetened cocoa* |
| *75 g/3 oz blended white vegetable fat* | *6 tablespoons shortening* |
| *3 tablespoons milk* | *3 tablespoons milk* |
| *75 g/3 oz caster sugar* | *6 tablespoons sugar* |

Grease a 20 cm/8 inch round deep cake tin and line the bottom with greased greaseproof (waxed) paper. Heat the butter gently until melted, then leave until cool but still liquid. Sift the flour and cornflour (cornstarch) together twice. Put the eggs and sugar into a large heatproof bowl over a saucepan of hot water and whisk until the mixture is very thick and pale and the whisk leaves a trail when lifted. Remove from the heat and whisk until cool. (If using an electric mixer, no heat is needed.) Using a metal spoon, fold in half of the sifted flour and then the cooled butter. Finally fold in the remaining flour and turn into the prepared tin. Bake towards the top of a moderately hot oven (190°C/375°F, Gas Mark 5) for about 30 minutes or until well risen and just firm to the touch. Turn out onto a wire rack and leave to cool.

For the frosting, sift the sugar and cocoa into a bowl. Put the fat (shortening), milk and sugar into a small pan and heat gently until well mixed. Bring to the boil, then pour over the sugar mixture. Beat until fluffy and beginning to cool. Spread over the top and sides of the cake using a round-bladed knife and pull the surface into peaks. Leave to set.

# CHOCOLATE ORANGE CAKE

This moist chocolate sponge cake has a strong orange flavouring and chocolate icing (frosting).

| Metric/Imperial | American |
|---|---|
| 2 tablespoons cocoa powder | 2 tablespoons unsweetened cocoa |
| 2 tablespoons hot water | 2 tablespoons hot water |
| 100 g/4 oz butter or margarine | ½ cup butter or margarine |
| 125 g/5 oz caster sugar | ⅔ cup sugar |
| 2 large eggs, beaten | 2 eggs, beaten |
| 100 g/4 oz self-raising flour | 1 cup self-rising flour |
| grated rind of 1 orange | grated rind of 1 orange |
| 1 tablespoon orange juice | 1 tablespoon orange juice |
| few orange jelly slices for decoration | few orange candy slices for decoration |
| CHOCOLATE ICING: | CHOCOLATE FROSTING: |
| 50 g/2 oz plain chocolate | 2 squares semisweet chocolate |
| 25 g/1 oz butter | 2 tablespoons butter |
| 25 g/1 oz icing sugar, sifted | ¼ cup confectioners' sugar, sifted |

Grease an 18 cm/7 inch round deep cake tin and line the bottom and sides with greased greaseproof (waxed) paper. Dissolve the cocoa in the water and leave to cool. Cream the butter or margarine and sugar together until light and fluffy and pale in colour. Beat in the eggs one at a time, followed by the cocoa mixture. Sift in the flour and fold in, followed by the orange rind and juice. Turn into the prepared tin. Bake in a moderate oven (180°C/350°F, Gas Mark 4) for 40 to 45 minutes or until firm to the touch. Turn out onto a wire rack to cool.

To make the icing (frosting), melt the chocolate in a heatproof bowl over hot water, then stir in the butter until melted and well mixed. Beat in the icing (confectioners') sugar until smooth and remove from the heat. Quickly spread over the top of the cake making a swirling design. Decorate with orange jelly (candy) slices. Leave to set.

# BUTTERSCOTCH SPONGE CAKE

This is a one-stage sponge cake with butterscotch flavouring and a soft butterscotch icing (frosting).

| Metric/Imperial | American |
|---|---|
| 100 g/4 oz self-raising flour | 1 cup self-rising flour |
| pinch of salt | pinch of salt |
| 1 teaspoon baking powder | 1 teaspoon baking powder |
| 75 g/3 oz soft (luxury) margarine | 6 tablespoons soft margarine |
| 100 g/4 oz soft brown sugar | ⅔ cup light brown sugar |
| 2 eggs | 2 eggs |
| 1 tablespoon water | 1 tablespoon water |
| little crushed butterscotch for decoration | little crushed butterscotch for decoration |
| ICING: | FROSTING: |
| 50 g/2 oz soft margarine | ¼ cup soft margarine |
| 1 tablespoon golden syrup | 1 tablespoon light corn syrup |
| 100 g/4 oz icing sugar, sifted | 1 cup confectioners' sugar, sifted |

Grease a 20 cm/8 inch square deep cake tin and line the bottom with greased greaseproof (waxed) paper. Sift the flour, salt and baking powder into a bowl. Add the other ingredients, mix well until incorporated, then beat hard for about 3 minutes until smooth and pale in colour. Turn into the prepared tin, level the top and bake in a moderate oven (160°C/325°F, Gas Mark 3) for about 45 minutes or until well risen and firm to the touch. Turn out onto a wire rack to cool.

To make the icing (frosting), cream the margarine and syrup together, then gradually beat in the icing (confectioners') sugar. If too stiff add a few drops of water, then spread over the top of the cake, making an attractive pattern with a fork or round-bladed knife. Sprinkle with crushed butterscotch.

*Left: Chocolate Orange Cake*
*Opposite: Coffee Fudge Cake*

# COFFEE FUDGE CAKE

An unusual light coffee-flavoured cake made with brown sugar, this has an apricot jam filling and rich coffee icing.

**Metric/Imperial**
150 g/6 oz butter or margarine
150 g/6 oz dark soft brown sugar
3 large eggs, beaten
150 g/6 oz self-raising flour
1 tablespoon coffee essence
4–6 tablespoons apricot jam
½ recipe quantity coffee Butter Cream (see page 104)
40 g/1½ oz walnuts, finely chopped
icing sugar for dredging

**American**
¾ cup butter or margarine
1 cup dark brown sugar
3 eggs, beaten
1½ cups self-rising flour
1 tablespoon strong black coffee
4–6 tablespoons apricot jam
½ recipe quantity coffee Butter Cream (see page 104)
⅓ cup finely chopped walnuts
confectioners' sugar for dredging

Grease two fairly deep 20 cm/8 inch sandwich tins (layer cake pans) and line the bottoms with greased greaseproof (waxed) paper. Cream the butter or margarine and sugar together until very pale in colour and fluffy. Beat in the eggs one at a time, following each with a spoonful of flour. Sift in the remaining flour and fold in with the coffee essence (strong black coffee) and divide between the tins. Level the tops and bake in a moderately hot oven (190°C/375°F, Gas Mark 5) for 20 to 25 minutes or until well risen, golden brown and firm to the touch. Turn out onto a wire rack to cool. When cold, sandwich the cakes together with the jam.

Spread a little of the butter cream around the sides of the cake and roll in the chopped nuts. Dredge the top of the cake heavily with icing (confectioners') sugar and then decorate with piped butter cream using a small star tube to make a wheel design and shell edging.

11

# CHOCOLATE RAISIN SPONGE CAKE

A speedy moist chocolate cake, this has a lightness achieved by folding in beaten egg whites.

**Metric/Imperial**
150 g/5 oz self-raising flour
25 g/1 oz cocoa powder
150 g/5 oz caster sugar
5 tablespoons corn or
   vegetable oil
5 tablespoons water
2 large eggs, separated
50 g/2 oz seedless raisins
ICING:
300 g/10 oz icing sugar
3 tablespoons corn or
   vegetable oil
2–3 tablespoons top-of-the-
   milk
rum essence
DECORATION:
few chocolate drops
few seedless raisins

**American**
$1\frac{1}{4}$ cups self-rising flour
$\frac{1}{4}$ cup unsweetened cocoa
$\frac{2}{3}$ cup sugar
$\frac{1}{3}$ cup corn oil
$\frac{1}{3}$ cup water
2 eggs, separated
$\frac{1}{3}$ cup seedless raisins
FROSTING:
$2\frac{1}{2}$ cups confectioners' sugar
3 tablespoons corn oil
2–3 tablespoons half-and-
   half
rum flavoring
DECORATION:
few chocolate chips
few seedless raisins

Grease two 18 cm/7 inch sandwich tins (layer cake pans) and line the bottoms with greased greaseproof (waxed) paper. Sift the flour and cocoa into a bowl. Add the sugar and mix well. Then add the oil, water and egg yolks and beat very thoroughly, for about 2 minutes with an electric mixer or 3 minutes by hand, until smooth and glossy. Whisk the egg whites stiffly and fold evenly through the mixture with the raisins. Pour into the prepared tins and bake in a moderate oven (180°C/350°F, Gas Mark 4) for about 30 minutes or until firm to the touch. Turn out onto a wire rack to cool.

To make the icing (frosting), sift the icing (confectioners') sugar into a bowl and add the oil and sufficient top-of-the-milk (half-and-half) to mix to a spreading consistency. Flavour with rum and use half to sandwich the cakes together. Spread the remainder over the top of the cake and decorate with chocolate drops (chips) and raisins.

*Variations*
*Coffee:* use 175 g/6 oz ($1\frac{1}{2}$ cups) self-raising (self-rising) flour; omit the cocoa and raisins and replace 1 tablespoon water with coffee essence (strong black coffee).
*Orange or lemon:* use 175 g/6 oz ($1\frac{1}{2}$ cups) self-raising (self-rising) flour; omit the cocoa and raisins, add the grated rind of 1 orange or lemon and replace 1 tablespoon water with fruit juice.

# COCONUT FEATHER SPONGE CAKE

This coconut-flavoured cake has toasted coconut around the edges and a feather-iced top.

**Metric/Imperial**
100 g/4 oz butter or
   margarine
100 g/4 oz caster sugar
2 large eggs, beaten
75 g/3 oz self-raising flour
25 g/1 oz desiccated
   coconut
1 tablespoon water
apricot jam
3–4 tablespoons desiccated
   coconut, toasted
GLACÉ ICING (WHITE):
100 g/4 oz icing sugar,
   sifted
about 1 tablespoon warm
   water
GLACÉ ICING (ORANGE):
50 g/2 oz icing sugar, sifted
little orange food colouring
1–2 teaspoons warm water

**American**
$\frac{1}{2}$ cup butter or margarine
$\frac{1}{2}$ cup sugar
2 eggs, beaten
$\frac{3}{4}$ cup self-rising flour
$\frac{1}{3}$ cup shredded coconut
1 tablespoon water
apricot jam
3–4 tablespoons shredded
   coconut, toasted
GLACÉ ICING (WHITE):
1 cup confectioners' sugar,
   sifted
about 1 tablespoon warm
   water
GLACÉ ICING (ORANGE):
$\frac{1}{2}$ cup confectioners' sugar,
   sifted
little orange food coloring
1–2 teaspoons warm water

Grease two 18 cm/7 inch sandwich tins (layer cake pans) and line the bottoms and sides with greased greaseproof (waxed) paper. Cream the butter or margarine and sugar together until light and fluffy. Beat in the eggs one at a time, following each with a spoonful of the flour. Sift in the remaining flour and fold in with the coconut, followed by the water. Divide between the tins, level the tops and bake in a moderately hot oven (190°C/375°F, Gas Mark 5) for 15 to 20 minutes or until well risen, golden brown and just firm to the touch. Turn onto a wire rack and leave to cool.

Sandwich the cakes together with jam. Then heat 2 tablespoons jam with 1 teaspoon water and brush around the sides of the cake. Roll in toasted coconut and place on a plate.

Make up the white and orange glacé icings (see page 105). Spread the white icing over the top of the cake. Put the orange icing into a paper piping bag (see page 126), cut off the tip and pipe straight lines across the cake at 1 cm/$\frac{1}{2}$ inch intervals. Immediately, before it has time to set, run a skewer or sharp knife backwards and forwards across the orange lines to give a feathered effect. Leave to set.

# APRICOT SWISS (JELLY) ROLL

The usual plain Swiss (jelly) roll, which is a favourite with everyone, is filled here with apricot jam.

**Metric/Imperial**
*3 eggs*
*75 g/3 oz caster sugar*
*75 g/3 oz plain flour, sifted*
*few drops of vanilla essence (optional)*
*1 tablespoon hot water*
*caster sugar for dredging*
*about 6 tablespoons apricot jam, warmed*

**American**
*3 eggs*
*6 tablespoons sugar*
*¾ cup all-purpose flour, sifted*
*few drops of vanilla extract (optional)*
*1 tablespoon hot water*
*sugar for dredging*
*about 6 tablespoons apricot jam, warmed*

Line a Swiss (jelly) roll tin, about 34 × 23 cm/13 × 9 inches, with greaseproof (waxed) paper and brush lightly with oil. Put the eggs and sugar into a large heatproof bowl and mix together. Place the bowl over a saucepan of hot water and whisk until the mixture is light and creamy and leaves a trail for a few seconds when the whisk is lifted. Remove the bowl from the heat and whisk until cold. (If using an electric mixer no heat is required.) Sift half the flour over the mixture and fold in lightly using a metal spoon. Repeat with the remaining flour and the vanilla essence (extract) and water. Pour into the prepared tin, spreading lightly where necessary so that the corners are evenly filled. Bake in a hot oven (220°C/425°F, Gas Mark 7) for 7 to 9 minutes or until a light golden brown, well risen and spongy.

Meanwhile, sprinkle a sheet of greaseproof (waxed) paper liberally with sugar. (If using non-stick parchment the sugar is not necessary.) Turn the cake quickly onto the paper and peel off the lining paper. Trim off the crusty edges with a very sharp knife. Spread the jam over the cake. Roll up quickly and evenly with the help of the paper. Dredge with more sugar and leave to cool on a wire rack.

*Filling Variations*
Most jams can be used in a Swiss (jelly) roll so long as they are not full of large pieces of fruit. Butter creams or fresh whipped cream can also be used either on their own or with jam.

*Note:* The cake can be rolled up without the jam, but with the paper inside, and left for a few minutes to cool. Then unroll and spread with the jam.

# LEMON SPONGE CAKE

A simple lemon-flavoured whisked sponge cake, this has a lemon curd filling and a glacé icing topping.

**Metric/Imperial**
*2 large eggs*
*100 g/4 oz caster sugar*
*100 g/4 oz plain flour*
*¼ teaspoon lemon essence*
*3–4 tablespoons lemon curd or apricot jam*
GLACÉ ICING:
*125 g/5 oz icing sugar*
*2–3 teaspoons lemon juice*
DECORATION:
*few mimosa balls*
*few candied angelica 'leaves'*

**American**
*2 eggs*
*½ cup sugar*
*1 cup all-purpose flour*
*¼ teaspoon lemon flavoring*
*3–4 tablespoons lemon curd or apricot jam*
GLACÉ ICING:
*1¼ cups confectioners' sugar*
*2–3 teaspoons lemon juice*
DECORATION:
*few mimosa balls*
*few candied angelica 'leaves'*

Grease a 20 cm/8 inch round deep cake tin and line the bottom with greased greaseproof (waxed) paper. Whisk the eggs and sugar together in a heatproof bowl over a pan of hot water, until the mixture is thick and pale and leaves a thick trail for a few seconds when the whisk is lifted. Remove from the heat. (If using an electric mixer, no heat is required.) Sift the flour twice and fold lightly and evenly into the egg mixture with the lemon essence (flavoring). Turn into the prepared tin and bake in a moderate oven (180°C/350°F, Gas Mark 4) for about 30 minutes or until firm to the touch. Turn out carefully onto a wire rack and leave to cool.

Split the cake into two layers and fill with the lemon curd or jam. Sift the icing (confectioners') sugar into a bowl and add sufficient lemon juice to mix to a thick pouring consistency. Spread the glacé icing evenly over the top of the cake and decorate with mimosa balls and angelica 'leaves'. Leave to set. (This cake is best eaten the day made or the following day.)

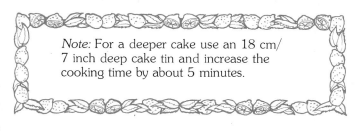

*Note:* For a deeper cake use an 18 cm/ 7 inch deep cake tin and increase the cooking time by about 5 minutes.

# BATTENBURG CAKE

Battenburg or 'window' cake is made from a basic Victoria sandwich (layer) cake mix in two colours. The cake is cut into blocks, reassembled and covered completely in marzipan to give a chequered effect when sliced.

**Metric/Imperial**
150 g/6 oz butter or margarine
150 g/6 oz caster sugar
3 large eggs
150 g/6 oz self-raising flour
1 tablespoon water
pink food colouring
raspberry flavouring (optional)
about 100 g/4 oz apricot jam
½ recipe quantity Marzipan (see page 104), or 225 g/8 oz bought
caster sugar for dredging

**American**
¾ cup butter or margarine
¾ cup sugar
3 eggs
1½ cups self-rising flour
1 tablespoon water
pink food coloring
raspberry flavoring (optional)
about ⅓ cup apricot jam
½ recipe quantity Marzipan (see page 104), or ½ lb bought
sugar for dredging

Grease a deep oblong cake tin, about 28 × 18 cm/11 × 7 inches, and line the bottom with greased greaseproof (waxed) paper. Make a division across the centre of the tin with a double thickness of foil.

Cream the butter or margarine and sugar together until light and fluffy. Beat in the eggs one at a time, following each with a spoonful of flour. Sift in the remaining flour and fold in, followed by the water. Spread half the mixture into one side of the cake tin. Add a few drops of pink food colouring and raspberry flavouring, if liked, to the remaining mixture. Put it into the other side of the tin. Bake in a moderately hot oven (190°C/375°F. Gas Mark 5) for about 25 minutes or until well risen and firm to the touch. Turn out onto a wire rack to cool.

Trim the cakes to an even size and cut in half lengthways. Spread the top of one white and one pink piece of cake with jam and top with alternate coloured pieces. Spread the sides of one double layer with jam and stick the two pieces together to give the chequered effect. Use the remaining jam to brush all around the outside of the cake.

Roll out the marzipan on a surface sprinkled with a little caster sugar, to an oblong large enough to enclose the whole cake (approx. 35 × 25 cm/14 × 10 inches). Place the cake in the centre. Wrap the marzipan around the cake to cover it completely and trim. Crimp or decorate the outer edges of the marzipan to give an even shape and mark a criss-cross pattern on top with a sharp knife. Sprinkle with a little more sugar and leave to set. Serve cut in slices.

*Opposite: Preparing a Walnut Raspberry Roll*
*Below: Battenburg Cake; Walnut Raspberry Roll*

# WALNUT RASPBERRY ROLL

Ground walnuts and cinnamon flavour this feather light Swiss (jelly) roll. Serve it at teatime or as a special occasion dessert, filled with fresh raspberries and whipped cream.

**Metric/Imperial**
4 large eggs
75 g/3 oz caster sugar
40 g/1½ oz plain flour
large pinch of ground
   cinnamon
40 g/1½ oz walnuts, ground
25 g/1 oz butter, melted
icing sugar for sprinkling
8 walnut halves for
   decoration
FILLING:
about 75 g/3 oz seedless
   raspberry jam
50 g/2 oz butter
100 g/4 oz icing sugar,
   sifted
large pinch of ground
   cinnamon

**American**
4 eggs
6 tablespoons sugar
6 tablespoons all-purpose
   flour
large pinch of ground
   cinnamon
⅓ cup ground walnuts
2 tablespoons butter, melted
confectioners' sugar for
   sprinkling
8 walnut halves for
   decoration
FILLING:
about ¼ cup raspberry jelly
¼ cup butter
1 cup confectioners' sugar,
   sifted
large pinch of ground
   cinnamon

Grease and line a Swiss (jelly) roll tin, about 30 × 25 cm/ 12 × 10 inches, and dust lightly with flour. Put the eggs and sugar into a large heatproof bowl. Place the bowl over a saucepan of hot water and whisk the eggs and sugar together, until the mixture is thick and pale in colour and the whisk leaves a thick trail when lifted. Remove from the heat. (If using an electric mixer, no heat is needed.) Sift the flour and cinnamon together twice and mix in the ground walnuts. Fold carefully into the whisked mixture using a metal spoon. Finally fold in the cooled melted butter. Pour into the prepared tin and spread lightly. Bake in a moderately hot oven (190°C/375°F, Gas Mark 5) for 15 to 20 minutes or until just firm and springy.

Turn out onto a sheet of greaseproof (waxed) paper sprinkled with icing (confectioners') sugar. Peel off the lining paper and trim the edges. While still warm, roll up with the greaseproof (waxed) paper inside the roll. Leave to cool.

Unroll and spread with the jam (jelly). Cream the butter and icing (confectioners') sugar together and flavour with the cinnamon. Spread half this butter cream over the jam and reroll the cake. Remove from the paper and dredge with icing (confectioners') sugar. Using a piping bag fitted with a star tube, pipe the remaining butter cream down the centre of the cake. Decorate with the walnuts.

# LEMON PRALINE SANDWICH (LAYER) CAKE

This is a one-stage sponge sandwich (layer) cake, filled and decorated with lemon butter cream with a praline coating.

| Metric/Imperial | American |
|---|---|
| 150 g/6 oz soft (luxury) margarine | $\frac{3}{4}$ cup soft margarine |
| 150 g/6 oz caster sugar | $\frac{3}{4}$ cup sugar |
| 3 eggs | 3 eggs |
| 150 g/6 oz self-raising flour, sifted | $1\frac{1}{2}$ cups self-rising flour, sifted |
| $1\frac{1}{2}$ teaspoons baking powder | $1\frac{1}{2}$ teaspoons baking powder |
| grated rind of 1 lemon | grated rind of 1 lemon |
| PRALINE: | PRALINE: |
| 140 g/$5\frac{1}{2}$ oz caster sugar | $\frac{3}{4}$ cup less 1 tablespoon sugar |
| 100 g/4 oz blanched almonds, finely chopped | 1 cup finely chopped blanched almonds |
| BUTTER CREAM: | BUTTER CREAM: |
| 125 g/5 oz butter | $\frac{1}{2}$ cup plus 2 tablespoons butter |
| 250 g/10 oz icing sugar, sifted | $2\frac{1}{2}$ cups confectioners' sugar, sifted |
| grated rind of 1 lemon | grated rind of 1 lemon |
| about 1 tablespoon lemon juice | about 1 tablespoon lemon juice |

Grease a 20 cm/8 inch round deep cake tin and line the bottom with greased greaseproof (waxed) paper. Put the margarine, sugar, eggs, flour, baking powder and lemon rind into a bowl. Mix well, then beat for about 3 minutes until smooth. Transfer to the prepared tin and level the top. Bake in a moderate oven (160°C/325°F, Gas Mark 3) for 50 to 60 minutes until well risen, golden brown and firm to the touch. Turn out onto a wire rack and leave to cool.

For the praline, put the sugar into a heavy-based saucepan and heat very gently until dissolved. Boil until a pale caramel colour, then add the almonds and stir in with a metal spoon. Turn quickly onto an oiled surface. Using a lemon or an oiled jam jar, roll out the praline thinly. Before the praline sets, cut out four 4 cm/$1\frac{1}{2}$ inch rounds and four to six 2 cm/$\frac{3}{4}$ inch rounds, using a warmed and oiled plain cutter. Cut the 4 cm/$1\frac{1}{2}$ inch rounds in half. Leave to set, then remove the rounds and crush the remaining pieces.

For the butter cream, cream the butter and sugar together, then beat in the lemon rind and juice to give a spreading consistency. Split the cake into three layers and use half the butter cream to sandwich them together. Spread the sides of the cake thinly with butter cream and roll in the crushed praline. Spread the remaining butter cream on top of the cake and decorate with piped rosettes using a star tube. Top with the reserved rounds of praline.

# ORANGE LAYER CAKE

Mandarin oranges and cream complete this layered sponge cake, to serve at a party tea or as a dinner party dessert.

| Metric/Imperial | American |
|---|---|
| 3 eggs | 3 eggs |
| 75 g/3 oz caster sugar | $\frac{1}{3}$ cup sugar |
| grated rind of 1 orange | grated rind of 1 orange |
| 90 g/$3\frac{1}{2}$ oz plain flour | $\frac{3}{4}$ cup plus 2 tablespoons all-purpose flour |
| few blanched pistachio nuts for decoration | few blanched pistachio nuts for decoration |
| FILLING: | FILLING: |
| 1 tablespoon orange liqueur | 1 tablespoon orange liqueur |
| 312 g/11 oz can mandarin oranges | 11 oz can mandarin oranges |
| 300 ml/$\frac{1}{2}$ pint double cream | $1\frac{1}{4}$ cups heavy cream |
| 2 tablespoons top-of-the-milk | 2 tablespoons half-and-half |
| finely grated rind of $\frac{1}{2}$ orange | finely grated rind of $\frac{1}{2}$ orange |

Grease a 20 cm/8 inch round deep cake tin and line with greased greaseproof (waxed) paper. Put the eggs and sugar into a bowl and whisk until very thick and pale in colour. Beat in the orange rind. Fold the sifted flour into the mixture. turn into the prepared tin and bake in a moderate oven (180°C/350°F, Gas Mark 4) for 35 to 40 minutes or until well risen and firm to the touch. Turn out and cool on a wire rack.

Split the cake in half and sprinkle the bottom layer with the liqueur and 2 tablespoons mandarin juice. Whip the cream and milk together until stiff and fold in the orange rind. Spread about one-third over the liqueur-soaked layer of cake. Drain the mandarins and arrange about three-quarters over the cream. Cover with the top cake layer and spread with half of the remaining cream. Put the rest of the cream into a piping bag fitted with a 5 mm/$\frac{1}{4}$ inch plain vegetable tube and decorate the top with a piped lattice pattern. Finish the decoration using the remaining mandarins and the pistachio nuts.

*Orange Layer Cake*

# ORANGE CARAWAY RING

This moist spongy orange cake is flavoured with caraway seeds. The caraway seeds can be omitted if preferred.

**Metric/Imperial**
100 g/4 oz butter or
    margarine
25 g/1 oz light soft brown
    sugar
75 g/3 oz caster sugar
2 eggs, separated
grated rind and juice of 1
    medium orange
150 g/6 oz self-raising flour,
    sifted
1 teaspoon caraway seeds
1 recipe quantity orange
    Glacé Icing (see page
    105)
DECORATION (OPTIONAL):
few orange jelly slices
few candied angelica 'leaves'

**American**
½ cup butter or margarine
2½ tablespoons light brown
    sugar
6 tablespoons sugar
2 eggs, separated
grated rind and juice of 1
    medium orange
1½ cups self-rising flour,
    sifted
1 teaspoon caraway seeds
1 recipe quantity orange
    Glacé Icing (see page
    105)
DECORATION (OPTIONAL):
few orange candy slices
few candied angelica 'leaves'

Grease a 1 litre/2 pint (5 cup) ring mould (tube pan) and put a strip of greaseproof (waxed) paper in the bottom of the ring. Cream the butter or margarine and sugars together until light and fluffy. Beat in the egg yolks one at a time, then stir in the orange rind, flour, caraway seeds and 3 tablespoons orange juice. Finally, whisk the egg whites until stiff and fold evenly through the mixture. Turn into the prepared tin and bake in a moderately hot oven (190°C/375°F, Gas Mark 5) for about 30 minutes or until well risen, golden brown and firm to the touch. Turn out very carefully and leave to cool.

Drizzle the icing over the ring and allow it to run down the sides of the cake. Leave to set. If liked, decorate with pieces of orange jelly (candy) slices and candied angelica.

# SHERRIED SPICE CAKE

An unusual soft-textured sponge cake, this is full of nuts and sultanas (white raisins), flavoured with sherry and spice, with a strong sherry-flavoured rich butter cream.

**Metric/Imperial**
200 g/8 oz sultanas
125 ml/¼ pint water
100 g/4 oz butter or
    margarine
125 g/5 oz soft brown sugar
1 large egg, beaten
150 g/6 oz plain flour
1 teaspoon bicarbonate of
    soda
½ teaspoon ground cloves
½ teaspoon grated nutmeg
¼ teaspoon ground
    cinnamon
75 g/3 oz walnuts, chopped
3 tablespoons sherry
1 recipe quantity Rich Butter
    Cream (see page 107)
few walnut halves for
    decoration

**American**
1⅓ cups seedless white
    raisins
⅔ cup water
½ cup butter or margarine
¾ cup light brown sugar
1 egg, beaten
1½ cups all-purpose flour
1 teaspoon baking soda
½ teaspoon ground cloves
½ teaspoon grated nutmeg
¼ teaspoon ground
    cinnamon
¾ cup chopped walnuts
3 tablespoons sherry
1 recipe quantity Rich Butter
    Cream (see page 107)
few walnut halves for
    decoration

Grease two 20 cm/8 inch round deep cake tins and line the bottoms with greased greaseproof (waxed) paper. Put the sultanas (raisins) and water into a small pan and bring to the boil. Simmer gently for 15 minutes. Strain off the liquid and make up to 100 ml/4 fl oz (½ cup) with cold water. Leave to cool.

Cream the butter or margarine and sugar together until very pale and fluffy, then beat in the egg. Sift the flour with the soda and spices and fold into the mixture alternating with the sultana (raisin) liquid. Add the walnuts, sultanas (raisins) and 2 tablespoons sherry and mix lightly but evenly. Divide between the tins and level the tops. Bake in a moderate oven (180°C/350°F, Gas Mark 4) for 30 to 35 minutes or until firm. Cool for a few minutes in the tin, then loosen the edges and turn out very carefully onto a wire rack to cool.

Beat the remaining sherry into the butter cream. Use to sandwich the cake layers together, then cover the top. Decorate with the walnut halves.

# CHOCOLATE COATED ROLLS

These miniature vanilla Swiss (jelly) rolls are filled with jam, completely coated in plain chocolate and then decorated with milk chocolate.

| **Metric/Imperial** | **American** |
| --- | --- |
| 50 g/2 oz plain flour | ½ cup all-purpose flour |
| 2 large eggs | 2 eggs |
| 50 g/2 oz caster sugar | ¼ cup sugar |
| 6 tablespoons jam, beaten smooth | 6 tablespoons jam, beaten smooth |
| COATING: | COATING: |
| about 175 g/6 oz plain chocolate | about 6 squares semisweet chocolate |
| 40 g/1½ oz milk chocolate | about 1½ squares milk chocolate |

Grease a shallow rectangular cake tin, about 33 × 23 cm/13 × 9 inches and line with greased greaseproof (waxed) paper. Sift the flour twice. Put the eggs and sugar into a heatproof bowl and place over a saucepan of hot water. Whisk until the mixture is very thick and pale and the whisk leaves a trail when lifted. (If using an electric mixer, no heat is needed.) Remove from the heat. Sift half the flour over the egg mixture and fold in, using a metal spoon. Sift the remaining flour and fold in. Pour into the prepared tin and spread out lightly until smooth and even. Bake in a hot oven (220°C/425°F, Gas Mark 7) for 7 to 8 minutes or until a pale biscuit colour and just firm.

Lay a sheet of non-stick parchment over a damp tea (dish) towel and turn the sponge onto it. Remove the lining paper. Trim the edges and spread the cake with jam. Cut the sponge in half lengthways and then cut each piece into four even-sized pieces crossways. Quickly roll up each piece of sponge to make a mini Swiss (jelly) roll and leave to cool on a wire rack.

Melt the two chocolates separately in heatproof bowls over hot water and beat until smooth. Dip each roll in the plain (semisweet) chocolate, using a paint brush to cover all the awkward parts. Put onto non-stick parchment or waxed paper and leave until set. As the chocolate sets, decorate with wavy lines made with a fork. Put the milk chocolate into a paper piping bag (see page 126) and cut off just the very tip of the bag. Drizzle the chocolate over the rolls and leave to set.

MAKES 8

*Variations*
The miniature Swiss (jelly) rolls can be dredged in caster sugar and served without the chocolate coating.
*For chocolate-flavoured rolls:* sift 1 tablespoon cocoa powder (unsweetened cocoa) with the flour and continue as above. Fill with vanilla or chocolate Butter Cream (see page 104) in place of the jam.

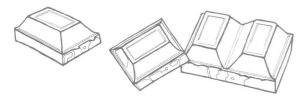

# MARBLE CAKE

This cake is made using a sponge sandwich (layer) cake mixture of three colours which gives a marbled effect to the cut cake.

| **Metric/Imperial** | **American** |
| --- | --- |
| 100 g/4 oz butter or margarine | ½ cup butter or margarine |
| 100 g/4 oz caster sugar | ½ cup sugar |
| 2 large eggs, beaten | 2 eggs, beaten |
| 150 g/6 oz self-raising flour | 1½ cups self-rising flour |
| 2–3 tablespoons milk | 2–3 tablespoons milk |
| few drops of vanilla essence | few drops of vanilla extract |
| few drops of cochineal or green food colouring | few drops of pink or green food coloring |
| 2 teaspoons cocoa powder, sifted | 2 teaspoons unsweetened cocoa, sifted |
| 2–3 glacé cherries for decoration | 2–3 candied cherries for decoration |
| MOCHA ICING: | MOCHA FROSTING: |
| 50 g/2 oz butter or margarine | ¼ cup butter or margarine |
| 75 g/3 oz icing sugar, sifted | ¾ cup confectioners' sugar, sifted |
| 25 g/1 oz cocoa powder | ¼ cup unsweetened cocoa |
| 2–3 teaspoons coffee essence | 2–3 teaspoons strong black coffee |

Grease an 18 cm/7 inch round deep cake tin and line the bottom with greased greaseproof (waxed) paper. Cream the butter or margarine and sugar together until very light and fluffy. Beat in the eggs one at a time, following each with a spoonful of flour. Sift the remaining flour and fold in alternately with the milk to give a soft dropping consistency.

Beat in the vanilla essence (extract), then divide the mixture equally into three and put into separate bowls. Beat food colouring into one bowl, the sifted cocoa into another and leave the third plain. Put alternate spoonfuls of the mixtures into the cake tin, arranging colours so they overlap and make a pattern. Bake in the centre of a moderately hot oven (190°C/375°F, Gas Mark 5) for 40 to 50 minutes or until well risen and firm to the touch. Turn out and cool on a wire rack.

To make the icing (frosting), beat the butter or margarine and icing (confectioners') sugar together until creamy, then beat in the cocoa and coffee essence (strong black coffee) to give a spreading consistency. Spread most of the icing (frosting) over the top of the cake (and sides if liked) and pipe rosettes around the top edge. Decorate with pieces of glacé (candied) cherry.

*Note:* Other colours and flavours can be used for this cake.

# LITTLE CAKES

## SPONGE (LADY) FINGERS

Spongy-textured cakes made into fingers or drops, these can be served either plain or sandwiched together with cream, butter cream or jam. They are a good accompaniment to fruit salad.

**Metric/Imperial**
3 large eggs
75 g/3 oz caster sugar
vanilla essence
75 g/3 oz plain flour, sifted
    twice
300 ml/½ pint whipping
    cream
icing sugar for dredging

**American**
3 eggs
6 tablespoons sugar
vanilla extract
¾ cup all-purpose flour,
    sifted twice
1¼ cups whipping cream
confectioners' sugar for
    dredging

Grease two baking sheets or line them with non-stick parchment. Whisk the eggs and sugar together until really thick and creamy and the whisk leaves a trail when lifted. This can be done with an electric mixer or by hand in a heatproof bowl over a pan of hot water. Add a few drops of vanilla essence (extract) and then gradually fold in the flour. Put the mixture into a large forcing bag fitted with a 1 cm/½ inch plain tube. Pipe fingers or small dots of the mixture onto the baking sheets, well apart to allow for spreading. Bake just above the centre of a hot oven (220°C/425°F, Gas Mark 7) for about 7 minutes or until an even pale brown. Remove carefully to a wire rack to cool. When cold, store in an airtight container.

To serve, whip the cream until stiff and use to sandwich either fingers or drops together. Dredge lightly with icing (confectioners') sugar.

MAKES ABOUT 40 (20 PAIRS)

*Variations*
The fingers or drops can also be filled with butter cream or jam, if preferred. The single fingers or drops can be half dipped in melted chocolate instead of sandwiching them together; or the tops simply drizzled with melted chocolate.

# ROCKY BUNS

Traditional rocky-textured buns, these can be baked in heaps on a baking sheet or in patty (muffin) tins for a more even shape.

*Rocky Buns; Sponge (Lady) Fingers*

| Metric/Imperial | American |
| --- | --- |
| 200 g/8 oz self-raising flour | 2 cups self-rising flour |
| ½ teaspoon mixed spice | ½ teaspoon apple pie spice |
| ½ teaspoon ground cinnamon | ½ teaspoon ground cinnamon |
| pinch of ground mace | pinch of ground mace |
| 100 g/4 oz butter or margarine | ½ cup butter or margarine |
| 50 g/2 oz currants | ⅓ cup currants |
| 50 g/2 oz sultanas | ⅓ cup seedless white raisins |
| 50 g/2 oz mixed candied peel, chopped | ⅓ cup chopped mixed candied peel |
| 100 g/4 oz demerara sugar | ⅔ cup light brown sugar |
| grated rind of ½ lemon or orange | grated rind of ½ lemon or orange |
| 1 large egg, beaten | 1 egg, beaten |
| 2–3 tablespoons milk | 2–3 tablespoons milk |

Grease two baking sheets or 16–18 patty (shallow muffin) tins. Sift the flour and spices into a bowl, add the butter or margarine and rub in until the mixture resembles fine breadcrumbs. Add the currants, sultanas (raisins), peel, sugar and lemon or orange rind and mix well. Add the egg and sufficient milk to mix to a stiff consistency. Put the mixture into 16–18 heaps on the baking sheets or divide between the patty (muffin) tins. Do not smooth the mixture. Bake in a moderately hot oven (200°C/400°F, Gas Mark 6) for about 20 minutes or until lightly browned and firm. Cool on a wire rack.

MAKES 16 TO 18

*Variation*
*For ginger rockies:* replace the spices with 1 teaspoon ground ginger and add 50 g/2 oz (¼ cup) chopped crystallized or stem (preserved) ginger instead of the candied peel.

# COCONUT BUNS

These are moist rocky-type coconut buns.

| Metric/Imperial | American |
|---|---|
| 125 g/4 oz self-raising flour | 1 cup self-rising flour |
| 50 g/2 oz butter or margarine | ¼ cup butter or margarine |
| 50 g/2 oz caster sugar | ¼ cup sugar |
| 50 g/2 oz desiccated coconut | ⅔ cup shredded coconut |
| 1 egg, beaten | 1 egg, beaten |
| little milk | little milk |

Grease 10 bun (muffin) tins. Sift the flour into a bowl, add the butter or margarine and rub in until the mixture resembles fine breadcrumbs. Mix in the sugar and coconut. Add the egg and a little milk, if necessary, to mix to a soft dropping consistency. Divide between the tins and bake in a moderately hot oven (190°C/375°F, Gas Mark 5) for 20 minutes. Cool on a wire rack.

MAKES ABOUT 10

Variation
25 g/1 oz (2½ tablespoons) glacé (candied) cherries, finely chopped and well rinsed and dried, can be added to the dry ingredients.

# BAKEWELL TARTS

These are moist almond sponge tarts baked in pastry cases with a layer of jam beneath the sponge.

| Metric/Imperial | American |
|---|---|
| ½ recipe quantity Shortcrust Pastry (see page 109) | ½ recipe quantity Pie Pastry (see page 109) |
| icing sugar for dredging | confectioners' sugar for dredging |
| FILLING: | FILLING: |
| 50 g/2 oz butter or margarine | ¼ cup butter or margarine |
| 50 g/2 oz caster sugar | ¼ cup sugar |
| 1 large egg, beaten | 1 egg, beaten |
| almond essence | almond extract |
| 40 g/1½ oz self-raising flour, sifted | 6 tablespoons self-rising flour, sifted |
| 15 g/½ oz ground almonds | 2 tablespoons ground almonds |
| raspberry jam | raspberry jam |

Lightly grease or dampen 16 to 18 patty (shallow muffin) tins. For the filling, cream together the butter or margarine and sugar until light and fluffy. Beat in the egg and a few drops of almond essence (extract), then fold in the flour and ground almonds.

Roll out the dough and cut out 16 to 18 circles using a 7.5 cm/3 inch cutter. Use to line the patty (muffin) tins. Spread a little raspberry jam in each pastry case and cover with the filling. Bake in a moderately hot oven (200°C/400°F, Gas Mark 6) for 15 to 20 minutes or until well risen and golden brown. Cool on a wire rack and dredge with icing (confectioners') sugar.

MAKES 16 TO 18

# MADELEINES

The traditional French Madeleines are made with a genoese sponge cake mixture (see page 8), baked in the special fluted madeleine moulds, sandwiched together with jam and/or cream and dusted with icing (confectioners') sugar. This better known version is a sponge cake mixture baked in dariole moulds, coated in jam and rolled in coconut.

| Metric/Imperial | American |
|---|---|
| 100 g/4 oz butter or margarine | ½ cup butter or margarine |
| 100 g/4 oz caster sugar | ½ cup sugar |
| 2 eggs, beaten | 2 eggs, beaten |
| 100 g/4 oz self-raising flour | 1 cup self-rising flour |
| 4 tablespoons seedless raspberry jam or redcurrant jelly | ¼ cup raspberry or redcurrant jelly |
| 2 teaspoons water | 2 teaspoons water |
| desiccated coconut for coating | shredded coconut for coating |
| DECORATION: | DECORATION: |
| about 6 glacé cherries | about 6 candied cherries |
| about 12 candied angelica 'leaves' | about 12 candied angelica 'leaves' |

Grease 10 to 12 dariole moulds. Cream the butter or margarine and sugar together until light and fluffy, then beat in the eggs one at a time, following each with a spoonful of the flour. Sift in the remaining flour and fold in. Divide the mixture between the tins, filling them not more than three-quarters full. Stand on a baking sheet and bake in a moderate oven (180°C/350°F, Gas Mark 4) for about 20 minutes or until firm to the touch and browned. Turn out to cool on a wire rack. When cold, trim the base of each cake so it stands evenly.

Warm the jam or jelly with the water until liquid and brush over the madeleines. (The best way to do this is by holding the cake on a fork or skewer.) Quickly roll the cakes in coconut until evenly coated. Leave on a plate until cold, then decorate the top of each with pieces of glacé (candied) cherry and angelica.

MAKES 10 TO 12

# CHOCOLATE BUTTERFLIES

Chocolate sponge cake buns filled with butter cream, these are topped with 'wings' made from a slice cut off the top of each bun.

| **Metric/Imperial** | **American** |
|---|---|
| 100 g/4 oz butter or margarine | $\frac{1}{2}$ cup butter or margarine |
| 100 g/4 oz caster sugar | $\frac{1}{2}$ cup sugar |
| 2 eggs, beaten | 2 eggs, beaten |
| 100 g/4 oz plain flour | 1 cup all-purpose flour |
| $\frac{1}{2}$ teaspoon baking powder | $\frac{1}{2}$ teaspoon baking powder |
| 25 g/1 oz cocoa powder | $\frac{1}{4}$ cup unsweetened cocoa |
| 1 tablespoon water | 1 tablespoon water |
| $\frac{1}{2}$ recipe quantity Butter Cream (see page 104) | $\frac{1}{2}$ recipe quantity Butter Cream (see page 104) |
| icing sugar for dredging | confectioners' sugar for dredging |

Line 16 to 18 bun (muffin) tins with paper cases or grease them well. Cream the butter or margarine and sugar together until light and fluffy. Beat in the eggs one at a time, following each with a spoonful of flour. Sift the flour, baking powder and cocoa together and fold into the mixture with the water. Divide between the tins and bake in a moderately hot oven (190°C/375°F, Gas Mark 5) for 15 to 20 minutes or until firm to the touch. Turn out onto a wire rack to cool.

Put the butter cream into a piping bag fitted with a small star tube. Slice the tops off the cakes and cut these pieces in half to make two 'wings'. Pipe butter cream onto each cake, position the wings and pipe a little more butter cream in the centre of the wings. Dredge lightly with icing (confectioners') sugar.

MAKES 16 TO 18

*Variations*
Plain Victoria sandwich (layer) cake mixture (see page 6) or other variations can be used for these buns with different flavoured butter creams.

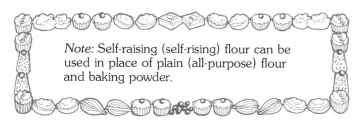

*Note:* Self-raising (self-rising) flour can be used in place of plain (all-purpose) flour and baking powder.

# SHELL CAKES

An easy type of cake to make when a large number is required, these piped shell shapes are made from a type of shortbread dough and sandwiched together with lemon curd or jam.

| **Metric/Imperial** | **American** |
|---|---|
| 75 g/3 oz butter or margarine | 6 tablespoons butter or margarine |
| 75 g/3 oz caster sugar | 6 tablespoons sugar |
| $\frac{1}{2}$ large egg, beaten | $\frac{1}{2}$ egg, beaten |
| 125 g/5 oz plain flour, sifted | $1\frac{1}{4}$ cups all-purpose flour, sifted |
| lemon curd or jam | lemon curd or jam |
| icing sugar for dredging | confectioners' sugar for dredging |

Grease two or three baking sheets. Cream the butter or margarine and sugar together until light and fluffy, then beat in the egg. Fold in the flour and mix well. Place the mixture in a piping bag fitted with a large star vegetable tube and pipe small shell shapes onto the baking sheets. Bake in a moderately hot oven (200°C/400°F, Gas Mark 6) for 10 to 15 minutes or until lightly coloured. Cool on a wire rack. When cold, sandwich together in pairs with lemon curd or jam and dredge with icing (confectioners') sugar.

MAKES 12 TO 14

# CHOCOLATE TRUFFLE CAKES

Chocolate cases filled with a sherry- or rum-flavoured sponge cake mixture and cream topping, these are an ideal way to use up stale sponge cake.

| **Metric/Imperial** | **American** |
|---|---|
| 225 g/8 oz plain chocolate | 8 squares semisweet chocolate |
| 100 g/4 oz sponge cake crumbs | 2 cups sponge cake crumbs |
| 1 tablespoon apricot jam | 1 tablespoon apricot jam |
| 1–2 tablespoons sherry or rum | 1–2 tablespoons sherry or rum |
| 150 ml/$\frac{1}{4}$ pint double cream | $\frac{2}{3}$ cup heavy cream |
| 8 maraschino or glacé cherries for decoration | 8 maraschino or candied cherries for decoration |

Melt the chocolate in a heatproof bowl over a pan of hot water. Using a pastry brush, coat the insides of 8 paper cake cases with the liquid chocolate. Chill in the refrigerator. When set, repeat with a second layer of chocolate. Chill in the refrigerator overnight.

Carefully peel off the paper and stand the chocolate cases on a plate. Mix together the cake crumbs, jam and sherry or rum and divide between the chocolate cases. Whip the cream until stiff and pipe a large whirl on each cake using a piping bag fitted with a large star tube. Decorate with cherries and serve chilled.

MAKES 8

# ALMOND SPONGE FANCIES

This is an almond-flavoured slab sponge cake cut into fancy shapes. The sides are coated in chopped toasted almonds and the tops decorated with butter cream, nuts and cherries.

**Metric/Imperial**
150 g/6 oz butter or
  margarine
150 g/6 oz caster sugar
3 eggs, beaten
150 g/6 oz self-raising flour
½–1 teaspoon almond
  essence
225 g/8 oz apricot jam
about 1 tablespoon water
150 g/6 oz blanched
  almonds, toasted and
  finely chopped
TOPPING:
1 recipe quantity Butter
  Cream (see page 104)
green food colouring
25 g/1 oz plain chocolate,
  melted
2 teaspoons coffee essence
DECORATION:
few split almonds, blanched
  or toasted
few pistachio nuts, blanched
few glacé cherries

**American**
¾ cup butter or margarine
¾ cup sugar
3 eggs, beaten
1½ cups self-rising flour
½–1 teaspoon almond
  extract
⅔ cup apricot jam
about 1 tablespoon water
1½ cups toasted and finely
  chopped almonds
TOPPING:
1 recipe quantity Butter
  Cream (see page 104)
green food coloring
1 square semisweet
  chocolate, melted
2 teaspoons strong black
  coffee
DECORATION:
few split almonds, blanched
  or toasted
few pistachio nuts, blanched
few candied cherries

Grease a deep oblong cake tin, about $33 \times 23$ cm/$13 \times 9$ inches, or two 20 cm/8 inch square deep sandwich tins (layer cake pans), and line the bottom(s) with greased greaseproof (waxed) paper. Cream the butter or margarine and sugar together until light and fluffy, then beat in the eggs one at a time, following each one with a spoonful of flour. Sift in the remaining flour and fold in with the almond essence (extract). Turn into the prepared tin(s) and level the tops. Bake in a moderate oven (180°C/350°F, Gas Mark 4) for about 30 minutes or until well risen, golden brown and firm to the touch. (The smaller tins will take a little less cooking time.) Turn out onto a wire rack to cool.

When cold, cut the cake into different shapes, using a 5 cm/ 2 inch plain round cutter and cutting others into 5 cm/2 inch squares or triangles. Warm the jam with the water and sieve (strain). Brush the sides of the cakes with jam, then roll in the chopped nuts.

Divide the butter cream into three small bowls. Colour one portion lightly with green food colouring; add the melted chocolate to the second bowl and the coffee essence (strong black coffee) to the third. Spread or pipe the butter cream over the tops of the cakes. Decorate with rosettes of a different coloured butter cream and with split almonds, pistachio nuts and pieces of glacé (candied) cherry.

MAKES ABOUT 20

*Almond Sponge Fancies; Honey Buns*

# COBURG CAKES

These traditional fluted spicy buns have a blanched almond baked into the top of each one.

| **Metric/Imperial** | **American** |
|---|---|
| 6 blanched almonds, split in half | 6 blanched almonds, split in half |
| 50 g/2 oz butter or margarine | ¼ cup butter or margarine |
| 50 g/2 oz caster sugar | ¼ cup sugar |
| 1 egg, beaten | 1 egg, beaten |
| 150 g/5 oz plain flour | 1¼ cups all-purpose flour |
| 1 teaspoon bicarbonate of soda | 1 teaspoon baking soda |
| ½ teaspoon ground ginger | ½ teaspoon ground ginger |
| ½ teaspoon ground cinnamon | ½ teaspoon ground cinnamon |
| ½ teaspoon grated nutmeg | ½ teaspoon grated nutmeg |
| 3 tablespoons milk | 3 tablespoons milk |
| 1 tablespoon golden syrup | 1 tablespoon light corn syrup |

Grease 12 deep fluted bun tins (cup cake pans). Place a halved almond in the bottom of each tin. Cream the butter or margarine and sugar together until light and fluffy, then beat in the egg. Sift together the flour, bicarbonate of soda (baking soda), ginger, cinnamon and nutmeg and fold into the creamed mixture alternating with the milk and syrup. Divide between the tins. Bake in a moderate oven (180°C/350°F, Gas Mark 4) for about 20 minutes or until firm to the touch. Turn out and cool on a wire rack, leaving the buns upside down with the nut on the 'top' of the cake.

MAKES 12

# HONEY BUNS

These are thin round spongy buns sandwiched together with thick honey or jam and dredged with sugar.

| **Metric/Imperial** | **American** |
|---|---|
| 50 g/2 oz butter | ¼ cup butter |
| 50 g/2 oz whipped white fat | ¼ cup shortening |
| 75 g/3 oz light soft brown sugar | ½ cup light brown sugar |
| 1 large egg, beaten | 1 egg, beaten |
| 2 tablespoons clear honey | 2 tablespoons clear honey |
| 175 g/7 oz plain flour | 1¾ cups all-purpose flour |
| ½ teaspoon bicarbonate of soda | ½ teaspoon baking soda |
| jam or thick honey | jam or thick honey |
| icing sugar for dredging | confectioners' sugar for dredging |

Grease two baking sheets. Cream the fats together until mixed, then add the sugar and continue to beat until very light and fluffy. Beat in the egg, followed by the honey. Sift the flour and soda together and work into the mixture. Chill until firm.

Shape the dough into small balls about the size of a walnut and place well apart on the baking sheets. Bake in a moderate oven (180°C/350°F, Gas Mark 4) for about 12 minutes or until well risen and lightly coloured. Remove carefully to a wire rack to cool. When cold, sandwich together with a little jam or thick honey and dredge lightly with icing (confectioners') sugar.

MAKES 10 TO 12

# CHOCOLATE DOT BUNS

These are one-stage sponge buns full of little pieces of chocolate which do not melt during cooking.

**Metric/Imperial**
100 g/4 oz self-raising flour
1 teaspoon baking powder
100 g/4 oz soft margarine
100 g/4 oz caster sugar
2 eggs, beaten
50 g/2 oz chocolate dots

**American**
1 cup self-rising flour
1 teaspoon baking powder
½ cup soft margarine
½ cup sugar
2 eggs, beaten
⅓ cup chocolate chips

Line 16 to 18 bun (muffin) tins with paper cases. Sift the flour and baking powder into a bowl. Add all the other ingredients, except the chocolate dots (chips), and mix well. Beat thoroughly for 2 to 3 minutes until smooth, then stir in the chocolate dots (chips). Divide the mixture between the paper cases. Bake in a moderate oven (180°C/350°F, Gas Mark 4) for 20 to 25 minutes or until well risen and golden. Cool on a wire rack.

MAKES 16 TO 18

*Variations*
*For fairy cakes:* omit the chocolate and replace with currants or sultanas (seedless white raisins).
*For mixed fruit buns:* replace the chocolate with a mixture of currants, chopped mixed candied peel and chopped glacé (candied) cherries.
*For chocolate cherry buns:* use 25 g/1 oz of both chocolate and glacé (candied) cherries.

# CUP CAKES

These little sponge cakes are topped with a thick, soft chocolate icing (frosting).

**Metric/Imperial**
100 g/4 oz butter or
    margarine
100 g/4 oz caster sugar
2 eggs, beaten
100 g/4 oz self-raising flour
1 tablespoon water
few drops of vanilla essence
    or grated rind of ½ orange
    or lemon
ICING:
115 g/4½ oz cooking
    chocolate
40 g/1½ oz butter
4 tablespoons single cream
    or top-of-the-milk
75 g/3 oz icing sugar, sifted

**American**
½ cup butter or margarine
½ cup sugar
2 eggs, beaten
1 cup self-rising flour
1 tablespoon water
few drops of vanilla extract
    or grated rind of ½ orange
    or lemon
FROSTING:
4½ squares semisweet
    chocolate
3 tablespoons butter
¼ cup light cream or half-
    and-half
¾ cup confectioners' sugar,
    sifted

Line 24 to 30 deep bun tins (cup cake pans) with paper cases. (If you use two cases together the extra stiffness will help keep the shape of the cakes and the thick icing.) Cream the butter or margarine and sugar together until light and fluffy, then beat in the eggs one at a time, adding a spoonful of flour after each one. Sift in the remaining flour and fold in, followed by the water and either vanilla essence (extract) or grated fruit rind. Divide between the paper cases, filling them not more than half full. Bake in a moderately hot oven (190°C/375°F, Gas Mark 5) for about 12 minutes or until well risen and light brown. Remove from the tins to a wire rack and leave to cool.

For the icing (frosting), melt the chocolate in a heatproof bowl over a pan of hot water, then beat in the butter until melted. Add the cream and the icing (confectioners') sugar and mix until smooth. Remove from the heat and cool until the icing (frosting) begins to thicken. Spoon the icing (frosting) over each cup cake so that it comes right up to the top of the paper cases. Leave to set. Remove surplus cake cases to use again.

The cakes can be left plain or covered with a little whipped cream or vanilla butter cream, if liked.

MAKES 24 TO 30

*Variations*
*For coffee cup cakes:* replace the water with coffee essence (strong black coffee) and omit other flavourings.
*For chocolate sponge cakes:* replace 20 g/¾ oz (3 tablespoons) of the flour with cocoa powder (unsweetened cocoa).

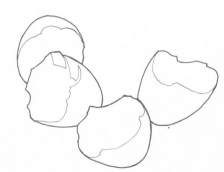

# COFFEE MERINGUE NESTS

Meringue nests flavoured with instant coffee powder and filled with cream or butter cream and fruit, these are suitable for a tea party if made small or for a dessert if made larger.

| Metric/Imperial | American |
|---|---|
| 2 large egg whites | 2 egg whites |
| 100 g/4 oz caster sugar | $\frac{1}{2}$ cup superfine sugar |
| 2 teaspoons instant coffee powder | 2 teaspoons instant coffee powder |
| 300 ml/$\frac{1}{2}$ pint double cream | 1$\frac{1}{4}$ cups whipping cream |
| 1 tablespoon coffee liqueur (optional) | 1 tablespoon coffee liqueur (optional) |
| 225 g/8 oz raspberries | $\frac{1}{2}$ lb raspberries |
| chocolate matchstick sweets for decoration | chocolate matchstick candies for decoration |

Line two baking sheets with non-stick parchment and draw six 9–10 cm/3$\frac{1}{2}$–4 inch circles on them. For smaller nests draw nine to ten 5 cm/2 inch circles. Whisk the egg whites until stiff, dry and standing in peaks. Whisk in half the sugar a little at a time, making sure the meringue is stiff again before adding more sugar. Whisk in the remaining sugar and instant coffee until no speckles remain.

Put the meringue mixture into a piping bag fitted with a large vegetable tube – plain or star – and pipe nest shapes onto the circles on the paper-lined baking sheets. First fill in the circle with meringue, then pipe one or two layers around the edge to make a nest shape. Dry out in a very cool oven (110°C/225°F, Gas mark $\frac{1}{4}$), or the lowest setting on the oven, for 2 to 3 hours or until crisp and firm. Cool, then peel off the paper. Put the meringue nests onto a serving plate.

Whip the cream until stiff and fold in the liqueur, if used. Pipe or spoon into the nests and decorate with raspberries and pieces of chocolate matchstick.

MAKES 6 LARGE OR 9 TO 10 SMALL NESTS

*Variations*
If preferred, the raspberries and chocolate matchsticks can be replaced with coarsely grated plain chocolate. The coffee can be omitted from the meringue to make plain nests and they can be shaped with a spoon if you do not have any piping equipment.

# HAZELNUT MERINGUES

Crisp nutty meringue rounds with a slightly sticky centre, eat these plain or with whipped cream and a variety of toppings.

| Metric/Imperial | American |
|---|---|
| 2 egg whites | 2 egg whites |
| 150 g/5 oz icing sugar, sifted | 1$\frac{1}{4}$ cups confectioners' sugar, sifted |
| 50 g/2 oz hazelnuts, toasted and finely chopped | $\frac{1}{2}$ cup toasted and finely chopped hazelnuts |
| TOPPING (OPTIONAL): | TOPPING (OPTIONAL): |
| whipped cream | whipped cream |
| fresh soft fruit or toasted hazelnuts and Chocolate Curls (see page 118) | fresh soft fruit or toasted hazelnuts and Chocolate Curls (see page 118) |

Cover two baking sheets with non-stick parchment or rice paper. Put the egg whites and sugar into a heatproof bowl and place over a saucepan of gently simmering water. Whisk the mixture until it stands in stiff peaks. Remove from the heat and beat in the nuts. Spoon the mixture into rounds, about 7 cm/2$\frac{1}{2}$ inches in diameter, on the lined baking sheets. Bake in a cool oven (150°C/300°F, Gas Mark 2) for about 30 minutes or until pale cream in colour and easily removed from the sheet. Cool.

Serve each meringue as it is, or topped with whipped cream and a piece of fresh soft fruit or a toasted hazelnut and chocolate curls.

MAKES 9 TO 10

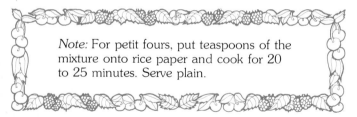

*Note:* For petit fours, put teaspoons of the mixture onto rice paper and cook for 20 to 25 minutes. Serve plain.

# CREAM SLICES

**Metric/Imperial**
¼ recipe quantity Puff Pastry
  (see page 110)
1 recipe quantity
  Confectioners' Custard
  (see page 105)
6–8 tablespoons raspberry
  jam
1 recipe quantity Glacé Icing
  (see page 105)
yellow or pink food
  colouring

**American**
¼ recipe quantity Puff Pastry
  (see page 110)
1 recipe quantity
  Confectioners' Custard
  (see page 105)
6–8 tablespoons raspberry
  jam
1 recipe quantity Glacé Icing
  (see page 105)
yellow or pink food coloring

Lightly grease one or two baking sheets or dampen with cold water. Roll out the dough on a floured surface and trim to a rectangle, 30 × 25 cm/12 × 10 inches. Cut this in half lengthways and transfer to the baking sheets. Leave for 20 minutes. (Alternatively, cut the dough into 12 strips, 13 × 5 cm/ 5 × 2 inches.) Meanwhile, make the confectioners' custard. Cover and cool.

Bake the dough rectangles in a very hot oven (230°C/450°F, Gas Mark 8) for 15 to 20 minutes or until well risen and golden brown. Cool on a wire rack.

To assemble, spread one rectangle of pastry with half the jam and then the confectioners' custard. Spread the remaining jam on the base of the second piece of pastry and place on the custard, jam side down.

Transfer 1 tablespoon of the glacé icing to a small bowl. Colour this fairly strongly with yellow or pink food colouring and put into a greaseproof paper piping bag (see page 126). Spread the white icing over the top of the pastry. Cut the tip off the piping bag and pipe lines across the icing at 1 cm/½ inch intervals. Quickly draw a skewer down the length of the slice at 1 cm/½ inch intervals first from one end and then the other to make feathering. Leave to set. Serve cut into slices.

MAKES 6

*Opposite: Preparing Almond Squares*
*Below: Cream Slices; Almond Squares; Orange Meringue Bars*

# ALMOND SQUARES

These sweet pastry-based cakes have a moist almond and glacé (candied) cherry topping.

| Metric/Imperial | American |
|---|---|
| 75 g/3 oz plain flour | ¾ cup all-purpose flour |
| pinch of salt | pinch of salt |
| 25 g/1 oz caster sugar | 2 tablespoons sugar |
| 50 g/2 oz butter or | ¼ cup butter or margarine |
| margarine | ½ cup halved candied |
| 75 g/3 oz glacé cherries, | cherries, rinsed and dried |
| halved, rinsed and dried | confectioners' sugar for |
| icing sugar for dredging | dredging |
| TOPPING: | TOPPING: |
| 50 g/2 oz butter or | ¼ cup butter or margarine |
| margarine | ¼ cup sugar |
| 50 g/2 oz caster sugar | 1 egg, beaten |
| 1 large egg, beaten | ½ cup ground almonds |
| 50 g/2 oz ground almonds | almond extract |
| almond essence | |

Lightly grease a shallow 20 cm/8 inch square cake tin. Sift the flour and salt into a bowl and mix in the sugar. Add the butter or margarine and rub in until the mixture binds together. Press the dough into the bottom of the tin and arrange the cherries over it.

For the topping, cream the butter or margarine and sugar together until light and fluffy, then beat in the egg. Mix in the ground almonds and a few drops of almond essence (extract) and spread over the cherries. Bake in a moderately hot oven (190°C/375°F, Gas Mark 5) for about 40 minutes or until just set and golden brown. Cool in the tin for a few minutes, then turn carefully onto a wire rack. When cold, dredge with icing (confectioners') sugar and cut into squares.

MAKES 12

# ORANGE MERINGUE BARS

These bars have an orange-flavoured spongy base, a layer of nuts and a crisp meringue topping.

| Metric/Imperial | American |
|---|---|
| 100 g/4 oz butter or | ½ cup butter or margarine |
| margarine | ½ cup sugar |
| 100 g/4 oz caster sugar | 3 eggs, separated |
| 3 eggs, separated | grated rind of 1 orange |
| grated rind of 1 orange | 2 tablespoons orange juice |
| 2 tablespoons orange juice | 2 cups self-rising flour, sifted |
| 200 g/8 oz self-raising flour, | ½ cup chopped walnuts |
| sifted | 1½ cups confectioners' sugar, |
| 50 g/2 oz walnuts, chopped | sifted |
| 150 g/6 oz icing sugar, | |
| sifted | |

Line a shallow oblong cake tin, about 28 × 18 cm/11 × 7 inches, with non-stick parchment. Cream the butter or margarine and sugar together until light and fluffy, then beat in the egg yolks, orange rind and juice. Add the flour and mix to a fairly stiff consistency. Press evenly into the prepared tin and sprinkle all over with the chopped walnuts.

Whisk the egg whites until very stiff and whisk in half of the icing (confectioners') sugar a little at a time. Fold in all but 1 tablespoon of the remaining sugar. Spread evenly over the nuts, pulling the meringue up into peaks. Sprinkle with the reserved icing (confectioners') sugar and bake in a moderate oven (160°C/325°F, Gas Mark 3) for about 45 minutes or until pale brown. Leave in the tin until cold and cut into fingers (bars).

MAKES 12 TO 14

*Variation*
*For lemon meringue bars:* replace the orange rind and juice with lemon.

# MERINGUES

Crisp and crunchy, meringues are always a favourite whether served plain or filled with whipped cream.

**Metric/Imperial**
2 egg whites
50 g/2 oz granulated sugar
50 g/2 oz caster sugar
FILLING:
150 ml/¼ pint double cream
25 g/1 oz hazelnuts, toasted
  and chopped, or a few
  pistachio nuts, blanched
  and chopped

**American**
2 egg whites
¼ cup sugar
¼ cup superfine sugar
FILLING:
⅔ cup whipping cream
¼ cup toasted and chopped
  hazelnuts, or a few
  pistachio nuts, blanched
  and chopped

Line two baking sheets with non-stick parchment. Use a very clean grease-free bowl for making meringues. Whisk the egg whites until very stiff, dry and standing in peaks. Whisk in the granulated sugar, a little at a time, making sure the mixture is stiff again before adding more sugar. Fold in the caster (superfine) sugar; the mixture should still be very stiff.

Put into a large piping bag fitted with a large vegetable tube – either plain or star – and pipe whirls, fingers, shells or other shapes onto the prepared baking sheets. The meringue can also be spooned if preferred. Dry out towards the bottom of a very cool oven (110°C/225°F, Gas Mark ¼) or the lowest setting on the oven for 2 to 3 hours or until set, still white and easily removed from the paper. Leave to cool. Store in an airtight container.

To fill the meringues, whip the cream until stiff and pipe or spread onto the base of one meringue. Sandwich together with another and put onto a plate or into a paper case. Sprinkle nuts over the cream.

MAKES ABOUT 15

*Variations*
*For coloured meringues:* add a few drops of cochineal (red), yellow, orange or green food colouring, using the tip of a skewer to prevent over-colouring.
*For coffee meringues:* whisk in 1 teaspoon instant coffee powder.
*For chocolate meringues:* add 1½ teaspoons sifted cocoa powder (unsweetened cocoa).

# CHOCOLATE ÉCLAIRS

This is the traditional choux pastry éclair, filled with whipped cream and topped with chocolate.

**Metric/Imperial**
1 recipe quantity Choux
  Paste (see page 111)
FILLING:
150 ml/¼ pint double cream
2 tablespoons top-of-the-
  milk
TOPPING:
100 g/4 oz plain chocolate
25 g/1 oz butter

**American**
1 recipe quantity Choux
  Paste (see page 111)
FILLING:
⅔ cup whipping cream
2 tablespoons half-and-half
TOPPING:
4 squares semisweet
  chocolate
2 tablespoons butter

Grease two baking sheets. Put the choux paste into a piping bag fitted with a plain 1 cm/½ inch tube. Pipe the mixture into éclairs on the baking sheets – straight lines about 6 cm/2½ inches long – trimming the mixture from the tube with a knife. Space them fairly well apart to allow for spreading. Bake in a hot oven (220°C/425°F, Gas Mark 7) for 20 to 25 minutes or until well risen and a pale golden brown. Make a slit in the side of each éclair to allow the steam to escape and return to the oven for a few minutes. Cool on a wire rack.

Just before serving, whip the cream and milk (half-and-half) together and use to fill the éclairs. Melt the chocolate in a heatproof bowl over hot water, then stir in the butter until melted. Cool until beginning to thicken, then dip the top of each éclair into the chocolate. Leave to set.

MAKES ABOUT 24

*Variations*
*For coffee éclairs:* use coffee Glacé Icing (see page 105) in place of the melted chocolate.
*For profiteroles:* pipe the mixture into small bun shapes and fill and ice as for éclairs. Alternatively, fill the choux buns with cream then pile into a pyramid shape on a plate. Dredge with icing (confectioners') sugar and serve with a separate rich chocolate sauce.

MAKES 30 PROFITEROLES

# PALMIERS

Sugar-crusted flaky or puff pastry cakes, palmiers are often sandwiched together with whipped cream but are equally good eaten plain.

| **Metric/Imperial** | **American** |
|---|---|
| $\frac{1}{4}$ recipe quantity Puff or Flaky Pastry (see page 110) | $\frac{1}{4}$ recipe quantity Puff or Flaky Pastry (see page 110) |
| caster sugar | sugar |
| FILLING: | FILLING: |
| 250 ml/8 fl oz double cream | 1 cup whipping cream |
| 1 teaspoon sugar | 1 teaspoon sugar |
| vanilla essence | vanilla extract |
| little jam (optional) | little jam (optional) |

Lightly grease one or two baking sheets. Roll out the dough very thinly on a floured surface and trim to a rectangle, approx. $30 \times 25$ cm/$12 \times 10$ inches. Dredge with caster sugar. Fold the long sides halfway to the centre. Dredge with sugar again and fold the folded sides right to the centre. Dredge with sugar and fold in half lengthways to hide the other folds. Press together lightly. Cut right through into 12 even-sized slices. Place the palmiers, cut sides down and well apart, on the baking sheets. Open the tip of each a little and flatten slightly with a round-bladed knife. Dredge with a little more sugar and bake in a hot oven (220°C/425°F, Gas Mark 7) for about 7 minutes or until golden brown. Turn over carefully and continue baking for a further 4 to 5 minutes or until golden brown. Transfer to a wire rack to cool.

Whip the cream until stiff and add sugar and a few drops of vanilla essence (extract) to taste. Pipe or spread the cream over six of the palmiers and top each with another one. If liked, a thin layer of jam can also be added.

MAKES 6 PAIRS OR 12 PLAIN PALMIERS

*Variation*
*For spicy palmiers:* mix $\frac{1}{2}$ teaspoon ground cinnamon or mixed spice (apple pie spice) with sugar before dredging the pastry.

# SACRISTANS

Sacristans are knots, circles, twists and other shapes of puff pastry coated in nuts and spices. This is a good way of using up leftover puff pastry.

| **Metric/Imperial** | **American** |
|---|---|
| $\frac{1}{8}$ recipe quantity Puff Pastry (see page 110) or equivalent in trimmings | $\frac{1}{8}$ recipe quantity Puff Pastry (see page 110) or equivalent in trimmings |
| 1 egg white, lightly beaten | 1 egg white, lightly beaten |
| 25 g/1 oz blanched almonds, chopped | $\frac{1}{4}$ cup chopped blanched almonds |
| 25 g/1 oz caster sugar | 2 tablespoons sugar |
| $1\frac{1}{2}$ teaspoons ground cinnamon or mixed spice | $1\frac{1}{2}$ teaspoons ground cinnamon or apple pie spice |

Grease two baking sheets. Roll out the dough to an oblong, approx. $10 \times 35$ cm/$4 \times 14$ inches. Brush all over with lightly beaten egg white. Sprinkle first with the nuts and then with the sugar mixed with the spice. Cut into strips about 1 cm/$\frac{1}{2}$ inch wide and place on the baking sheets. These strips can also be twisted, tied into knots, shaped into circles, etc. Bake in a hot oven (220°C/425°F, Gas Mark 7) for about 10 minutes or until puffy and well browned. Cool on a wire rack.

MAKES ABOUT 25

# BROWNIES

These chewy nut and chocolate squares have a crisp and crumbly top.

| **Metric/Imperial** | **American** |
|---|---|
| 50 g/2 oz plain chocolate | 2 squares semisweet chocolate |
| 65 g/$2\frac{1}{2}$ oz butter or margarine | $\frac{1}{4}$ cup plus 1 tablespoon butter or margarine |
| 150 g/6 oz caster sugar | $\frac{3}{4}$ cup sugar |
| $\frac{1}{2}$ teaspoon vanilla essence | $\frac{1}{2}$ teaspoon vanilla extract |
| 65 g/$2\frac{1}{2}$ oz self-raising flour | $\frac{1}{2}$ cup plus 2 tablespoons self-rising flour |
| large pinch of salt | large pinch of salt |
| 50 g/2 oz walnuts, chopped | $\frac{1}{2}$ cup chopped walnuts |
| 2 eggs, beaten | 2 eggs, beaten |

Grease and flour a shallow 20 cm/8 inch square cake tin. Put the broken-up chocolate and butter or margarine into a heatproof bowl over a saucepan of hot water. Stir until melted, then beat in the sugar and vanilla essence (extract). Remove from the heat. Sift the flour and salt into a bowl and add the walnuts. Add the eggs and the chocolate mixture and beat until smooth. Pour into the prepared tin and bake in a moderate oven (180°C/350°F, Gas Mark 4) for 35 to 40 minutes or until well risen and just beginning to shrink away from the sides of the tin. Cool in the tin. When cold, cut into 12 squares.

MAKES 12

*Above: Coconut Pyramids. Opposite: Eccles Cakes*

# MATRIMONIAL CAKES

These date and oat cakes, flavoured with brown sugar and lemon, are served at 'shower' parties for the bride-to-be given by her girl friends.

| Metric/Imperial | American |
|---|---|
| 150 g/5 oz plain flour | 1¼ cups all-purpose flour |
| 1 teaspoon bicarbonate of soda | 1 teaspoon baking soda |
| 125 g/4½ oz rolled oats | 1⅓ cups rolled oats |
| 250 g/9 oz soft brown sugar | 1½ cups dark brown sugar |
| 1 teaspoon lemon essence | 1 teaspoon lemon flavoring |
| 175 g/6 oz butter, melted | ¾ cup butter, melted |
| FILLING: | FILLING: |
| 225 g/8 oz stoned dates, chopped | 1¼ cups chopped pitted dates |
| 2 tablespoons soft brown sugar | 2 tablespoons dark brown sugar |
| 1 teaspoon lemon essence | 1 teaspoon lemon flavoring |
| ½ teaspoon grated lemon rind | ½ teaspoon grated lemon rind |
| 150 ml/¼ pint water | ⅔ cup water |

Grease a shallow rectangular cake tin, about 33 × 23 cm/13 × 9 inches. For the filling, put the dates into a small saucepan with the sugar, lemon essence (flavoring), lemon rind and water and bring to the boil. Simmer gently, uncovered, until thick and smooth but not too dry. Stir occasionally. Remove from the heat and cool.

Sift the flour and soda together and mix in the oats and sugar. Bind together with the lemon essence (flavoring) and melted butter. Press half the oat mixture into the tin. Cover with the date filling, spreading it evenly, then cover with the remaining oat crumble. Press down evenly with a round-bladed knife and bake in a moderately hot oven (190°C/375°F, Gas Mark 5) for about 30 minutes or until lightly browned. Cool in the tin and cut into squares.

MAKES ABOUT 20

# COCONUT PYRAMIDS

| Metric/Imperial | American |
|---|---|
| 2 egg whites | 2 egg whites |
| 100 g/4 oz caster sugar | ½ cup sugar |
| 150 g/6 oz desiccated coconut | 2 cups shredded coconut |
| pink or green food colouring | pink or green food coloring |
| glacé cherries for decoration | candied cherries for decoration |

Line one or two baking sheets with rice paper. Whisk the egg whites until stiff and standing in peaks, then whisk in the sugar a little at a time until stiff again. Fold in the coconut. Divide the mixture in half. Using one portion, place seven to eight spoonfuls on the rice paper, placing them fairly well apart and shaping each spoonful into a pyramid. Tint the second portion with a little pink or green food colouring, using the tip of a skewer to prevent over-colouring. Form into seven to eight more pyramids on the rice paper. Bake in a cool oven (150°C/300°F, Gas Mark 2) for about 1 hour or until lightly tinged pale brown. Cool, trim off the surplus rice paper and decorate with halved cherries.

MAKES 14 TO 16

# ECCLES CAKES

| Metric/Imperial | American |
|---|---|
| 25 g/1 oz butter, softened | 2 tablespoons butter, softened |
| 25 g/1 oz soft brown sugar | 2½ tablespoons dark brown sugar |
| 25 g/1 oz mixed candied peel, chopped | 3 tablespoons chopped mixed candied peel |
| 50 g/2 oz currants | ⅓ cup currants |
| ¼ teaspoon mixed spice | ¼ teaspoon apple pie spice |
| ¼ recipe quantity Puff or Flaky Pastry (see page 110) | ¼ recipe quantity Puff or Flaky Pastry (see page 110) |
| 1 egg white | 1 egg white |
| caster sugar for dredging | sugar for dredging |

Grease one or two baking sheets. Mix together the butter, sugar, candied peel, currants and spice. Roll out the dough thinly and cut into 10 cm/4 inch plain rounds. Place a spoonful of the fruit mixture in the centre of each round, moisten the edges of the dough with water and draw up the edges of each to meet in the centre and completely enclose the filling. Press well together and turn over so the join is underneath. Roll out lightly until the currants just show through the dough and the cake is about 0.75 cm/⅓ inch thick. Place on the baking sheets and leave for 10 minutes in a cool place.

Make three slits in the top of each cake, then brush all over with egg white and dredge with sugar. Bake in a hot oven (230°C/450°F, Gas Mark 8) for about 15 minutes or until golden brown and crisp. Cool on a wire rack.

MAKES 8 TO 10

# MINCEMEAT SLICES

This short-textured munchy pastry has a spicy mincemeat layer in the centre.

| Metric/Imperial | American |
|---|---|
| 225 g/8 oz self-raising flour | 2 cups self-rising flour |
| 100 g/4 oz butter or margarine | ½ cup butter or margarine |
| 100 g/4 oz caster sugar | ½ cup sugar |
| 1 egg, beaten | 1 egg, beaten |
| 2–3 tablespoons milk | 2–3 tablespoons milk |
| 5–6 tablespoons mincemeat | 5–6 tablespoons mincemeat |
| 2 tablespoons demerara sugar | 2 tablespoons light brown sugar |

Lightly grease a shallow 20 cm/8 inch square cake tin. Sift the flour, add the fat and rub in until the mixture resembles fine breadcrumbs. Stir in the sugar. Add the beaten egg and sufficient milk to mix to a fairly soft dough. Divide the dough in half and press one portion into the tin to cover the bottom evenly. Spread with the mincemeat, leaving a small margin around the edges plain. Roll out the remaining dough and place over the mincemeat. Press down well, particularly at the edges. Brush lightly with milk and sprinkle with the demerara (light brown) sugar.

Bake in a moderately hot oven (190°C/375°F, Gas Mark 5) for 35 to 40 minutes or until well risen and firm. Cool in the tin for 5 minutes, then cut into fingers (bars) or squares. When cold, remove from the tin and store in an airtight container.

MAKES 12 TO 14

# CREAM HORNS

| Metric/Imperial | American |
|---|---|
| ¼ recipe quantity Puff Pastry (see page 110) | ¼ recipe quantity Puff Pastry (see page 110) |
| 1 egg, beaten | 1 egg, beaten |
| lemon curd, raspberry jam or blackberry jelly | lemon curd, raspberry jam or blackberry jelly |
| 200 ml/8 fl oz double cream, whipped | 1 cup whipping cream, whipped |
| icing sugar for dredging | confectioners' sugar for dredging |

Lightly grease 8 cream horn tins and a baking sheet. Roll out the dough thinly to a long strip, approx. 60 × 11 cm/25 × 4½ inches, and brush all over with beaten egg. Cut into eight long strips about 1 cm/½ inch wide. Wind one strip carefully around each tin, starting at the tip, with the glazed side outwards and overlapping slightly each time. Cut off the dough when the metal is covered. Place on baking sheets with the join underneath. Bake towards the top of a hot oven (220°C/425°F, Gas Mark 7) for 8 to 10 minutes or until well puffed up and golden brown. Cool for a few minutes until the pastry begins to shrink a little, then ease out the tins and leave the pastry horns to cool on a wire rack. When cold, fill the tips of each horn with a little lemon curd, jam or jelly and then fill up with cream. Dredge with sugar before serving.

MAKES 8

# MAIDS OF HONOUR

These little tartlets originated during the reign of Henry VIII at his palace Hampton Court and became favourites with the Queen's maids of honour. The recipe was a closely guarded secret through the ages and for many years they were made only by one shop in Richmond, Surrey. There are now several versions, this being one using curd (cottage) cheese, brandy and mashed potato.

| Metric/Imperial | American |
|---|---|
| ¼ recipe quantity Puff Pastry (see page 110) | ¼ recipe quantity Puff Pastry (see page 110) |
| 100 g/4 oz curd cheese | ½ cup cottage cheese |
| 75 g/3 oz butter, softened | 6 tablespoons butter, softened |
| 2 egg yolks | 2 egg yolks |
| 1 tablespoon brandy | 1 tablespoon brandy |
| 75 g/3 oz caster sugar | 6 tablespoons sugar |
| 40 g/1½ oz cold mashed potato | ¼ cup cold mashed potato |
| 40 g/1½ oz ground almonds | 4½ tablespoons ground almonds |
| grated rind of ½ lemon | grated rind of ½ lemon |
| 1 tablespoon lemon juice | 1 tablespoon lemon juice |
| ¼ teaspoon grated nutmeg | ¼ teaspoon grated nutmeg |

Lightly grease or dampen 16 to 18 patty (shallow muffin) tins. Roll out the dough thinly and cut into 16 to 18 rounds to fit the tins. Line the tins with the dough. Beat the curd (cottage) cheese and butter together until smooth, then gradually beat in the egg yolks and brandy, followed by the sugar, potato, almonds, lemon rind and juice and nutmeg. Beat well until smooth. Spoon into the pastry cases and bake in a moderately hot oven (190°C/375°F, Gas Mark 5) for about 30 minutes or until well risen and golden brown. Cool on a wire rack.

MAKES 16 TO 18

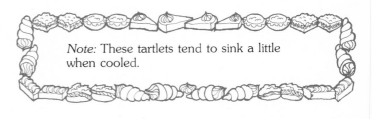

*Note:* These tartlets tend to sink a little when cooled.

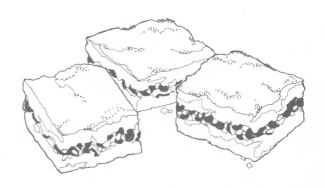

# CREAM PUFFS

Crisp-textured puffy choux buns are achieved by baking the pastry in its own steam. These are filled with whipped cream and coated with toasted almonds or icing (confectioners') sugar.

**Metric/Imperial**
1 recipe quantity Choux
  Paste (see page 111)
300 ml/½ pint double or
  whipping cream
little apricot jam, warmed
50 g/2 oz flaked almonds,
  toasted

**American**
1 recipe quantity Choux
  Paste (see page 111)
1¼ cups whipping cream
little apricot jam, warmed
½ cup flaked almonds,
  toasted

You will need a large shallow tin with a tight fitting lid, or baking sheets with roasting tins or loaf tins to invert over the buns, to keep in the all-important steam. Grease the tin or baking sheets.

Put the choux paste into a piping bag fitted with a plain 1 cm/½ inch tube. Pipe the paste into small buns, leaving plenty of space around them – only three or four per baking sheet – and cover tightly with the lid or tins. If the fit is bad, seal with a flour and water paste. Bake in a moderately hot oven (200°C/400°F, Gas Mark 6) for 40 to 50 minutes or until the buns move when the tin is gently shaken. Do not remove the lid or tins during the cooking time or the steam will escape and the buns sink. Cool on a wire rack.

Just before serving, whip the cream until stiff and put into a piping bag fitted with a small plain tube. Make a small hole in the side of each bun and pipe in the cream. Brush the tops of the buns with a little jam and sprinkle with nuts.

MAKES 12 TO 16

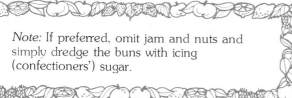

Note: If preferred, omit jam and nuts and simply dredge the buns with icing (confectioners') sugar.

# APPLE CRUNCH

Slices of apple baked into an almond and sugar topping over a rich pastry base, this is equally good as a cake or dessert.

**Metric/Imperial**
150 g/6 oz self-raising flour
pinch of salt
1 tablespoon caster sugar
75 g/3 oz butter
2 large eggs
75 g/3 oz ground almonds
75 g/3 oz demerara sugar
1½ teaspoons mixed spice or
  ground cinnamon
3 eating apples, peeled,
  cored and sliced
2 tablespoons apricot jam
1 teaspoon water

**American**
1½ cups self-rising flour
pinch of salt
1 tablespoon sugar
6 tablespoons butter
2 eggs
¾ cup ground almonds
½ cup light brown sugar
1½ teaspoons apple pie spice
  or ground cinnamon
3 eating apples, peeled,
  cored and sliced
2 tablespoons apricot jam
1 teaspoon water

Grease a deep oblong cake tin, about 28 × 18 cm/11 × 7 inches. Sift together the flour, salt and sugar, then rub in the butter until the mixture resembles fine breadcrumbs. Add one beaten egg and mix to a firm but pliable dough. Put into the tin and press out to cover the bottom evenly. Beat the other egg and use all of it to glaze the pastry.

Mix the almonds, demerara (brown) sugar and spice together and sprinkle over the egg. Arrange the apple slices in overlapping rows across the sugar topping, leaving about 1 cm/½ inch between each row. Heat the jam with the water and brush carefully over the apple slices. Bake in a moderate oven (180°C/350°F, Gas Mark 4) for about 1 hour. Leave to cool in the tin for 10 minutes, then cut into squares. Leave until cold before removing from the tin.

MAKES ABOUT 18

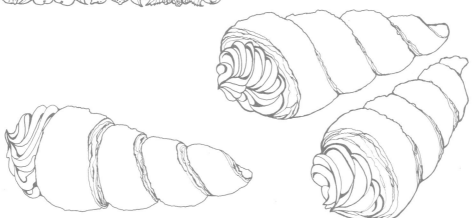

# FAMILY CAKES

## FRENCH ALMOND CAKE

This is a very moist almond-flavoured cake with a sugar topping.

**Metric/Imperial**
100 g/4 oz butter or
  margarine
150 g/5½ oz caster sugar
3 large eggs, beaten
75 g/3 oz ground almonds
40 g/1½ oz plain flour, sifted
almond essence
caster sugar for sprinkling

**American**
½ cup butter or margarine
¾ cup less 1 tablespoon
  sugar
3 eggs, beaten
¾ cup ground almonds
6 tablespoons all-purpose
  flour, sifted
almond extract
sugar for sprinkling

Grease an 18 cm/7 inch deep sandwich tin (layer cake pan) or round cake tin (springform pan) and grease the bottom and sides with greased greaseproof (waxed) paper. Cream the butter or margarine until very soft, then beat in the sugar until light and fluffy. Beat the eggs in one at a time, following each with a little of the ground almonds. Fold in the flour and a few drops of almond essence (extract) and turn the mixture into the prepared tin.

Bake in the centre of a moderate oven (180°C/350°F, Gas Mark 4) for about 50 minutes or until golden brown and firm to the touch. Turn out onto a wire rack, sprinkle with caster sugar and leave to cool.

# CRUNCHY TOPPED ALMOND CAKE

This 'cut-and-come-again' light fruit cake has a crunchy topping of flaked almonds and sugar lumps.

**Metric/Imperial**
175 g/6 oz butter or
    margarine
175 g/6 oz caster sugar
225 g/8 oz plain flour
1½ teaspoons baking powder
50 g/2 oz ground almonds
3 large eggs
350 g/12 oz mixed dried
    fruit
50 g/2 oz mixed candied
    peel, chopped
1 teaspoon instant coffee
    powder
1 tablespoon boiling water
TOPPING:
25 g/1 oz flaked almonds
25 g/1 oz lump sugar,
    roughly crushed

**American**
¾ cup butter or margarine
¾ cup sugar
2 cups all-purpose flour
1½ teaspoons baking powder
½ cup ground almonds
3 eggs
2 cups mixed dried fruit
⅓ cup chopped mixed
    candied peel
1 teaspoon instant coffee
    powder
1 tablespoon boiling water
TOPPING:
¼ cup flaked almonds
3 tablespoons roughly
    crushed sugar lumps

Grease a 20 cm/8 inch square cake tin and line the bottom and sides with greased greaseproof (waxed) paper. Cream the fat and sugar together until light and fluffy. Sift the flour and baking powder together and mix in the ground almonds. Beat the eggs into the creamed mixture one at a time, following each with a spoonful of the flour mixture. Fold in the remaining flour, followed by the mixed fruit and peel. Dissolve the instant coffee in the boiling water, cool a little, then add to the cake mixture. Turn into the prepared tin, level the top and sprinkle first with the nuts and then the sugar.

Bake in a moderate oven (160°C/325°F, Gas Mark 3) for 2 to 2¼ hours or until firm to the touch and a light golden brown. Cool in the tin for about 10 minutes then turn out onto a wire rack. This cake is best if wrapped in foil and kept for 2 to 3 days before cutting.

*Variations*
Replace the coffee liquid with orange juice and add the grated rind of 1 large orange to the mixture. Or omit the dried fruit; add an extra 100 g/4 oz (1 cup) ground almonds to the flour and replace the coffee liquid with milk. Bake for about 1½ hours.

# PARKIN

This type of gingerbread is made with oatmeal and golden syrup (light corn syrup).

| Metric/Imperial | American |
|---|---|
| 100 g/4 oz butter or margarine | $\frac{1}{2}$ cup butter or margarine |
| 100 g/4 oz soft brown sugar | $\frac{2}{3}$ cup dark brown sugar |
| 100 g/4 oz golden syrup | $\frac{1}{3}$ cup light corn syrup |
| 100 g/4 oz oatmeal, medium or fine | $\frac{2}{3}$ cup oatmeal, medium or fine |
| 100 g/4 oz plain flour | 1 cup all-purpose flour |
| $\frac{1}{2}$ teaspoon salt | $\frac{1}{2}$ teaspoon salt |
| 1 teaspoon ground cinnamon and 1 teaspoon mixed spice or 2 teaspoons ground ginger | 1 teaspoon ground cinnamon and 1 teaspoon apple pie spice or 2 teaspoons ground ginger |
| 4 tablespoons milk | $\frac{1}{4}$ cup milk |
| 1 egg, beaten | 1 egg, beaten |
| $\frac{1}{2}$ teaspoon bicarbonate of soda | $\frac{1}{2}$ teaspoon baking soda |

Grease a 20 cm/8 inch square cake tin and line the bottom and sides with greased greaseproof (waxed) paper. Put the butter or margarine, sugar and syrup into a pan and heat until melted and dissolved, then allow to cool a little. Put the oatmeal into a bowl and sift in the flour, salt and spices. Mix well. Add the syrup mixture, 3 tablespoons of the milk and the egg and beat well. Dissolve the soda in the remaining milk, add to the batter and beat well. Pour into the prepared tin and bake in a moderate oven (160°C/325°F, Gas Mark 3) for 1 to 1¼ hours or until golden brown and firm. Turn onto a wire rack to cool. Wrap in foil or store in an airtight container for 3 to 4 days before use.

# FRUITED GINGERBREAD

Raisins and pieces of stem (preserved) ginger are baked into this gingerbread. It can be covered with a lemon glacé icing or served in slices spread with butter.

| Metric/Imperial | American |
|---|---|
| 100 g/4 oz butter | $\frac{1}{2}$ cup butter |
| 100 g/4 oz demerara sugar | $\frac{2}{3}$ cup light brown sugar |
| 100 g/4 oz black treacle | $\frac{1}{3}$ cup molasses |
| 200 g/8 oz plain flour | 2 cups all-purpose flour |
| pinch of salt | pinch of salt |
| 1–1½ teaspoons ground ginger | 1–1½ teaspoons ground ginger |
| 75 g/3 oz raisins or sultanas | $\frac{1}{2}$ cup raisins or seedless white raisins |
| 25 g/1 oz stem ginger, chopped | 3 tablespoons chopped preserved ginger |
| 4 tablespoons milk | $\frac{1}{4}$ cup milk |
| 1 egg, beaten | 1 egg, beaten |
| $\frac{1}{2}$ teaspoon bicarbonate of soda | $\frac{1}{2}$ teaspoon baking soda |

Grease a shallow rectangular cake tin, about 25 × 18 cm/10 × 7 inches, and line with greased greaseproof (waxed) paper. Put the butter, sugar and treacle (molasses) into a pan and heat gently until melted, then cool. Sift the flour, salt and ground ginger into a bowl and mix in the dried fruit and chopped ginger. Add the melted mixture and 3 tablespoons of the milk to the dry ingredients with the egg and mix well. Dissolve the soda in the remaining milk and beat quickly into the batter.

Pour into the prepared tin and bake in a moderate oven (160°C/325°F, Gas Mark 3) for about 1 hour or until firm to the touch. Turn onto a wire rack and cool. Either wrap in foil or store in an airtight container for 3 to 4 days before cutting.

*Variations*
*Lemon or orange:* replace the ground ginger with the finely grated rind of 1 lemon or orange and omit the chopped ginger; cover the top with lemon or orange glacé icing.
*Spiced orange or lemon:* as above but add 1 teaspoon mixed spice (apple pie spice) or ground ginger as well.

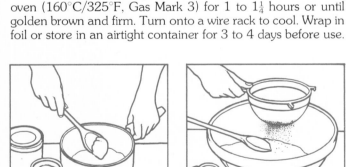

Melt the fat, sugar and syrup

Sift the flour, salt and spices

Add syrup to dry ingredients

Pour into the prepared tin

Bake until well risen and firm

Cool in the tin, then turn out

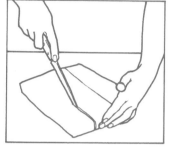
Cut into squares

Decorate with glacé icing

# GOLDEN GINGERBREAD

This is for those who prefer a mild golden gingerbread without the sometimes bitter taste caused by a lot of black treacle (molasses).

| Metric/Imperial | American |
|---|---|
| 225 g/8 oz plain flour | 2 cups all-purpose flour |
| 1½ teaspoons ground ginger | 1½ teaspoons ground ginger |
| large pinch of bicarbonate of soda | large pinch of baking soda |
| 100 g/4 oz light soft brown sugar | ⅔ cup light brown sugar |
| 125 ml/¼ pint milk | ⅔ cup milk |
| 100 g/4 oz butter or margarine | ½ cup butter or margarine |
| 2 eggs | 2 eggs |
| 100 g/4 oz golden syrup | ⅓ cup light corn syrup |
| 1½ tablespoons black treacle | 1½ tablespoons molasses |
| grated rind of 1 lemon | grated rind of 1 lemon |

Grease a rectangular cake tin, 28 × 18 × 4 cm/11 × 7 × 1½ inches and line with greased greaseproof (waxed) paper. Sift the flour, ginger and soda into a bowl and mix in the sugar. Warm the milk, add the fat and heat until it melts – but do not boil. Add the eggs, syrup, black treacle (molasses), lemon rind and warmed milk mixture to the dry ingredients and beat well to give a smooth batter. Pour into the prepared tin and bake in a cool oven (150°C/300°F, Gas Mark 2) for 35 minutes.

Reduce the oven temperature to 140°C/275°F, Gas Mark 1 and continue baking for a further 35 minutes or until well risen and just firm to the touch. Cool in the tin. Turn out, wrap in foil and store for 2 to 3 days before cutting. Serve in squares either plain or drizzled with lemon Glacé Icing (see page 105).

# OLD-FASHIONED GINGER CAKE

This light-textured spicy ginger cake can be served plain or with a glacé icing.

| Metric/Imperial | American |
|---|---|
| 225 g/8 oz plain flour | 2 cups all-purpose flour |
| 1 teaspoon mixed spice | 1 teaspoon apple pie spice |
| 2 teaspoons ground ginger | 2 teaspoons ground ginger |
| 1 teaspoon bicarbonate of soda | 1 teaspoon baking soda |
| 100 g/4 oz butter or margarine | ½ cup butter or margarine |
| 50 g/2 oz soft brown sugar | ⅓ cup dark brown sugar |
| 50 g/2 oz black treacle | 3 tablespoons molasses |
| 150 g/6 oz golden syrup | ½ cup light corn syrup |
| 2 eggs, beaten | 2 eggs, beaten |
| 125 ml/¼ pint milk | ⅔ cup milk |

Grease an 18 cm/7 inch square deep cake tin and line with greased greaseproof (waxed) paper. Sift the flour, spice, ginger and soda into a bowl. Melt the butter or margarine, sugar, treacle (molasses) and syrup in a small pan until melted and dissolved, then cool until lukewarm. Stir the melted mixture into the dry ingredients with the eggs and milk and beat until smooth.

Pour into the prepared tin and bake in a cool oven (150°C/300°F, Gas Mark 2) for 1¼ to 1½ hours or until a skewer inserted into the centre of the cake comes out clean. Cool in the tin, then turn out. Either leave plain or serve covered with a layer of lemon or plain Glacé Icing (see page 105) and a few slices of crystallized (candied) ginger.

# GRANNY'S TEA CAKE

A very good everyday fruited cake, this keeps well for 1 to 2 weeks.

**Metric/Imperial**
350 g/12 oz plain flour
1½ teaspoons bicarbonate of soda
pinch of salt
1 teaspoon mixed spice
½ teaspoon ground cinnamon or grated nutmeg
175 g/6 oz butter or margarine
175 g/6 oz demerara sugar
175 g/6 oz currants
100 g/4 oz sultanas
300 ml/½ pint milk
grated rind of 1 lemon
2 tablespoons lemon juice

**American**
3 cups all-purpose flour
1½ teaspoons baking soda
pinch of salt
1 teaspoon apple pie spice
½ teaspoon ground cinnamon or grated nutmeg
¾ cup butter or margarine
1 cup light brown sugar
1 cup currants
⅔ cup seedless white raisins
1¼ cups milk
grated rind of 1 lemon
2 tablespoons lemon juice

Grease a 900 g/2 lb (9 × 5 × 3 inch) loaf tin and line with greased greaseproof (waxed) paper. Sift the flour, soda, salt and spices into a bowl. Add the butter or margarine and rub in until the mixture resembles breadcrumbs. Stir in the sugar, currants and sultanas (white raisins). Combine the milk, lemon rind and juice (this will make the milk turn sour and form into clots). Add to the dry ingredients and mix to form a soft dropping consistency. If possible, leave the mixture for a couple of hours.

Turn into the prepared tin, level the top and bake in a moderate oven (160°C/325°F, Gas Mark 3) for 1¾ to 2 hours or until well risen and firm to the touch. Cool in the tin for 5 minutes before turning onto a wire rack. Wrap in foil or store in an airtight container for 2 to 3 days before use.

# COFFEE LOAF CAKE

The mild coffee flavour mingles well with currants and walnuts in this family loaf cake.

**Metric/Imperial**
200 g/8 oz self-raising flour
100 g/4 oz butter or margarine
100 g/4 oz demerara sugar
100 g/4 oz currants
50 g/2 oz walnuts, chopped
2 eggs, beaten
2 tablespoons coffee essence
3–4 tablespoons milk

**American**
2 cups self-rising flour
½ cup butter or margarine
⅔ cup light brown sugar
⅔ cup currants
½ cup chopped walnuts
2 eggs, beaten
2 tablespoons strong black coffee
3–4 tablespoons milk

Grease a 900 g/2 lb (9 × 5 × 3 inch) loaf tin and line the bottom and sides with greased greaseproof (waxed) paper. Sift the flour into a bowl. Add the fat and rub in until the mixture resembles fine breadcrumbs. Mix in the sugar, currants and walnuts. Add the eggs, coffee essence (strong black coffee) and sufficient milk to mix to a soft dropping consistency. Turn into the prepared tin and bake in a moderate oven (180°C/350°F, Gas Mark 4) for 1 to 1¼ hours or until well risen and firm to the touch. Turn out onto a wire rack to cool.

*Granny's Tea Cake*

# FARMHOUSE CHERRY CAKE

A plain lemon-flavoured cake, this is filled with cherries.

| Metric/Imperial | American |
|---|---|
| 100 g/4 oz glacé cherries | 2/3 cup candied cherries |
| 250 g/10 oz self-raising flour | 2½ cups self-rising flour |
| pinch of salt | pinch of salt |
| 100 g/4 oz butter or margarine | ½ cup butter or margarine |
| 2 teaspoons grated lemon rind | 2 teaspoons grated lemon rind |
| 100 g/4 oz caster sugar | ½ cup sugar |
| 2 eggs, beaten | 2 eggs, beaten |
| 3 tablespoons milk | 3 tablespoons milk |

Grease a 15 cm/6 inch round deep cake tin and line the bottom and sides with greased greaseproof (waxed) paper. Cut the cherries into small pieces, rinse well and dry very thoroughly. Sift the flour and salt into a bowl. Add the fat and rub in until the mixture resembles fine breadcrumbs. Stir in the lemon rind, sugar and cherries, then add the eggs and milk and mix well. Put into the prepared tin and bake in a moderately hot oven (190°C/375°F, Gas Mark 5) for about 1 hour or until well risen, firm to the touch and golden brown. Cover with foil after 45 minutes if sufficiently browned. Turn out onto a wire rack and leave to cool.

*Variations*
*Coconut:* replace 25 g/1 oz (¼ cup) flour with desiccated (shredded) coconut.
*Date:* replace the cherries with chopped dates or dried fruit.

# EVERYDAY FRUIT LOAF

A good basic loaf flavoured with nutmeg and ginger; the top is strewed with slivers of almonds.

| Metric/Imperial | American |
|---|---|
| 75 g/3 oz plain flour | ¾ cup all-purpose flour |
| 75 g/3 oz self-raising flour | ¾ cup self-rising flour |
| ½ teaspoon grated nutmeg | ½ teaspoon grated nutmeg |
| ¾ teaspoon ground ginger | ¾ teaspoon ground ginger |
| 40 g/1½ oz ground almonds | 4½ tablespoons ground almonds |
| grated rind of ½ lemon (optional) | grated rind of ½ lemon (optional) |
| 100 g/4 oz butter or margarine | ½ cup butter or margarine |
| 100 g/4 oz caster sugar | ½ cup sugar |
| 3 large eggs, beaten | 3 eggs, beaten |
| 250 g/9 oz mixed dried fruit | 1½ cups mixed dried fruit |
| 25 g/1 oz whole blanched almonds | ¼ cup whole blanched almonds |

Grease a 900 g/2 lb (9 × 5 × 3 inch) loaf tin and line the bottom and sides with greased greaseproof (waxed) paper. Sift the flours, nutmeg and ginger into a bowl and mix in the almonds and lemon rind, if used. Cream the butter or margarine and sugar together until light and fluffy, then beat in the eggs one at a time, following each with a spoonful of the flour mixture. Fold in the remaining flour, followed by the dried fruit, and turn into the tin. Level the top. Cut the almonds into slivers and sprinkle over the top. Bake in a moderate oven (180°C/350°F, Gas Mark 4) for 45 minutes.

Reduce the temperature to 160°C/325°F, Gas Mark 3 and continue baking for 40 to 50 minutes or until a skewer inserted into the centre comes out clean. Cool on a wire rack.

# OLD-FASHIONED PLUM CAKE

This traditional British fruit cake used to be served with a glass of wine or sherry to unexpected guests. It is a rich cake which is not usually covered with marzipan or icing.

| Metric/Imperial | American |
|---|---|
| 200 g/8 oz butter or margarine | 1 cup butter or margarine |
| 100 g/4 oz soft brown sugar | $\frac{2}{3}$ cup light brown sugar |
| 4 tablespoons golden syrup | $\frac{1}{4}$ cup light corn syrup |
| 4 eggs | 4 eggs |
| 225 g/9 oz plain flour | $2\frac{1}{4}$ cups all-purpose flour |
| 2 teaspoons mixed spice | 2 teaspoons apple pie spice |
| 1 teaspoon grated nutmeg | 1 teaspoon grated nutmeg |
| pinch of salt | pinch of salt |
| finely grated rind of 1 orange and 1 lemon | finely grated rind of 1 orange and 1 lemon |
| 50 g/2 oz ground almonds | $\frac{1}{2}$ cup ground almonds |
| 450 g/1 lb raisins | $2\frac{1}{2}$ cups raisins |
| 350 g/12 oz sultanas | 2 cups seedless white raisins |
| 450 g/1 lb currants | $2\frac{1}{2}$ cups currants |
| 100 g/4 oz mixed candied peel, chopped | $\frac{2}{3}$ cup chopped mixed candied peel |
| 1 tablespoon sherry | 1 tablespoon sherry |

Grease a 23 cm/9 inch square deep cake tin and line the bottom and sides with greased greaseproof (waxed) paper. Cream the fat, sugar and syrup together until light and fluffy. Beat in the eggs one at a time, following each with a spoonful of flour. Sift the remaining flour with the spices and salt and fold into the mixture with the fruit rind and ground almonds. Finally fold in the dried fruit, peel and sherry. Turn into the prepared tin and slightly hollow the centre.

Wrap several thicknesses of newspaper round the outside of the tin and secure with string. Stand the tin on a folded newspaper. Bake in a cool oven (150°C/300°F, Gas Mark 2) for $4\frac{1}{2}$ to 5 hours or until a skewer inserted into the centre of the cake comes out clean. Cool in the tin for 10 minutes, then turn onto a wire rack to cool completely. Store wrapped in foil or in an airtight container. This cake improves with keeping.

# DARK CHOCOLATE CAKE

A moist chocolate cake with a slightly bitter taste, this is very quick to make.

| Metric/Imperial | American |
|---|---|
| 175 g/6 oz plain flour | $1\frac{1}{2}$ cups all-purpose flour |
| 2 tablespoons cocoa powder | 2 tablespoons unsweetened cocoa |
| 1 teaspoon bicarbonate of soda | 1 teaspoon baking soda |
| 1 teaspoon baking powder | 1 teaspoon baking powder |
| 125 g/5 oz caster sugar | $\frac{1}{2}$ cup plus 2 tablespoons sugar |
| 2 tablespoons black treacle | 2 tablespoons molasses |
| 2 eggs | 2 eggs |
| 125 ml/scant $\frac{1}{4}$ pint corn oil | $\frac{2}{3}$ cup corn oil |
| 125 ml/scant $\frac{1}{4}$ pint milk | $\frac{2}{3}$ cup milk |
| $\frac{1}{2}$–1 recipe quantity Chocolate Icing (see page 106) | $\frac{1}{2}$–1 recipe quantity Chocolate Frosting (see page 106) |
| mimosa balls for decoration | mimosa balls for decoration |

Grease an 18 cm/7 inch round or square deep cake tin and line the bottom and sides with greased greaseproof (waxed) paper. Sift the flour, cocoa, soda and baking powder into a bowl. Add the sugar. Make a well in the centre and add the treacle (molasses) and eggs. Gradually beat in the oil and milk and beat well until smooth. Pour the batter into the prepared tin and bake in a moderate oven (160°C/325°F, Gas Mark 3) for 1 to $1\frac{1}{4}$ hours or until well risen and just firm to the touch. The cake should also just begin to shrink from the sides of the tin. Turn onto a wire rack to cool.

Make up the rich chocolate icing (frosting) and spread over the top of the cake. (If liked, cover the sides as well.) Decorate with mimosa balls and leave to set.

*Note:* Golden syrup (light corn syrup) can be used in place of black treacle (molasses) to give a sweeter cake.

# ROSE CAKE

The rose water gives a mellow 'scented' taste and aroma to this lightly fruited layer cake.

**Metric/Imperial**
200 g/8 oz butter or margarine
200 g/8 oz caster sugar
3 large eggs
250 g/10 oz self-raising flour
½ teaspoon grated nutmeg
75 g/3 oz sultanas
75 g/3 oz currants
2 teaspoons triple-strength rose water or rose flavouring
silver balls for decoration
FILLING:
150 g/6 oz butter
300 g/12 oz icing sugar, sifted
1–2 teaspoons triple-strength rose water or rose flavouring
pink food colouring (optional)

**American**
1 cup butter or margarine
1 cup sugar
3 eggs
2½ cups self-rising flour
½ teaspoon grated nutmeg
½ cup seedless white raisins
½ cup currants
2 teaspoons triple-strength rose water or rose flavoring
silver balls for decoration
FILLING:
¾ cup butter
2⅔ cups confectioners' sugar, sifted
1–2 teaspoons triple-strength rose water or flavoring
pink food coloring (optional)

Grease two fairly deep 23 cm/9 inch sandwich tins (layer cake pans) and line the bottoms and sides with greased greaseproof (waxed) paper. Cream the fat and sugar together until light and fluffy, then beat in the eggs one at a time, following each with a spoonful of flour. Sift the remaining flour with the nutmeg and fold into the mixture, followed by the sultanas (white raisins), currants and rose water. Divide between the tins, slightly hollowing out the centres. Bake in a moderately hot oven (190°C/375°F, Gas Mark 5) for 30 to 40 minutes or until well risen and firm to the touch. Turn out and cool on a wire rack.

For the filling, cream the butter and sugar together until light and fluffy, adding the rose water and a little water, if necessary, to give a soft spreading consistency. A little pink food colouring can be added if liked. Use some of this butter cream to sandwich the cakes together. Put the remainder in a piping bag fitted with a large star tube. Decorate the top with lines of rosettes or zig-zags and silver balls. Crystallized or sugar roses can also be used for decoration.

# APPLE CAKE

This moist fruit cake is improved by storing in foil for 2 to 3 days before use.

**Metric/Imperial**
225 g/8 oz plain flour
½ teaspoon bicarbonate of soda
1 teaspoon mixed spice
½ teaspoon ground cinnamon
100 g/4 oz butter or margarine
150 g/6 oz caster sugar
2 eggs, beaten
150 g/6 oz currants
100 g/4 oz sultanas
50 g/2 oz mixed candied peel, chopped
225 g/8 oz cooking apples, peeled, cored and coarsely grated

**American**
2 cups all-purpose flour
½ teaspoon baking soda
1 teaspoon apple pie spice
½ teaspoon ground cinnamon
½ cup butter or margarine
¾ cup sugar
2 eggs, beaten
1 cup currants
⅔ cup seedless white raisins
⅓ cup chopped mixed candied peel
½ lb cooking apples, peeled, cored and coarsely grated

Grease a 20 cm/8 inch round deep cake tin and line the bottom and sides with greased greaseproof (waxed) paper. Sift the flour, soda and spices together in a bowl. Cream the fat and sugar together until light and fluffy, then beat in the eggs one at a time, following each with a spoonful of flour. Fold in the remaining flour, followed by the dried fruits, peel and grated apple. Turn into the prepared tin and level the top. Bake in a moderate oven (180°C/350°F, Gas Mark 4) for 1¼ to 1½ hours or until golden brown and firm to the touch. Cool in the tin for about 10 minutes before turning out onto a wire rack to cool.

# DEVIL'S FOOD CAKE

Dark, rich and very chocolatey, this cake is filled and iced with American (boiled) frosting.

| Metric/Imperial | American |
|---|---|
| 100 g/4 oz butter or margarine | ½ cup butter or margarine |
| 100 g/4 oz soft brown sugar | ⅔ cup dark brown sugar |
| 100 g/4 oz golden syrup | ⅓ cup light corn syrup |
| 150 g/6 oz plain flour | 1½ cups all-purpose flour |
| 65 g/2½ oz cocoa powder | ⅔ cup unsweetened cocoa |
| 1 egg, beaten | 1 egg, beaten |
| 1 teaspoon bicarbonate of soda | 1 teaspoon baking soda |
| 150 ml/¼ pint warm milk | ⅔ cup warm milk |
| 1 recipe quantity American Frosting (see page 106) | 1 recipe quantity Boiled Frosting (see page 106) |

Grease two 20 cm/8 inch sandwich tins (layer cake pans) and line the bottoms with greased greaseproof (waxed) paper. Put the fat, sugar and syrup into a saucepan and heat gently until melted. Sift the flour and cocoa into a bowl, add the melted ingredients and mix until smooth. Add the egg and beat in. Dissolve the soda in the milk, add to the mixture and beat very thoroughly. Pour into the prepared tins and bake in a moderate oven (180°C/350°F, Gas Mark 4) for about 30 minutes or until firm. Turn out onto a wire rack and leave to cool.

Make up the American (boiled) frosting. Use a little to sandwich the cakes together and the remainder to mask the whole cake. Pull the frosting up into small peaks with a palette knife and leave to set.

# MADEIRA CAKE

This traditional British cake is flavoured with lemon and has a piece of citron peel baked into the top.

| Metric/Imperial | American |
|---|---|
| 150 g/6 oz butter | ¾ cup butter |
| 150 g/6 oz caster sugar | ¾ cup sugar |
| 3 eggs, beaten | 3 eggs, beaten |
| 150 g/6 oz self-raising flour | 1½ cups self-rising flour |
| 75 g/3 oz plain flour | ¾ cup all-purpose flour |
| grated rind of 1 large lemon | grated rind of 1 large lemon |
| 1 tablespoon lemon juice | 1 tablespoon lemon juice |
| piece of candied citron peel | piece of candied citron peel |

Grease an 18 cm/7 inch round deep cake tin and line the bottom with greased greaseproof (waxed) paper. Cream the butter and sugar together until light and fluffy and very pale in colour. Beat in the eggs one at a time. Sift the flours together and fold into the mixture, followed by the lemon rind and juice. Turn into the prepared tin and top with a few thin slices of citron peel. Bake in a moderate oven (160°C/325°F, Gas Mark 3) for about 1¼ hours or until well risen, firm and browned. Cool in the tin for 10 minutes, then turn out onto a wire rack.

*Opposite: White Chiffon Cake; Devil's Food Cake*
*Right: Madeira Cake*

# WHITE CHIFFON CAKE

An angel cake mixture, this may be baked in a ring mould (tube pan) or round cake tin.

| Metric/Imperial | American |
|---|---|
| 40 g/1½ oz plain flour | 6 tablespoons all-purpose flour |
| 40 g/1½ oz cornflour | 6 tablespoons cornstarch |
| pinch of salt | pinch of salt |
| 1 teaspoon baking powder | 1 teaspoon baking powder |
| 1 teaspoon cream of tartar | 1 teaspoon cream of tartar |
| 5 egg whites | 5 egg whites |
| 140 g/5 oz caster sugar | ½ cup plus 2 tablespoons sugar |
| vanilla essence | vanilla extract |
| 1 recipe quantity chocolate American Frosting (see page 106) | 1 recipe quantity chocolate Boiled Frosting (see page 106) |
| DECORATION: | DECORATION: |
| few pieces of candied angelica | few pieces of candied angelica |
| few glacé cherries (optional) | few candied cherries (optional) |

Lightly grease a 1.2–1.5 litre/2–2½ pint (5–6 cup) ring mould (tube pan) or a 20 cm/8 inch round deep cake tin (springform pan). Sift the flour, cornflour (cornstarch), salt, baking powder and cream of tartar together two or three times. Beat the egg whites to a stiff froth (not as stiff as for meringue), then fold in the sugar lightly and carefully, followed by the dry ingredients and a few drops of vanilla essence (extract). Spoon into the prepared tin and bake in the centre of a moderate oven (180°C/350°F, Gas Mark 4) for about 45 minutes or until well risen and firm to the touch. After 30 minutes lay a sheet of greaseproof (waxed) paper over the cake to prevent over browning.

Turn onto a wire rack and leave with the tin on the cake until it is cool and slips out easily. Cover with American (boiled) frosting and decorate with pieces of angelica and cherry, if liked.

Chop half the almonds and mix with the fruit

Mix to a dropping consistency

Arrange the almonds in circles all over the top

Test the cake by inserting a skewer into the centre

## BOILED FRUIT CAKE

The texture and flavour of this cake are excellent but it can have a tendency to sink very slightly in the centre, particularly if the door of the oven is opened too soon during cooking. The toasted marzipan topping is optional.

**Metric/Imperial**
275 ml/½ pint water
100 g/4 oz margarine
125 g/5 oz soft brown sugar
325 g/12 oz mixed dried
   fruit
2 teaspoons mixed spice
½ teaspoon grated nutmeg
275 g/10 oz plain flour
2 teaspoons bicarbonate of
   soda
1 teaspoon baking powder
1 egg
finely grated rind of 1
   orange
TOPPING (OPTIONAL):
little clear honey
½ recipe quantity Marzipan
   (see page 104) or
   225 g/8 oz bought

**American**
1¼ cups water
½ cup margarine
¾ cup plus 1 tablespoon light
   brown sugar
2 cups mixed dried fruit
2 teaspoons apple pie spice
½ teaspoon grated nutmeg
2½ cups all-purpose flour
2 teaspoons baking soda
1 teaspoon baking powder
1 egg
finely grated rind of 1
   orange
TOPPING (OPTIONAL):
little clear honey
½ recipe quantity Marzipan
   (see page 104) or ½ lb
   bought

Grease a 20 cm/8 inch round deep cake tin and line the bottom and sides with greased greaseproof (waxed) paper. Put the water into a saucepan. Add the margarine, sugar, dried fruit and spices. Bring to the boil and simmer gently for 20 minutes. Cool, then fold in the flour sifted with the soda and baking powder, the egg and orange rind. Turn into the prepared tin and bake in a moderate oven (180°C/350°F, Gas Mark 4) for about 1¼ hours or until a skewer inserted into the centre comes out clean. Turn the cake onto a wire rack to cool.

If adding the topping, brush the top of the cake with honey. Roll out the marzipan to fit the top of the cake, place in position and crimp the edges. Mark a criss-cross pattern on the marzipan and put under a moderate grill (broiler) until lightly tinged brown. Leave to cool.

## DUNDEE CAKE

This fairly light fruit cake has a traditional topping of blanched almonds.

**Metric/Imperial**
150 g/6 oz plain flour
100 g/4 oz self-raising flour
pinch of salt
75 g/3 oz blanched almonds
200 g/8 oz currants
200 g/8 oz raisins
200 g/8 oz sultanas
100 g/4 oz mixed candied
   peel, chopped
grated rinds of 1 orange and
   1 lemon
200 g/8 oz butter
200 g/8 oz light soft brown
   sugar
4 large eggs
little lemon or orange juice

**American**
1½ cups all-purpose flour
1 cup self-rising flour
pinch of salt
¾ cup blanched almonds
1⅓ cups currants
1⅓ cups raisins
1⅓ cups seedless white raisins
⅔ cup chopped mixed
   candied peel
grated rinds of 1 orange and
   1 lemon
1 cup butter
1⅓ cups light brown sugar
4 eggs
little lemon or orange juice

Grease a 20 cm/8 inch round deep cake tin and line the bottom and sides with greased greaseproof (waxed) paper. Sift the flours and salt together. Chop half of the almonds and mix with the dried fruits, peel and fruit rinds. Cream the butter until soft, then add the sugar and continue creaming until very light and fluffy and pale in colour. Beat in the eggs one at a time, following each with a spoonful of flour. Fold in the remaining flour followed by the fruits and a little fruit juice, if necessary, to give a dropping consistency.

Turn the mixture into the prepared tin and make a slight hollow in the centre. Split the remaining almonds in half (dip briefly in boiling water if they are too hard) and arrange in concentric circles all over the top of the cake. Bake in a moderate oven (160°C/325°F, Gas Mark 3) for 3 to 3½ hours or until a skewer inserted into the centre of the cake comes out clean. Cover the top of the cake with a piece of foil if it becomes too brown. Cool in the tin for 10 to 15 minutes, then turn out onto a wire rack to cool completely.

# DATE AND WALNUT CAKE

**Metric/Imperial**
150 g/6 oz margarine
75 g/3 oz caster sugar
3 tablespoons clear honey
3 eggs, beaten
175 g/7 oz self-raising flour
½ teaspoon ground
    cinnamon (optional)
grated rind of ½ lemon
75 g/3 oz stoned dates,
    chopped
40 g/1½ oz walnuts, halved

**American**
¾ cup margarine
6 tablespoons sugar
3 tablespoons clear honey
3 eggs, beaten
1¾ cups self-rising flour
½ teaspoon ground
    cinnamon (optional)
grated rind of ½ lemon
½ cup chopped pitted dates
⅓ cup walnut halves

Grease a 20 cm/8 inch square cake tin and line the bottom and sides with greased greaseproof (waxed) paper. Cream the margarine, sugar and honey together until light and fluffy. Beat in the eggs one at a time, following each with a spoonful of flour. Sift the remaining flour with the cinnamon and fold into the mixture, followed by the lemon rind and dates. Turn into the prepared tin, level the top and cover with the walnut halves. Bake in a moderately hot oven (190°C/375°F, Gas Mark 5) for 40 to 45 minutes or until well risen and firm to the touch. Cool in the tin for a few minutes, then turn out onto a wire rack to cool completely.

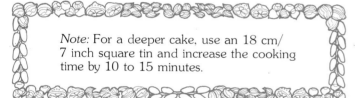

*Note:* For a deeper cake, use an 18 cm/7 inch square tin and increase the cooking time by 10 to 15 minutes.

# WHOLEWHEAT FRUIT CAKE

The brown flour in this recipe gives an interesting nutty taste.

**Metric/Imperial**
100 g/4 oz self-raising flour
½ teaspoon grated nutmeg
½ teaspoon ground
    cinnamon
large pinch of salt
100 g/4 oz wholemeal flour
100 g/4 oz butter or
    margarine
150 g/6 oz demerara sugar
300 g/10 oz mixed dried
    fruit
50 g/2 oz mixed candied
    peel, chopped
2 eggs, beaten
about 5 tablespoons milk

**American**
1 cup self-rising flour
½ teaspoon grated nutmeg
½ teaspoon ground
    cinnamon
large pinch of salt
1 cup wholewheat or
    graham flour
½ cup butter or margarine
1 cup light brown sugar
1⅔ cups mixed dried fruit
⅓ cup chopped mixed
    candied peel
2 eggs, beaten
about ⅓ cup milk

Grease an 18 cm/7 inch square deep cake tin and line the bottom and sides with greased greaseproof (waxed) paper. Sift the self-raising (self-rising) flour with the spices and salt into a bowl and mix in the brown flour. Add the fat and rub in until the mixture resembles breadcrumbs. Stir in the sugar, dried fruit and peel, then add the eggs and sufficient milk to give a fairly soft dropping consistency.

Turn the mixture into the prepared tin and bake in a moderate oven (180°C/350°F, Gas Mark 4) for 1¼ to 1½ hours or until well risen and firm to the touch. Turn out onto a wire rack to cool.

*Above: Preparing a Rich Cherry Cake
Below: Cherry and Walnut Loaf*

# NO-COOK CHOCOLATE CAKE

| Metric/Imperial | American |
|---|---|
| 175 g/6 oz digestive biscuits, crushed | 1½ cups crushed graham crackers |
| 50 g/2 oz walnuts, chopped | ½ cup chopped walnuts |
| 50 g/2 oz raisins, roughly chopped | ⅓ cup roughly chopped raisins |
| 50 g/2 oz plain chocolate, coarsely grated | 2 squares semisweet chocolate, coarsely grated |
| 50 g/2 oz soft brown sugar | ⅓ cup dark brown sugar |
| 75 g/3 oz butter or margarine | 6 tablespoons butter or margarine |
| 75 g/3 oz golden syrup | ¼ cup light corn syrup |
| TOPPING: | TOPPING: |
| 50 g/2 oz plain chocolate | 2 squares semisweet chocolate |

Place a greased 15–18 cm/6–7 inch plain or fluted deep flan ring on a flat plate, or grease a loose-bottomed deep cake tin of the same size.

Mix the biscuits (graham crackers), walnuts, raisins, grated chocolate and sugar together. Melt the fat and syrup together and add to the rest of the ingredients. Mix well and press into the flan ring or cake tin. Chill overnight or until thoroughly set.

Remove the ring carefully or press out of the tin. For the topping, melt the chocolate in a heatproof bowl over a pan of hot water. Beat until smooth, then spread over the top of the cake. As it sets mark the chocolate into a pattern with a round-bladed knife or a fork. Leave until completely set.

# RICH CHERRY CAKE

| Metric/Imperial | American |
|---|---|
| 150 g/6 oz glacé cherries, quartered, rinsed and well dried | 1 cup quartered candied cherries, rinsed and well dried |
| 1 tablespoon cornflour | 1 tablespoon cornstarch |
| 150 g/6 oz self-raising flour | 1½ cups self-rising flour |
| 75 g/3 oz plain flour | ¾ cup all-purpose flour |
| 150 g/6 oz butter or margarine | ¾ cup butter or margarine |
| 150 g/6 oz caster sugar | ¾ cup sugar |
| 3 eggs, beaten | 3 eggs, beaten |
| 1 tablespoon milk | 1 tablespoon milk |
| 1 recipe quantity lemon Glacé Icing (see page 105) | 1 recipe quantity lemon Glacé Icing (see page 105) |

Grease an 18 cm/7 inch round deep cake tin and line the bottom and sides with greased greaseproof (waxed) paper. Coat the cherries in the cornflour (cornstarch) and shake off the surplus. Sift the flours together. Cream the fat and sugar together until light and fluffy. Beat in the eggs one at a time, adding a spoonful of flour after each one. Fold in the remaining flour alternating with the milk. Finally fold in the cherries and turn into the tin. Bake in a moderate oven (160°C/325°F, Gas Mark 3) for 1¼ to 1½ hours or until well risen, light brown and firm to the touch. Turn out onto a wire rack to cool.

Pour the icing over the top of the cake and allow to run down the sides. Decorate the top with halved cherries, if you like.

# CHERRY AND WALNUT LOAF

*No-cook Chocolate Cake; Rich Cherry Cake*

A one-stage cake, this is very quick and easy to make.

**Metric/Imperial**
150 g/6 oz soft (luxury) margarine
150 g/6 oz caster sugar
3 eggs, beaten
75 g/3 oz glacé cherries, quartered, rinsed and well dried
200 g/8 oz plain flour
½ teaspoon baking powder
40 g/1½ oz walnuts, roughly chopped
TOPPING:
100 g/4 oz glacé cherries, halved
3 tablespoons apricot jam

**American**
¾ cup soft margarine
¾ cup sugar
3 eggs, beaten
½ cup quartered candied cherries, rinsed and well dried
2 cups all-purpose flour
½ teaspoon baking powder
⅓ cup roughly chopped walnuts
TOPPING:
⅔ cup halved candied cherries
3 tablespoons apricot jam

Grease a 900 g/2 lb (9 × 5 × 3 inch) loaf tin and line the bottom and sides with greased greaseproof (waxed) paper. Put all the ingredients for the cake together in a mixing bowl and beat well with a wooden spoon for 4 to 5 minutes or until well mixed and smooth. (An electric mixer will take 2 to 3 minutes.) Turn into the prepared tin and smooth the top. Arrange the halved cherries over the top of the cake. Bake in a moderate oven (160°C/325°F, Gas mark 3) for 1½ to 1¾ hours or until well risen and firm to the touch. Cool in the tin for 5 minutes, then turn out onto a wire rack.

Heat the apricot jam and sieve (strain), then brush over the cherry topping. Leave to cool.

*Variation*
*For a one-stage mixed fruit cake:* replace the quartered cherries with 250 g/10 oz (1½ cups) dried mixed fruit and 50 g/2 oz (⅓ cup) each of chopped mixed candied peel and chopped glacé (candied) cherries. Bake in a greased and lined 18 cm/ 7 inch round deep cake tin for 1¾ to 2 hours or until well risen and firm to the touch.

# CARAWAY FRUIT RING

The flavour of caraway seeds blends well with chopped cherries and peel in this cake.

**Metric/Imperial**
150 g/6 oz butter or margarine
150 g/6 oz caster sugar
3 large eggs, beaten
200 g/8 oz self-raising flour, sifted
100 g/4 oz glacé cherries, quartered, rinsed and dried
75 g/3 oz mixed candied peel, chopped
2–3 teaspoons caraway seeds
1–2 tablespoons milk
TOPPING:
½ recipe quantity white Glacé Icing (see page 105)
50–75 g/2–3 oz glacé cherries, halved

**American**
¾ cup butter or margarine
¾ cup sugar
3 eggs, beaten
2 cups self-rising flour, sifted
⅔ cup quartered candied cherries, rinsed and dried
½ cup chopped mixed candied peel
2–3 teaspoons caraway seeds
1–2 tablespoons milk
TOPPING:
½ recipe quantity white Glacé Icing (see page 105)
⅓–½ cup halved candied cherries

Grease a 1 litre/2 pint (2½ pint) ring mould (tube pan) or a 21 cm/8½ inch round loose-bottomed spring-release cake tin fitted with a fluted tubular base. Cream the fat and sugar together until very light and fluffy and pale in colour. Beat in the eggs one at a time, following each with a spoonful of flour. Fold in the remaining flour followed by the cherries, peel, caraway seeds and sufficient milk to give a dropping consistency. Turn into the tin and level the top. Bake in a moderate oven (180°C/350°F, Gas Mark 4) for 30 minutes.

Reduce the temperature to 160°C/325°F, Gas Mark 3 and continue baking for 30 to 35 minutes or until firm to the touch. Turn out onto a wire rack and leave to cool.

For the topping, make up the glacé icing and stir in the cherries. As it begins to thicken spoon the icing over the top of the ring and let it run down the sides of the cake. Leave to set.

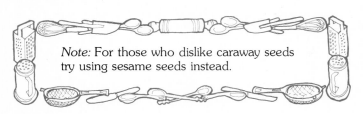

*Note:* For those who dislike caraway seeds try using sesame seeds instead.

# COCONUT STREUSEL CAKE

This moist, coconut-flavoured cake has a crunchy sugar topping.

**Metric/Imperial**
350 g/12 oz self-raising flour
pinch of salt
200 g/8 oz butter or margarine
150 g/6 oz caster sugar
100 g/4 oz desiccated coconut
3 eggs, beaten
about 75 ml/3 fl oz milk
STREUSEL TOPPING:
40 g/1½ oz butter or margarine
50 g/2 oz plain flour, sifted
50 g/2 oz demerara sugar
little coconut, strands or desiccated

**American**
3 cups self-rising flour
pinch of salt
1 cup butter or margarine
¾ cup sugar
1⅓ cups shredded coconut
3 eggs, beaten
about ⅓ cup milk
STREUSEL TOPPING:
3 tablespoons butter or margarine
½ cup all-purpose flour, sifted
⅓ cup light brown sugar
little coconut, strands or shredded

Grease a 20 cm/8 inch round or square cake tin and line the bottom and sides with greased greaseproof (waxed) paper. Sift the flour and salt into a bowl. Rub in the fat until the mixture resembles breadcrumbs. Stir in the sugar and coconut followed by the beaten eggs and sufficient milk to mix to a fairly stiff dropping consistency. Turn into the prepared tin and level the top.

For the topping, rub the fat into the flour, then mix in the sugar. Sprinkle over the top of the cake, followed by a little coconut.

Bake in a moderate oven (180°C/350°F, Gas mark 4) for 1¼ to 1½ hours or until well risen and firm to the touch. Turn the cake out carefully, putting a sheet of paper over the streusel topping to prevent any falling off. Cool on a wire rack.

# HONEY ORANGE CAKE

An unusual topping of syrupy orange slices decorates this honey-flavoured cake.

**Metric/Imperial**
150 g/6 oz butter or margarine
6 tablespoons clear honey
50 g/2 oz caster sugar
finely grated rind of 2 oranges
3 eggs
200 g/8 oz plain flour
1 teaspoon baking powder
pinch of salt
TOPPING:
1 orange, thinly sliced
150 ml/¼ pint water
100 g/4 oz sugar

**American**
¾ cup butter or margarine
6 tablespoons clear honey
¼ cup sugar
finely grated rind of 2 oranges
3 eggs
2 cups all-purpose flour
1 teaspoon baking powder
pinch of salt
TOPPING:
1 orange, thinly sliced
⅔ cup water
½ cup sugar

Grease an 18 cm/7 inch round deep cake tin and line the bottom and sides with greased greaseproof (waxed) paper. Cream the fat with the honey and sugar until light and fluffy. Beat in the orange rind and then the eggs, one at a time, following each with a spoonful of flour. Sift the remaining flour with the baking powder and salt and fold into the mixture. Turn into the prepared tin and bake in a moderate oven (160°C/325°F, Gas Mark 3) for about 1¼ hours or until well risen and firm to the touch. Turn out onto a wire rack and leave to cool.

For the topping, poach the orange slices in the water in a frying pan (skillet) for about 10 minutes. Stir in the sugar until dissolved and continue to simmer until the liquid is thick and syrupy. Cool a little, then arrange the orange slices around the top of the cake. Spoon or brush the syrup over both the top of the cake and the oranges and leave until cold.

# CRYSTALLIZED GINGER CAKE

This is a good plain cake flavoured with crystallized (preserved) ginger and raisins, with a sugar topping.

**Metric/Imperial**
250 g/10 oz self-raising flour
pinch of salt
1 teaspoon ground ginger
100 g/4 oz butter or margarine
100 g/4 oz soft brown sugar
50 g/2 oz crystallized or stem ginger, finely chopped
100 g/4 oz raisins
2 eggs, beaten
3 tablespoons milk
1 tablespoon coffee sugar crystals

**American**
2½ cups self-rising flour
pinch of salt
1 teaspoon ground ginger
½ cup butter or margarine
⅔ cup dark brown sugar
¼ cup finely chopped preserved ginger
⅔ cup raisins
2 eggs, beaten
3 tablespoons milk
1 tablespoon coffee sugar crystals

Grease a 15 cm/6 inch round deep cake tin and line the bottom and sides with greased greaseproof (waxed) paper. Sift the flour, salt and ginger into a bowl. Add the fat and rub in until the mixture resembles fine breadcrumbs. Stir in the sugar, ginger and raisins and mix to a soft dropping consistency with the eggs and milk. Turn into the prepared tin, level the top and sprinkle with coffee sugar crystals. Bake in a moderately hot oven (190°C/375°F, Gas Mark 5) for about 1 hour or until well risen, firm to the touch and browned. Cool on a wire rack.

# ORANGE MARMALADE CAKE

This orange-flavoured cake has pieces of marmalade peel in every slice.

**Metric/Imperial**
225 g/8 oz self-raising flour
½ teaspoon baking powder
pinch of salt
100 g/4 oz butter or margarine
50 g/2 oz caster sugar
grated rind of ½ orange
2 eggs, beaten
2 tablespoons orange marmalade (not jelly type)
about 2 tablespoons orange juice

**American**
2 cups self-rising flour
½ teaspoon baking powder
pinch of salt
½ cup butter or margarine
¼ cup sugar
grated rind of ½ orange
2 eggs, beaten
2 tablespoons orange marmalade (not jelly type)
about 2 tablespoons orange juice

Grease a 15 cm/6 inch round cake tin and line the bottom and sides with greased greaseproof (waxed) paper. Sift the flour, baking powder and salt into a bowl. Rub in the fat until the mixture resembles fine breadcrumbs, then stir in the sugar and orange rind. Add the eggs, marmalade and sufficient orange juice to mix to a soft dropping consistency. Turn into the prepared tin and level the top. Bake in a moderate oven (180°C/350°F, Gas Mark 4) for about 1 hour or until well risen and firm to the touch. Cool on a wire rack.

# SCONES AND TEA BREADS

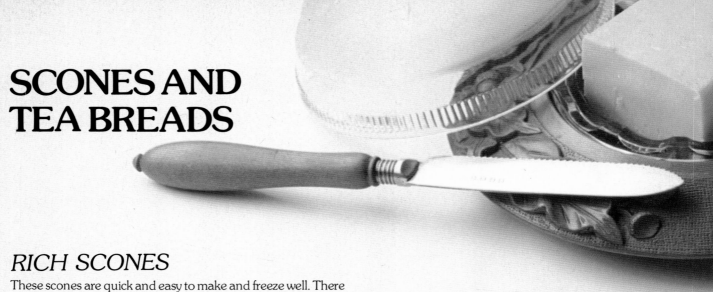

## RICH SCONES

These scones are quick and easy to make and freeze well. There are many ways to vary the flavours, from sweet to savoury.

*Floury Sultana (Raisin) Scones*

| Metric/Imperial | American |
|---|---|
| 200 g/8 oz self-raising flour | 2 cups self-rising flour |
| pinch of salt | pinch of salt |
| 50 g/2 oz butter or margarine | $\frac{1}{4}$ cup butter or margarine |
| 25 g/1 oz caster sugar | 2 tablespoons sugar |
| 1 egg, beaten | 1 egg, beaten |
| about 5 tablespoons milk or sour milk | about $\frac{1}{3}$ cup milk or sour milk |
| beaten egg or milk to glaze | beaten egg or milk to glaze |

Either grease a baking sheet or dredge liberally with flour. Sift the flour and salt into a bowl. Add the butter or margarine and rub in until the mixture resembles fine breadcrumbs. Stir in the sugar. Add the egg and sufficient milk to mix to a fairly soft dough.

Turn out onto a floured surface and gently flatten the dough out to about 2 to 2.5 cm/$\frac{3}{4}$ to 1 inch with your hand. Using a well floured 5 cm/2 inch plain cutter, stamp out the scones. Place on the baking sheet so each scone almost touches the next one and brush the tops with egg or milk.

Bake in a hot oven (230°C/450°C, Gas Mark 8) for 12 to 15 minutes or until well risen, golden brown and firm. Slide, in one piece, onto a clean cloth over a wire rack and wrap in the cloth. This is important for it pushes the steam back into the scones giving them their special texture. Leave to cool and pull apart as required. They can be served warm or cold.

MAKES 8 TO 10

*Variations*
*Fruit scones:* add 50 g/2 oz ($\frac{1}{3}$ cup) currants or sultanas (seedless white raisins) to the dry ingredients.
*Lemon scones:* add the finely grated rind of 1 lemon to the dry ingredients.
*Salty scones:* omit the sugar and sprinkle the tops of the scones with crushed sea (coarse) salt before cooking.
*Cheese scones:* omit the sugar and add a pinch of dry mustard and 40 to 50 g/1$\frac{1}{2}$ to 2 oz ($\frac{1}{3}$ to $\frac{1}{2}$ cup) finely grated mature Cheddar cheese, or 1 to 2 tablespoons finely grated Parmesan cheese, to the dry ingredients.
*Herb scones:* omit the sugar and add 1 to 2 teaspoons freshly chopped herbs or 1$\frac{1}{2}$ teaspoons dried herbs to the dry ingredients.

## FLOURY SULTANA (RAISIN) SCONES

| Metric/Imperial | American |
|---|---|
| 350 g/12 oz self-raising flour | 3 cups self-rising flour |
| pinch of salt | pinch of salt |
| 75 g/3 oz butter or margarine | 6 tablespoons butter or margarine |
| 40 g/1$\frac{1}{2}$ oz caster sugar | 3 tablespoons sugar |
| 50 g/2 oz sultanas | $\frac{1}{3}$ cup seedless white raisins |
| 1 large egg, beaten | 1 egg, beaten |
| about 150 ml/$\frac{1}{4}$ pint milk (preferably sour) | about $\frac{2}{3}$ cup milk (preferably sour) |
| flour for dredging | flour for dredging |

Dredge a baking sheet liberally with flour. Sift the flour and salt into a bowl. Add the fat and rub in until the mixture resembles fine breadcrumbs. Mix in the sugar and sultanas (white raisins). Add the egg and sufficient milk to mix to a fairly soft dough. Knead lightly, then turn onto a floured surface and roll out lightly to a square 1.5 to 2 cm/$\frac{1}{2}$ to $\frac{3}{4}$ inch thick. Dredge fairly thickly with flour and cut into triangles.

Place the scones on the prepared baking sheet so that they almost touch each other. Bake them in a hot oven (230°C/450°F, Gas Mark 8) for 12 to 15 minutes or until lightly browned and firm to the touch. Turn out onto a wire rack covered with a clean cloth. Wrap the scones in the cloth and leave until cold. Serve split and buttered.

MAKES 14 TO 16

*Variations*
*Plain scones:* leave out the sultanas (seedless white raisins).
*Spicy scones:* add 1$\frac{1}{2}$ teaspoons mixed spice (apple pie spice) to the dry ingredients and dredge the tops with a mixture of spice and flour.
*Cheese and onion scones:* omit the sugar and sultanas (seedless white raisins) and add 50 g/2 oz ($\frac{1}{2}$ cup) finely grated Cheddar cheese and 1 to 2 tablespoons finely grated raw onion to the dry ingredients.

# SPICED TREACLE (MOLASSES) SCONES

Black treacle (molasses) and spice give an unusual flavour to these scones.

**Metric/Imperial**
225 g/8 oz self-raising flour
1 teaspoon baking powder
¾ teaspoon mixed spice
pinch of salt
50 g/2 oz butter or
  margarine
25 g/1 oz caster sugar
25 g/1 oz sultanas
  (optional)
1 tablespoon black treacle
about 150 ml/¼ pint milk

**American**
2 cups self-rising flour
1 teaspoon baking powder
¾ teaspoon apple pie spice
pinch of salt
¼ cup butter or margarine
2 tablespoons sugar
3 tablespoons seedless white
  raisins (optional)
1 tablespoon molasses
about ⅔ cup milk

Lightly grease a baking sheet. Sift the flour, baking powder, spice and salt into a bowl. Add the butter or margarine and rub in until the mixture resembles fine breadcrumbs. Stir in the sugar and sultanas (white raisins), if used. Gently heat the treacle (molasses) in a pan and mix thoroughly with half the milk. Add to the dry ingredients with enough of the remaining milk to mix to a fairly soft dough.

Turn the dough onto a floured surface and flatten out to about 2 cm/¾ inch thick. Using a plain 5 cm/2 inch cutter stamp out about 10 scones. Place on the baking sheet and bake in a very hot oven (230°C/450°F, Gas Mark 8) for 10 to 12 minutes or until well risen and golden brown. Cool on a wire rack.

MAKES ABOUT 10

# SCONE ROUND

This sugar-topped plain scone mixture is made in minutes.

| Metric/Imperial | American |
|---|---|
| 200 g/8 oz self-raising flour | 2 cups self-rising flour |
| 1 teaspoon baking powder | 1 teaspoon baking powder |
| large pinch of salt | large pinch of salt |
| 1 tablespoon caster sugar | 1 tablespoon sugar |
| 50 g/2 oz butter or margarine | $\frac{1}{4}$ cup butter or margarine |
| about 6 tablespoons milk (preferably sour) | about 6 tablespoons milk (preferably sour) |
| granulated sugar for dredging | sugar for dredging |

Lightly grease a baking sheet. Sift the flour, baking powder and salt into a bowl. Mix in the sugar then add the butter or margarine and rub in until the mixture resembles fine breadcrumbs. Add sufficient milk to mix to a softish dough. Knead lightly on a floured surface and shape into a round about 20 cm/8 inches in diameter.

Transfer the dough round to the baking sheet and cut into 8 wedges. Brush with milk and sprinkle with granulated sugar. Bake towards the top of a very hot oven (230°C/450°F, Gas Mark 8) for 12 to 15 minutes or until golden brown and firm. Cool on a wire rack. Serve split open and buttered, either cold or warmed.

MAKES 8

*Variations*
*Sultana scones:* add 40 to 50 g/1$\frac{1}{2}$ to 2 oz ($\frac{1}{4}$ to $\frac{1}{3}$ cup) sultanas (seedless white raisins) to the dry mix.
*Walnut scones:* add 25 to 40 g/1 to 1$\frac{1}{2}$ oz ($\frac{1}{4}$ cup) finely chopped walnuts to the dry mix.
*Cheese scones:* omit the sugar and add 40 g/1$\frac{1}{2}$ oz ($\frac{1}{3}$ cup) finely grated mature Cheddar cheese to the dry ingredients. Sprinkle with a little more grated cheese before cooking.

# WHOLEWHEAT SCONES

For those who like wholemeal (wholewheat) bread, these scones are quite delicious.

| Metric/Imperial | American |
|---|---|
| 50 g/2 oz plain flour | $\frac{1}{2}$ cup all-purpose flour |
| pinch of salt | pinch of salt |
| 1 tablespoon baking powder | 1 tablespoon baking powder |
| 150 g/6 oz plain wholemeal flour | 1$\frac{1}{2}$ cups wholewheat or graham flour |
| 50 g/2 oz butter or margarine | $\frac{1}{4}$ cup butter or margarine |
| 25–40 g/1–1$\frac{1}{2}$ oz caster sugar | 2–3 tablespoons sugar |
| about 150 ml/$\frac{1}{4}$ pint milk (preferably sour) | about $\frac{2}{3}$ cup milk (preferably sour) |

Lightly grease a baking sheet and dredge liberally with flour. Sift the plain (all-purpose) flour, salt and baking powder into a bowl and mix in the wholemeal (wholewheat) flour. Rub in the butter or margarine until the mixture resembles breadcrumbs. Stir in the sugar. Add sufficient milk to mix to a fairly soft dough.

Turn onto a floured surface and roll out to about 2.5 cm/1 inch thick. Cut into plain or fluted rounds 4 to 7 cm/1$\frac{1}{2}$ to 2$\frac{1}{2}$ inches in diameter using a floured cutter. Place on the baking sheet. Brush with milk or beaten egg or dredge lightly with flour. Bake in a hot oven (230°C/450°F, Gas Mark 8) for 12 to 15 minutes or until well risen and golden brown. Cool on a wire rack and serve split and buttered.

MAKES 8 TO 10

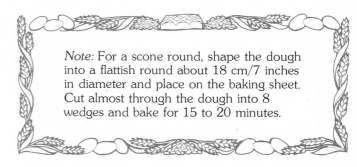

*Note:* For a scone round, shape the dough into a flattish round about 18 cm/7 inches in diameter and place on the baking sheet. Cut almost through the dough into 8 wedges and bake for 15 to 20 minutes.

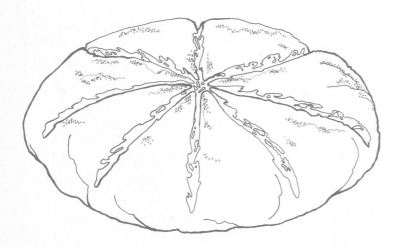

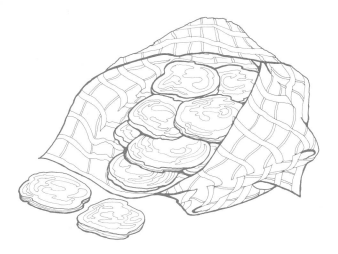

# DROP SCONES (SCOTCH PANCAKES)

A special favourite with children, these are usually eaten as soon as cooked with a thick spreading of butter, although they can also be served cold.

| Metric/Imperial | American |
|---|---|
| 100 g/4 oz self-raising flour | 1 cup self-rising flour |
| pinch of salt | pinch of salt |
| 1 tablespoon caster sugar | 1 tablespoon sugar |
| 1 egg | 1 egg |
| 150 ml/¼ pint milk | ⅔ cup milk |
| little lard or oil for cooking | little lard or oil for cooking |

Sift the flour and salt into a bowl and mix in the sugar. Make a well in the centre and add the egg and half the milk. Gradually work in the flour to give a smooth batter. Add the remaining milk and beat again until smooth.

Grease a griddle or large heavy-based frying pan (skillet) with a little lard or oil. Heat the pan until the fat gives off a blue haze, then wipe off any excess fat. Pour on spoonfuls of the batter, keeping well apart, and cook until bubbles rise to the surface of the scones. Turn over with a palette knife and cook for about 1 minute or until golden brown. Remove to a wire rack covered with a clean cloth and wrap up while cooking the remainder. Serve warm, thickly buttered and spread with syrup or jam.

MAKES ABOUT 16

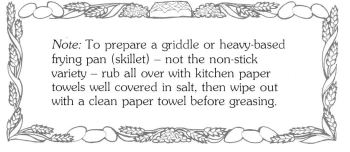

*Note:* To prepare a griddle or heavy-based frying pan (skillet) – not the non-stick variety – rub all over with kitchen paper towels well covered in salt, then wipe out with a clean paper towel before greasing.

# FRUITED GIRDLE SCONES

These can be cooked on a girdle, griddle, in a heavy-based frying pan (skillet) or on a special solid cooker hot plate. Serve hot or cold.

| Metric/Imperial | American |
|---|---|
| 200 g/8 oz plain flour | 2 cups all-purpose flour |
| 1 teaspoon bicarbonate of soda | 1 teaspoon baking soda |
| 2 teaspoons cream of tartar | 2 teaspoons cream of tartar |
| 1 teaspoon salt | 1 teaspoon salt |
| 25 g/1 oz lard or margarine | 2 tablespoons lard or margarine |
| 25 g/1 oz caster sugar | 2 tablespoons sugar |
| 40 g/1½ oz currants | ¼ cup currants |
| about 150 ml/¼ pint milk | about ⅔ cup milk |
| lard or oil for cooking | lard or oil for cooking |

Sift the flour, soda, cream of tartar and salt into a bowl. Add the fat and rub in until the mixture resembles breadcrumbs. Stir in the sugar and currants and mix to a soft dough with milk. Knead lightly on a floured surface, then divide the dough in half. Roll each piece into a round about 5 mm/¼ inch thick. Cut each round into 6 wedges.

Grease a girdle, griddle, hot plate or heavy-based frying pan (skillet) with lard or oil and heat. Cook one round at a time for about 5 minutes on each side or until well risen and an even golden brown. Wrap in a clean cloth on a wire rack and eat while fresh. Serve with butter, jam, honey or syrup.

MAKES 12

# HONEY WALNUT SCONES

| Metric/Imperial | American |
|---|---|
| 200 g/8 oz self-raising flour | 2 cups self-rising flour |
| ½ teaspoon salt | ½ teaspoon salt |
| 50 g/2 oz butter or margarine | ¼ cup butter or margarine |
| 1 tablespoon caster sugar | 1 tablespoon sugar |
| 25 g/1 oz walnuts, finely chopped | ¼ cup finely chopped walnuts |
| 1 egg, beaten | 1 egg, beaten |
| 1 tablespoon thin honey | 1 tablespoon thin honey |
| 2–3 tablespoons milk | 2–3 tablespoons milk |

Grease a baking sheet. Sift the flour and salt together into a bowl. Add the butter or margarine and rub into the flour until the mixture resembles fine breadcrumbs. Stir in the sugar and nuts, then add the egg, honey and sufficient milk to mix to a fairly soft dough.

Turn the dough onto a floured surface and roll out to 1.5 to 2 cm/½ to ¾ inch thick. Cut into ten to twelve 5 cm/2 inch rounds using a plain or fluted cutter. Put onto the baking sheet. Brush with milk and bake in a hot oven (220°C/425°F, Gas Mark 7) for 12 to 15 minutes or until well risen and golden brown. Cool on a wire rack.

MAKES 10 TO 12

# OAT AND TREACLE (MOLASSES) DROP SCONES

These oaty drop scones are made in a minute to disappear in seconds. Serve buttered with or without honey or syrup.

**Metric/Imperial**
*100 g/4 oz self-raising flour*
*1 tablespoon baking powder*
*pinch of salt*
*100 g/4 oz fine oatmeal*
*25 g/1 oz demerara sugar*
*50 g/2 oz margarine*
*2 tablespoons black treacle*
*1 egg, beaten*
*150 ml/¼ pint milk*
*lard for cooking*

**American**
*1 cup self-rising flour*
*1 tablespoon baking powder*
*pinch of salt*
*⅔ cup fine oatmeal*
*2½ tablespoons light brown sugar*
*¼ cup margarine*
*2 tablespoons molasses*
*1 egg, beaten*
*⅔ cup milk*
*lard for cooking*

Sift the flour, baking powder and salt into a bowl and stir in the oatmeal and sugar. Melt the margarine and treacle (molasses) and stir into the dry ingredients with the egg and the milk, adding a little at a time. Beat until smooth.

Grease a griddle or heavy-based frying pan (skillet). Heat the pan until the fat gives off a blue haze, then wipe off any excess fat. Drop tablespoons of the batter onto the hot griddle and cook gently for 3 to 4 minutes on each side or until browned. Keep warm wrapped in a clean cloth, while cooking the remainder. Serve warm or cold, spread with butter.

MAKES 25 TO 30

# ORANGE TEA LOAF

This tea loaf uses the part of the orange usually discarded and it gives an excellent flavour and texture to the loaf.

| Metric/Imperial | American |
| --- | --- |
| 50 g/2 oz butter or margarine | $\frac{1}{4}$ cup butter or margarine |
| 150 g/6 oz caster sugar | $\frac{3}{4}$ cup sugar |
| 3 tablespoons orange juice | 3 tablespoons orange juice |
| 1 orange shell, tough membrane removed and shell minced | 1 orange shell, tough membrane removed and shell minced |
| 1 egg, beaten | 1 egg, beaten |
| 200 g/8 oz plain flour | 2 cups all-purpose flour |
| 2$\frac{1}{2}$ teaspoons baking powder | 2$\frac{1}{2}$ teaspoons baking powder |
| pinch of salt | pinch of salt |

Grease a 450 g/1 lb loaf tin and line with greased greaseproof (waxed) paper. Beat the butter or margarine until soft, then add the sugar and beat in until well mixed and fluffy. Beat in the orange juice, minced rind and the egg. Sift the flour, baking powder and salt together and fold into the mixture.

Turn into the prepared tin and bake in a moderately hot oven (190°C/375°F, Gas Mark 5) for 45 to 50 minutes or until well risen and firm. Turn out and cool on a wire rack. Serve cut in slices, spread with butter and honey, or cream cheese.

# MALTED TEA LOAF

This malt-flavoured tea bread is full of sultanas (white raisins) and candied peel. After one or two days wrapped in foil it becomes more sticky.

| Metric/Imperial | American |
| --- | --- |
| 50 g/2 oz butter or margarine | $\frac{1}{4}$ cup butter or margarine |
| 100 g/4 oz golden syrup | $\frac{1}{3}$ cup light corn syrup |
| 100 g/4 oz malt extract | $\frac{1}{3}$ cup malt extract or molasses |
| 4 tablespoons milk | $\frac{1}{4}$ cup milk |
| 200 g/8 oz self-raising flour | 2 cups self-rising flour |
| pinch of salt | pinch of salt |
| 100 g/4 oz sultanas | $\frac{2}{3}$ cup seedless white raisins |
| 50 g/2 oz mixed candied peel, chopped | $\frac{1}{3}$ cup chopped mixed candied peel |
| 1 egg, beaten | 1 egg, beaten |

Grease a 900 g/2 lb (9 × 5 × 3 inch) loaf tin and line with greased greaseproof (waxed) paper. Put the butter or margarine, syrup, malt (or molasses) and milk into a small saucepan and heat gently until just melted. Sift the flour and salt into a bowl and mix in the sultanas (white raisins) and peel. Add the warmed mixture and egg to the dry ingredients and beat until smooth. Pour into the prepared tin and bake in a moderate oven (160°C/325°F, Gas Mark 3) for 1 to 1$\frac{1}{4}$ hours or until well risen and firm to the touch. Turn out onto a wire rack and leave to cool. Wrap in foil and store for 1 to 2 days before use. To serve, cut into slices and spread with butter.

*Opposite: Oat and Treacle (Molasses) Drop Scones*
*Above: Malted Tea Loaf. Right: Orange Tea Loaf*

# APRICOT TEA BREAD

Chopped dried apricots and almonds add a 'bite' to this moist tea bread.

| **Metric/Imperial** | **American** |
|---|---|
| 100 g/4 oz dried apricots, chopped | ⅔ cup chopped dried apricots |
| 150 ml/¼ pint water | ⅔ cup water |
| 25 g/1 oz butter | 2 tablespoons butter |
| 200 g/8 oz caster sugar | 1 cup sugar |
| ½ teaspoon salt | ½ teaspoon salt |
| 250 g/10 oz plain flour | 2½ cups all-purpose flour |
| 1 teaspoon bicarbonate of soda | 1 teaspoon baking soda |
| 1 egg, beaten | 1 egg, beaten |
| 1 teaspoon orange juice | 1 teaspoon orange juice |
| 50 g/2 oz blanched almonds, chopped | ½ cup chopped blanched almonds |

Grease a 900 g/2 lb (9 × 5 × 3 inch) loaf tin and line with greased greaseproof (waxed) paper. Put the apricots, water, butter, sugar and salt into a saucepan and bring to the boil, stirring until the sugar dissolves. Simmer for 5 minutes, then leave to cool.

Sift the flour and soda into a bowl. Add the apricot mixture, egg, orange juice and almonds and beat well. Turn into the prepared tin and bake in a moderate oven (180°C/350°F, Gas Mark 4) for about 1¼ hours or until firm to the touch. Turn out and leave to cool.

# CRANBERRY TEA BREAD

Cranberry sauce, orange rind, raisins and walnuts flavour this delicious tea bread.

| **Metric/Imperial** | **American** |
|---|---|
| 200 g/8 oz plain flour | 2 cups all-purpose flour |
| 1½ teaspoons baking powder | 1½ teaspoons baking powder |
| ½ teaspoon bicarbonate of soda | ½ teaspoon baking soda |
| large pinch of salt | large pinch of salt |
| 50 g/2 oz butter or margarine | ¼ cup butter or margarine |
| 150 g/6 oz light soft brown sugar | 1 cup light brown sugar |
| grated rind of 1 orange | grated rind of 1 orange |
| 75 g/3 oz walnuts, chopped | ¾ cup chopped walnuts |
| 50 g/2 oz raisins | ⅓ cup raisins |
| 4 tablespoons cranberry sauce, from a jar | ¼ cup cranberry sauce, from a jar |
| 4 tablespoons orange juice | ¼ cup orange juice |
| 1 large egg, beaten | 1 egg, beaten |

Grease a 900 g/2 lb (9 × 5 × 3 inch) loaf tin and line with greased greaseproof (waxed) paper. Sift the flour, baking powder, soda and salt into a bowl. Add the butter or margarine and rub in until the mixture resembles breadcrumbs. Stir in the sugar, orange rind, walnuts and raisins. Mix the cranberry sauce, orange juice and egg together and add to the dry ingredients. Mix lightly.

Turn into the prepared tin and bake in a moderate oven (180°C/350°F, Gas Mark 4) for 1 to 1¼ hours or until firm to the touch, well risen and golden brown. Turn out onto a wire rack to cool. Serve in slices, spread with butter.

# MARMALADE TEA BREAD

Pieces of marmalade peel give an interesting texture to this tea bread. It goes well with cottage, curd or cream cheese.

| **Metric/Imperial** | **American** |
|---|---|
| 200 g/8 oz self-raising flour | 2 cups self-rising flour |
| pinch of salt | pinch of salt |
| ½ teaspoon grated nutmeg | ½ teaspoon grated nutmeg |
| 100 g/4 oz butter or margarine | ½ cup butter or margarine |
| 100 g/4 oz soft brown or demerara sugar | ⅔ cup light brown sugar |
| 1 egg, beaten | 1 egg, beaten |
| 6 tablespoons chunky marmalade | 6 tablespoons chunky marmalade |
| 4 tablespoons milk | ¼ cup milk |

Grease a 900 g/2 lb (9 × 5 × 3 inch) loaf tin and line with greased greaseproof (waxed) paper. Sift the flour, salt and nutmeg into a bowl. Add the butter or margarine and rub in until the mixture resembles fine breadcrumbs. Stir in the sugar. Add the egg, 4 tablespoons of the marmalade and the milk and mix well.

Turn into the prepared tin and bake in a moderate oven (180°C/350°F, Gas Mark 4) for 50 to 60 minutes or until firm. Turn out onto a wire rack and, while still hot, spread the remaining marmalade over the top. Leave to cool, then wrap in foil or store in an airtight container for several days before use.

# DATE TEA BREAD

**Metric/Imperial**
200 g/8 oz plain flour
1 teaspoon baking powder
100 g/4 oz butter or
    margarine
100 g/4 oz soft brown sugar
100 g/4 oz stoned dates,
    chopped
grated rind of 1 lemon
1 teaspoon bicarbonate of
    soda
about 6 tablespoons milk

**American**
2 cups all-purpose flour
1 teaspoon baking powder
$\frac{1}{2}$ cup butter or margarine
$\frac{2}{3}$ cup dark brown sugar
$\frac{2}{3}$ cup chopped pitted dates
grated rind of 1 lemon
1 teaspoon baking soda
about 6 tablespoons milk

Grease a 900 g/2 lb (9 × 5 × 3 inch) loaf tin and line with greased greaseproof (waxed) paper. Sift the flour and baking powder into a bowl. Add the butter or margarine and rub in until the mixture resembles breadcrumbs. Stir in the sugar, dates and lemon rind. Dissolve the soda in 1 tablespoon of the milk and add to the dry ingredients together with enough of the remaining milk to mix to a stiff dropping consistency.

Turn into the prepared tin and bake in a moderate oven (180°C/350°F, Gas Mark 4) for 50 to 60 minutes or until well risen and just firm to the touch. Turn out onto a wire rack to cool. Serve in slices, spread with butter.

*Variation*
Orange rind can be used in place of lemon.

# SODA BREAD

Quick to make, soda bread can be served as an alternative to yeast bread. It is best eaten fresh from the oven.

**Metric/Imperial**
450 g/1 lb plain flour
2 teaspoons bicarbonate of
    soda
2 teaspoons cream of tartar
1 teaspoon salt
50 g/2 oz lard
300 ml/$\frac{1}{2}$ pint sour milk or
    fresh milk mixed with 1
    tablespoon lemon juice

**American**
4 cups all-purpose flour
2 teaspoons baking soda
2 teaspoons cream of tartar
1 teaspoon salt
$\frac{1}{4}$ cup lard
$1\frac{1}{4}$ cups sour milk or fresh
    milk mixed with 1
    tablespoon lemon juice

Dredge a baking sheet with flour. Sift the flour, soda, cream of tartar and salt into a bowl. Add the lard and rub in until the mixture resembles fine breadcrumbs. Add sufficient milk to mix to a soft manageable dough.

Turn the dough onto a floured surface and shape into a circle about 18 cm/7 inches in diameter. Transfer to the baking sheet, dredge with flour and mark into quarters with a sharp knife. Bake in a hot oven (220°C/425°F, Gas Mark 7) for about 30 minutes or until well risen and golden. Cool on a wire rack.

*Variation*
*For a brown soda loaf:* use half white and half wholemeal (wholewheat or graham) flour.

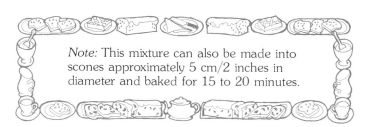

*Note:* This mixture can also be made into scones approximately 5 cm/2 inches in diameter and baked for 15 to 20 minutes.

# BANANA TEA LOAF

The soft mottled brown-skinned bananas which are rather over-ripe are ideal for this recipe.

**Metric/Imperial**
75 g/3 oz margarine
75 g/3 oz caster sugar
75 g/3 oz soft brown sugar
2 eggs, beaten
450 g/1 lb ripe bananas
  (about 3)
grated rind of ½ lemon
1 teaspoon lemon juice
25–40 g/1–1½ oz walnuts,
  chopped (optional)
175 g/7 oz self-raising flour
pinch of salt
¼ teaspoon bicarbonate of
  soda

**American**
6 tablespoons margarine
6 tablespoons sugar
½ cup dark brown sugar
2 eggs, beaten
1 lb ripe bananas (about 3)
grated rind of ½ lemon
1 teaspoon lemon juice
¼–⅓ cup chopped walnuts
  (optional)
1¾ cups self-rising flour
pinch of salt
¼ teaspoon baking soda

Grease a 900 g/2 lb (9 × 5 × 3 inch) loaf tin and line with greased greaseproof (waxed) paper. Beat the margarine until soft, then add the sugars and beat until light and fluffy. Beat in the eggs one at a time. Mash the bananas with the lemon rind and juice and beat into the mixture until smooth. Add the nuts, if used. Sift the flour, salt and soda together and fold into the mixture.

Turn into the prepared tin and bake in a moderate oven (180°C/350°F, Gas Mark 4) for about 1 hour or until firm to the touch. Cool in the tin for 10 minutes, then turn out onto a wire rack to cool completely. Wrap in foil and store for 24 hours before serving in slices, either plain or buttered.

*Cider Loaf Cake; Apple and Raisin Tea Bread*

# CIDER LOAF CAKE

Dried fruit soaked in cider is used for this delicious slightly crunchy tea loaf also flavoured with orange rind.

**Metric/Imperial**
350 g/12 oz mixed dried
    fruit
300 ml/½ pint sweet cider
275 g/10 oz self-raising
    flour, sifted
50 g/2 oz nuts, chopped
175 g/6 oz soft brown sugar
grated rind of 1 orange
2 large eggs, beaten

**American**
2 cups mixed dried fruit
1¼ cups hard sweet cider
2½ cups self-rising flour,
    sifted
½ cup chopped nuts
1 cup dark brown sugar
grated rind of 1 orange
2 eggs, beaten

Put the fruit into a bowl with the cider and leave to soak for at least 3 hours or overnight. Turn into a saucepan and bring to the boil. Remove from the heat and leave to cool.

Grease a 900 g/2 lb (9 × 5 × 3 inch) loaf tin and line the bottom and sides with greased greaseproof (waxed) paper. Mix the flour, nuts, sugar and orange rind together in a bowl. Add the cider mixture and eggs and mix thoroughly. Turn into the prepared tin and bake in a moderate oven (160°C/325°F, Gas Mark 3) for 1½ to 1¾ hours or until the loaf is well risen, golden brown and firm to the touch. Turn out onto a wire rack and leave to cool. Serve in slices, with or without butter.

# APPLE AND RAISIN TEA BREAD

The apple in this one-stage recipe gives a moist texture.

**Metric/Imperial**
100 g/4 oz soft (luxury)
    margarine
100 g/4 oz caster sugar
2 large eggs, beaten
1 tablespoon clear honey
150 g/6 oz raisins
200 g/8 oz self-raising flour
pinch of salt
1 teaspoon mixed spice
1 large cooking apple
    (150 g/6 oz), peeled,
    cored and coarsely grated
1–2 tablespoons clear honey
    to glaze

**American**
½ cup soft margarine
½ cup sugar
2 eggs, beaten
1 tablespoon clear honey
1 cup raisins
2 cups self-rising flour
pinch of salt
1 teaspoon apple pie spice
1 large cooking apple (6 oz),
    peeled, cored and
    coarsely grated
1–2 tablespoons clear honey
    to glaze

Grease a 900 g/2 lb (9 × 5 × 3 inch) loaf tin and line with greased greaseproof (waxed) paper. Put all the ingredients, except the honey, into a mixing bowl and beat with an electric mixer or wooden spoon for about 2 minutes until smooth. Turn into the prepared tin and level the top. Bake in a moderate oven (180°C/350°F, Gas Mark 4) for about 1¼ hours or until firm to the touch. Lay a sheet of greaseproof (waxed) paper or foil over the loaf after 1 hour. Turn out onto a wire rack and brush the top with honey. Leave to cool.

# BARA BRITH

A Welsh teatime favourite, this is full of sultanas (white raisins) and flavoured with black treacle (molasses).

| Metric/Imperial | American |
|---|---|
| 200 g/8 oz self-raising flour | 2 cups self-rising flour |
| pinch of salt | pinch of salt |
| ¾ teaspoon mixed spice | ¾ teaspoon apple pie spice |
| 50 g/2 oz butter | ¼ cup butter |
| 50 g/2 oz sugar | ¼ cup sugar |
| grated rind of 1 lemon | grated rind of 1 lemon |
| 100 g/4 oz sultanas | ⅔ cup seedless white raisins |
| 75 g/3 oz black treacle | ¼ cup molasses |
| 1 egg, beaten | 1 egg, beaten |
| ½ teaspoon bicarbonate of soda | ½ teaspoon baking soda |
| 100 ml/4 fl oz milk | ½ cup milk |

Grease a 900 g/2 lb (9 × 5 × 3 inch) loaf tin and line with greased greaseproof (waxed) paper. Sift the flour, salt and spice into a bowl. Add the butter and rub in until the mixture resembles fine breadcrumbs. Stir in the sugar, lemon rind and sultanas (white raisins). Add the treacle (molasses) and egg to the dry ingredients. Sprinkle the soda into the milk, add to the mixture and beat until evenly mixed.

Turn into the prepared tin and bake in a moderate oven (180°C/350°F, Gas Mark 4) for about 1¼ hours or until firm to the touch. Turn out onto a wire rack to cool. Store wrapped in foil for 24 hours before serving sliced and buttered.

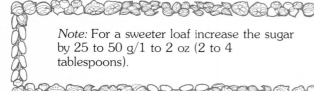

Note: For a sweeter loaf increase the sugar by 25 to 50 g/1 to 2 oz (2 to 4 tablespoons).

# BUN LOAF

A spicy 'current bun' tea loaf, this is flavoured with honey.

| Metric/Imperial | American |
|---|---|
| 300 g/12 oz self-raising flour | 3 cups self-rising flour |
| 1 teaspoon mixed spice | 1 teaspoon apple pie spice |
| pinch of salt | pinch of salt |
| 100 g/4 oz butter or margarine | ½ cup butter or margarine |
| 100 g/4 oz caster sugar | ½ cup sugar |
| 150 g/6 oz currants | 1 cup currants |
| 50 g/2 oz mixed candied peel, chopped | ⅓ cup chopped mixed candied peel |
| 1 egg, beaten | 1 egg, beaten |
| 150 ml/¼ pint milk | ⅔ cup milk |
| 2 tablespoons clear honey | 2 tablespoons clear honey |

Grease a 900 g/2 lb (9 × 5 × 3 inch) loaf tin and line with greased greaseproof (waxed) paper. Sift the flour, spice and salt into a bowl. Add the butter or margarine and rub in until the mixture resembles fine breadcrumbs. Stir in the sugar, currants and peel, then add the egg, milk and honey and beat well until smooth. Turn into the prepared tin and bake in a moderate oven (160°C/325°F, Gas Mark 3) for 1½ to 1¾ hours or until golden brown and firm to the touch. Cool on a wire rack.

# SAVOURY TEA LOAF

This cheese and peanut flavoured loaf is made by the one-stage method.

| Metric/Imperial | American |
|---|---|
| 225 g/8 oz self-raising flour | 2 cups self-rising flour |
| good pinch of salt and pepper | good pinch of salt and pepper |
| good pinch of dry mustard | good pinch of dry mustard |
| 100 g/4 oz soft (luxury) margarine | ½ cup soft margarine |
| 50 g/2 oz salted peanuts, chopped | ½ cup chopped salted peanuts |
| 1 egg | 1 egg |
| 75 g/3 oz mature Cheddar cheese, finely grated | ¾ cup finely grated Cheddar cheese |
| 100 ml/4 fl oz milk | ½ cup milk |

Grease and line a 900 g/2 lb (9 × 5 × 3 inch) loaf tin. Sift the flour with a good pinch of salt, pepper and mustard into a bowl. Add all the other ingredients and beat well for 2 to 3 minutes until quite smooth.

Turn into the prepared tin and level the top. Bake in a moderately hot oven (190°C/375°F, Gas Mark 5) for about 50 minutes or until well risen, golden brown and firm to the touch. Turn out onto a wire rack and leave to cool. Serve sliced and buttered, with cucumber and tomato, if liked.

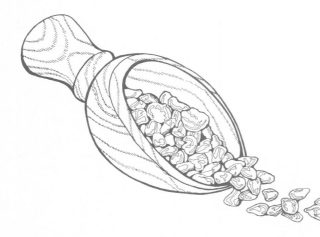

# LEMON AND DATE SCONE BAR

This lemon-flavoured scone bar is quickly made and baked.

| Metric/Imperial | American |
|---|---|
| 200 g/8 oz self-raising flour | 2 cups self-rising flour |
| pinch of salt | pinch of salt |
| 50 g/2 oz butter or margarine | $\frac{1}{4}$ cup butter or margarine |
| 50 g/2 oz caster sugar | $\frac{1}{4}$ cup sugar |
| grated rind of 1 lemon | grated rind of 1 lemon |
| 75 g/3 oz stoned dates, finely chopped | $\frac{1}{2}$ cup pitted dates, finely chopped |
| 1 egg, beaten | 1 egg, beaten |
| about 4 tablespoons milk (preferably sour) | about $\frac{1}{4}$ cup milk (preferably sour) |
| 1 tablespoon demerara sugar | 1 tablespoon light brown sugar |

Grease a baking sheet or dredge it with flour. Sift the flour and salt into a bowl. Add the butter or margarine and rub in until the mixture resembles fine breadcrumbs. Stir in the sugar, lemon rind and chopped dates. Add the egg and sufficient milk to mix to a fairly soft dough.

Turn onto the baking sheet and form into a brick shape about 2.5 cm/1 inch thick. Sprinkle with demerara (light brown) sugar. Bake in a hot oven (220°C/425°F, Gas Mark 7) for 20 to 25 minutes until well risen, golden brown and just firm to the touch. Turn onto a wire rack covered with a clean cloth, wrap up loosely in the cloth and leave to cool. Cut into bars or slices and serve plain or buttered.

*Variations*
Raisins or currants can be used in place of the dates.

# BARM BRACK

Use the leftovers of a freshly made pot of tea to soak the fruit for this Irish tea loaf.

| Metric/Imperial | American |
|---|---|
| 150 g/6 oz soft brown sugar | 1 cup dark brown sugar |
| 300 g/12 oz mixed dried fruit | 2 cups mixed dried fruit |
| 400 ml/$\frac{3}{4}$ pint freshly made tea, cold | 1 pint freshly made tea, cold |
| 1 egg, beaten | 1 egg, beaten |
| 300 g/12 oz self-raising flour, sifted | 3 cups self-rising flour, sifted |
| 1 teaspoon mixed spice (optional) | 1 teaspoon apple pie spice (optional) |

Put the sugar and mixed fruit in a bowl with the cold tea and leave for at least 6 hours or, preferably, overnight.

Grease and line a 900 g/2 lb (9 × 5 × 3 inch) loaf tin. Stir the beaten egg into the fruit mixture, followed by the flour and spice, if used. Turn into the prepared tin and bake in a moderate oven (180°C/350°F, Gas Mark 4) for about 1$\frac{1}{4}$ hours or until well risen and firm to the touch. Turn out onto a wire rack to cool.

# YEASTED FARE

## DOUGHNUTS

There is nothing to beat a homemade sugar-coated doughnut.

**Metric/Imperial**
225 g/8 oz strong plain
  white flour
½ teaspoon salt
15 g/½ oz fresh yeast, or 1½
  teaspoons dried yeast and
  1 teaspoon caster sugar
about 4 tablespoons warm
  milk (43°C/110°F)
15 g/½ oz butter or
  margarine, softened
1 egg, beaten
8 teaspoons thick red jam
fat or oil for deep frying
COATING:
50 g/2 oz caster sugar
½ teaspoon ground
  cinnamon (optional)

**American**
2 cups all-purpose flour
½ teaspoon salt
½ cake compressed yeast, or
  ¾ package active dry yeast
  and 1 teaspoon sugar
about ¼ cup warm milk
  (110°F)
1 tablespoon butter or
  margarine, softened
1 egg, beaten
8 teaspoons thick red jam
fat or oil for deep frying
COATING:
¼ cup sugar
½ teaspoon ground
  cinnamon (optional)

Grease two baking sheets and dredge lightly with flour. Sift the flour and salt into a bowl. Dissolve the fresh (compressed) yeast in the warm milk; or if using dried (active dry) yeast, dissolve the sugar in the milk, then sprinkle the yeast over the top and leave in a warm place for about 10 minutes or until frothy. Add the yeast liquid to the dry ingredients with the softened fat and egg and mix to form a fairly soft dough which leaves the sides of the bowl clean. Add a little more milk if necessary.

Turn the dough onto a floured surface and knead thoroughly until smooth – about 10 minutes by hand or 3 to 4 if using an electric mixer. Put the dough into a lightly floured bowl, cover with a piece of oiled polythene (plastic wrap) and put to rise in a warm place for about 1 hour or until doubled in size and the dough springs back when pressed with a floured finger.

Turn out onto a lightly floured surface and knock back (punch down). Knead the dough for 2 minutes until smooth. Divide into eight pieces and roll into rounds. Put 1 teaspoon jam in the centre of each and pull in the edges to enclose the jam and make a ball. Put onto the baking sheets, cover with oiled polythene (plastic wrap) and put to rise again for 10 to 20 minutes until puffy.

Heat the fat or oil to 182°C/360°F. Deep fry the doughnuts, three at a time, for 5 to 10 minutes or until golden brown all over, turning several times. Drain on crumpled absorbent kitchen paper and while still warm coat in a mixture of the sugar and cinnamon or just plain sugar. Leave to cool.
MAKES 8

Chelsea Buns

# CHELSEA BUNS

These are traditionally square buns which pull apart when cooked to give soft sides. They are made by the batter method of making yeast dough and the dough is rolled up Swiss (jelly) roll style with a filling of spiced dried fruit.

| Metric/Imperial | American |
|---|---|
| 225 g/8 oz strong plain white flour | 2 cups all-purpose flour |
| 15 g/½ oz fresh yeast, or 1½ teaspoons dried yeast | ½ cake compressed yeast, or ¾ package active dry yeast |
| 1 teaspoon caster sugar | 1 teaspoon sugar |
| 100 ml/4 fl oz warm milk (43°C/110°F) | ½ cup warm milk (110°F) |
| ½ teaspoon salt | ½ teaspoon salt |
| 15 g/½ oz butter or lard | 1 tablespoon butter or shortening |
| 1 egg, beaten | 1 egg, beaten |
| about 50 g/2 oz butter or margarine, melted | about ¼ cup butter or margarine, melted |
| 150 g/6 oz mixed dried fruit | 1 cup mixed dried fruit |
| 25 g/1 oz mixed candied peel, chopped | 3 tablespoons chopped mixed candied peel |
| ½ teaspoon mixed spice (optional) | ½ teaspoon apple pie spice (optional) |
| 50 g/2 oz soft brown sugar | ⅓ cup dark brown sugar |
| clear honey to glaze | clear honey to glaze |

Grease an 18 cm/7 inch square cake tin. Sift 50 g/2 oz (½ cup) of the flour into a bowl. Add the yeast, 1 teaspoon sugar and the milk and mix to a smooth batter. Put in a warm place and leave for 10 to 20 minutes or until frothy. Sift the remaining flour with the salt into a bowl and rub in the butter or shortening. Add to the yeast batter together with the egg and mix to form a soft dough which will leave the sides of the bowl clean after beating.

Turn out onto a lightly floured surface and knead until smooth – about 5 minutes. Shape into a ball, place in an oiled polythene (plastic) bag and put to rise in a warm place for 1 to 1½ hours or until doubled in size.

Remove from the bag and knead the dough until smooth. Roll out to an oblong, 30 × 24 cm/12 × 9 inches, and brush the whole surface with melted butter or margarine. Mix together the dried fruit, peel, spice, if used, and brown sugar and sprinkle over the dough. Starting from the longest side roll up Swiss (jelly) roll style and seal the end with water. Cut the roll into nine equal slices and place in the prepared tin, cut sides down, so they almost touch. Cover with oiled polythene (plastic wrap) and put to rise in a warm place for about 30 minutes or until doubled in size.

Remove the polythene (plastic wrap) and bake in a moderately hot oven (190°C/375°F, Gas Mark 5) for 30 to 35 minutes or until golden brown. Turn the buns out onto a wire rack all in one piece and while still warm brush the tops with a wet pastry brush dipped in honey. Leave to cool and pull apart as required.

MAKES 9

# WHITE BREAD ROLLS

This basic white bread dough can be used for loaves and rolls in assorted shapes and sizes as well as for variety breads such as Lardy Cake.

**Metric/Imperial**
700 g/1½ lb strong plain
   flour
2 teaspoons salt
15 g/½ oz lard
15 g/½ oz fresh yeast, or 1½
   teaspoons dried yeast and
   1 teaspoon caster sugar
400 ml/¾ pint warm water
   (43°C/110°F)
TOPPING:
beaten egg
poppy seeds or sesame
   seeds

**American**
6 cups all-purpose or bread
   flour
2 teaspoons salt
1 tablespoon shortening
½ cake compressed yeast, or
   ¾ package active dry yeast
   and 1 teaspoon sugar
1 pint warm water (110°F)
TOPPING:
beaten egg
poppy seeds or sesame
   seeds

Grease two or three baking sheets. Sift the flour and salt into a bowl and rub in the lard (shortening). Dissolve the fresh (compressed) yeast in the water; or for dried (active dry) yeast dissolve the sugar in the water, sprinkle the yeast on top and leave in a warm place for about 10 minutes or until frothy. Add the yeast liquid to the dry ingredients all at once and mix to a firm but not too stiff dough. Add a little extra flour, if necessary, until the dough leaves the sides of the bowl clean.

Turn out onto a lightly floured surface and knead until smooth and no longer sticky. This should take about 10 minutes by hand or 3 to 4 minutes if using an electric mixer fitted with a dough hook. Shape into a ball and place in an oiled polythene (plastic) bag. Put to rise in a warm place for about 1 hour or until doubled in size and the dough springs back when lightly pressed with a floured finger.

Remove the risen dough from the bag, knock back (punch down) and knead to knock out all the air bubbles and make the dough smooth and even – about 2 minutes. Divide into about 15 pieces, 50 to 75 g/2 to 3 oz. This bread dough can be twisted, plaited (braided) and tied into all sorts of shapes as well as rolled into round rolls, finger rolls etc. For soft-sided rolls, place the pieces of dough 1.5 to 2 cm/½ to ¾ inch apart on the baking sheet so they join up during cooking and can be pulled apart as required. For crisp rolls, place well apart so they do not touch at all. For extra crustiness, brush with salted water just before baking.

Cover all rolls with oiled polythene (plastic wrap) after shaping and put to rise in a warm place until doubled in size – about 15 to 30 minutes. Remove the polythene (plastic), brush with beaten egg (or milk) and sprinkle with poppy or sesame seeds or leave plain. Bake in a very hot oven (230°C/450°F, Gas Mark 8) for 10 to 20 minutes, depending on size, until well risen and browned. Cool on a wire rack.

MAKES ABOUT 15 ROLLS

# YORKSHIRE TEACAKES

Serve these large currant buns still warm from the oven, split open and spread with butter.

**Metric/Imperial**
15 g/½ oz fresh yeast, or 1½
   teaspoons dried yeast and
   1 teaspoon caster sugar
300 ml/½ pint warm milk
   (43°C/110°F)
450 g/1 lb strong plain
   white flour
1 teaspoon salt
40 g/1½ oz lard
25 g/1 oz caster sugar
100 g/4 oz currants
25 g/1 oz mixed candied
   peel, chopped
milk to glaze

**American**
½ cake compressed yeast, or
   ¾ package active dry yeast
   and 1 teaspoon sugar
1¼ cups warm milk (110°F)
4 cups all-purpose flour
1 teaspoon salt
3 tablespoons shortening
2 tablespoons sugar
⅔ cup currants
3 tablespoons chopped
   mixed candied peel
milk to glaze

Grease two or three baking sheets. Dissolve the fresh (compressed) yeast in the warm milk; or for dried (active dry) yeast, dissolve the 1 teaspoon sugar in the milk, sprinkle the yeast on top and leave in a warm place for about 10 minutes or until frothy. Sift the flour and salt into a bowl, add the lard (shortening) and rub in until the mixture resembles fine breadcrumbs. Stir in the sugar, currants and peel. Add the yeast liquid and mix to form a fairly soft dough, adding more flour if necessary until the dough leaves the sides of the bowl clean.

Turn out onto a floured surface and knead until smooth and elastic – about 10 minutes by hand or 3 to 4 minutes in an electric mixer. Form into a ball, place in an oiled polythene (plastic) bag and put to rise in a warm place for about 1 hour or until doubled in size.

Turn out onto a floured surface, knock back (punch down) and knead until smooth. Divide into six pieces. Shape each piece into a round, then roll out to a circle 15 to 18 cm/6 to 7 inches in diameter. Transfer to the baking sheets. Brush the tops with milk and cover with oiled polythene (plastic wrap). Put to rise in a warm place for about 40 minutes or until almost doubled in size.

Bake in a moderately hot oven (200°C/400°F, Gas Mark 6) for about 20 minutes or until well risen and golden brown. Remove to a wire rack and leave to cool. To serve, split open and spread thickly with butter. The teacakes are even better if eaten slightly warm.

MAKES 6

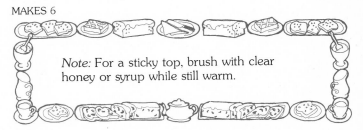

*Note:* For a sticky top, brush with clear honey or syrup while still warm.

# HOT CROSS BUNS

An Easter speciality, these rich spicy fruit buns may be served at any meal but are hard to beat when offered at breakfast, warmed and spread thickly with butter. The traditional 'cross' can be made with a sharp knife or with thin strips of pastry.

| Metric/Imperial | American |
| --- | --- |
| 450 g/1 lb strong plain white flour | 4 cups all-purpose flour |
| 25 g/1 oz fresh yeast, or 1 tablespoon dried yeast and 1 teaspoon caster sugar | 1 cake compressed yeast, or 1½ packages active dry yeast and 1 teaspoon sugar |
| 150 ml/¼ pint warm milk (43°C/110°F) | ⅔ cup warm milk (110 F) |
| 4 tablespoons warm water | ¼ cup warm water |
| 1 teaspoon salt | 1 teaspoon salt |
| ½ teaspoon mixed spice | ½ teaspoon apple pie spice |
| ½ teaspoon ground cinnamon | ½ teaspoon ground cinnamon |
| ½ teaspoon grated nutmeg | ½ teaspoon grated nutmeg |
| 50 g/2 oz caster sugar | ¼ cup sugar |
| 50 g/2 oz mixed candied peel, chopped | ⅓ cup chopped mixed candied peel |
| 100 g/4 oz currants | ⅔ cup currants |
| 50 g/2 oz butter or margarine, melted | ¼ cup butter or margarine, melted |
| 1 egg, beaten | 1 egg, beaten |
| SUGAR GLAZE: | SUGAR GLAZE: |
| 3 tablespoons caster sugar | 3 tablespoons sugar |
| 3 tablespoons mixed milk and water | 3 tablespoons mixed milk and water |

Grease two baking sheets. Put 100 g/4 oz (1 cup) of the flour into a bowl with the fresh (compressed) yeast, or dried yeast and 1 teaspoon sugar. Add the warm milk and water and mix well. Leave the batter in a warm place until frothy; fresh (compressed) yeast takes about 15 minutes, dried yeast about 25 minutes. Sift the remaining flour with the salt and spices, then add the sugar, peel and currants. Add the cooled melted fat and egg to the yeast batter followed by all the dry ingredients and mix to form a softish dough.

Turn out onto a lightly floured surface and knead until smooth and no longer sticky – about 10 minutes by hand or 3 to 4 minutes in an electric mixer. Shape into a ball and place in an oiled polythene (plastic) bag. Put to rise in a warm place for 1½ to 2 hours or until doubled in size and the dough springs back when pressed with a floured finger. (This dough takes longer to rise than usual because it is richly fruited.)

Turn out again onto a floured surface, knock back (punch down) and knead for 2 minutes until smooth. Divide into 12 or 14 pieces and shape into buns by rolling on a hard surface with the palm of your hand, first pressing down very hard then easing the pressure as the bun takes shape. Place well apart on the baking sheets. Either cut a cross in the top of each or, if using pastry crosses, leave as they are. Cover with oiled polythene (plastic wrap) and put to rise in a warm place until doubled in size – about 30 minutes.

For simple crosses, mark again with a sharp knife. For pastry crosses, roll out the pastry thinly and cut into narrow strips about 9 cm/3½ inches long. Brush with milk and lay two across each risen bun to make the cross. Bake in a moderately hot oven (190°C/375°F, Gas Mark 5) for 20 to 25 minutes or until golden brown. While the buns are baking, put the sugar and milk and water into a small pan and bring to the boil. Boil for 2 minutes. Remove the buns to a wire rack and while still hot brush the tops with the glaze two or three times. Leave to cool.

MAKES 14 TO 16

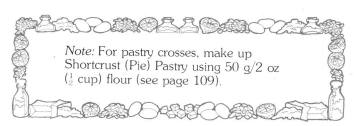

Note: For pastry crosses, make up Shortcrust (Pie) Pastry using 50 g/2 oz (½ cup) flour (see page 109).

# BATH BUNS

These are fruity buns with a crushed sugar topping.

| Metric/Imperial | American |
| --- | --- |
| 450 g/1 lb strong plain white flour | 4 cups all-purpose flour |
| 25 g/1 oz fresh yeast, or 1 tablespoon dried yeast | 1 cake compressed yeast, or 1½ packages active dry yeast |
| 50 g/2 oz plus 1 teaspoon caster sugar | ¼ cup plus 1 teaspoon sugar |
| 150 ml/¼ pint warm milk | ⅔ cup warm milk |
| 4 tablespoons warm water (43°C/110°F) | ¼ cup warm water (110°F) |
| 1 teaspoon salt | 1 teaspoon salt |
| 50 g/2 oz mixed candied peel, chopped | ⅓ cup chopped mixed candied peel |
| 150 g/6 oz sultanas | 1 cup seedless white raisins |
| 50 g/2 oz butter, melted | ¼ cup butter, melted |
| 2 eggs, beaten | 2 eggs, beaten |
| TOPPING: | TOPPING: |
| sugar lumps, lightly crushed | sugar lumps, lightly crushed |

Grease two baking sheets. Put 100 g/4 oz (1 cup) of the flour into a bowl with the yeast and 1 teaspoon sugar. Add the warm milk and water and mix to form a smooth batter. Leave in a warm place for 15 to 25 minutes or until frothy. Sift together the remaining flour and salt, then mix in the remaining sugar, peel and sultanas (white raisins). Stir the melted butter and most of the beaten eggs (reserve a little for glazing) into the yeast batter, then add the dry ingredients and mix well to form a soft dough.

Turn out onto a floured surface and knead for about 5 minutes until smooth. Place in a lightly floured bowl, cover with oiled polythene (plastic wrap) and put to rise in a warm place until doubled in size – this should take 45 to 60 minutes.

Remove the polythene (plastic wrap) and beat the dough with a wooden spoon or your hand to knock out all the air bubbles. Place tablespoons of the mixture, well apart, on the baking sheets. Cover lightly with oiled polythene (plastic wrap) and put to rise in a warm place until the buns have doubled in size. Remove the polythene (plastic wrap). Glaze lightly with the remaining egg and sprinkle with crushed sugar. Bake in a moderately hot oven (190°C/375°F, Gas Mark 5) for about 15 minutes or until well risen and golden. Cool on a wire rack.

MAKES 16 TO 18

# DEVONSHIRE SPLITS

These yeasted scone-like buns are split in half and filled with Devonshire, clotted or thick whipped cream and jam.

| Metric/Imperial | American |
| --- | --- |
| 15 g/½ oz fresh yeast, or 1½ teaspoons dried yeast and 1 teaspoon caster sugar | ½ cake compressed yeast, or ¾ package active dry yeast and 1 teaspoon sugar |
| about 300 ml/½ pint warm milk (43°C/110°F) | about 1¼ cups warm milk (110°F) |
| 450 g/1 lb strong plain white flour | 4 cups all-purpose flour |
| 1 teaspoon salt | 1 teaspoon salt |
| 50 g/2 oz butter or margarine | ¼ cup butter or margarine |
| 25 g/1 oz caster sugar | 2 tablespoons sugar |
| icing sugar for dredging | confectioners' sugar for dredging |
| FILLING: | FILLING: |
| Devonshire, clotted or whipped cream | whipped cream |
| raspberry jam | raspberry jam |

Grease two baking sheets. Dissolve the fresh (compressed) yeast in half the warm milk; or for dried (active dry) yeast, dissolve the 1 teaspoon sugar in half the milk, sprinkle the yeast on top and leave in a warm place for about 10 minutes or until frothy. Sift the flour and salt into a bowl. Melt the fat and sugar in the remaining milk, then cool to about 43°C/110°F. Add the milk and yeast liquid to the dry ingredients and mix to form a soft elastic dough.

Turn onto a floured surface and knead until smooth – about 10 minutes by hand or 3 to 4 minutes in an electric mixer. Shape into a ball, put into an oiled polythene (plastic) bag and leave to rise in a warm place until doubled in size – about 1 hour.

Turn out onto a floured surface and divide into about 15 equal pieces. Knead each piece lightly and shape into a ball. Put on the baking sheets and flatten slightly. Cover with oiled polythene (plastic wrap) and put to rise in a warm place until doubled in size – about 25 minutes.

Remove the polythene (plastic wrap) and bake in a hot oven (220°C/425°F, Gas Mark 7) for 15 to 20 minutes or until golden brown. Cool on a wire rack. To serve, split the buns open, spread with cream and jam, reassemble and dredge the tops with icing (confectioners') sugar.

MAKES 14 TO 15

*Opposite: Swiss Buns; Devonshire Splits; Bath Buns*

# SWISS BUNS

Long finger buns topped with pink or white glacé icing, these are a sticky treat.

**Metric/Imperial**
1 recipe quantity Devonshire
  Split dough (see opposite)
2 recipe quantities Glacé
  Icing (see page 105)
cochineal (optional)

**American**
1 recipe quantity Devonshire
  Split dough (see opposite)
2 recipe quantities Glacé
  Icing (see page 105)
pink food coloring (optional)

Grease two baking sheets. Make the dough as for Devonshire Splits and put to rise. Remove from the polythene (plastic) bag and turn onto a floured surface. Knock back (punch down) and

knead until smooth – about 2 minutes. Divide into about 12 equal pieces and roll each into a sausage shape by rolling backwards and forwards with the palms of your hands. Place on the baking sheets, cover with oiled polythene (plastic wrap) and put to rise in a warm place for about 25 minutes or until doubled in size.

Bake in a hot oven (220°C/425°F, Gas Mark 7) for about 15 minutes or until a pale golden brown. Cool on a wire rack.

Make up the glacé icing, with a few drops of cochineal (food coloring) if liked, to give a thick coating consistency. Spread a little icing over the top of each bun and leave to set.

MAKES ABOUT 12

# ICED FRUIT PLAIT (BRAID)

This attractive rich yeasted bread can be made into other shapes as well as a plait (braid). It is coated in glacé icing and sprinkled with nuts and glacé (candied) cherries.

**Metric/Imperial**
225 g/8 oz strong plain white flour
large pinch of salt
25 g/1 oz butter or margarine
50 g/2 oz caster sugar
75 g/3 oz mixed dried fruit
15 g/½ oz fresh yeast, or 1½ teaspoons dried yeast and 1 teaspoon caster sugar
5 tablespoons warm milk (43°C/110°F)
2 eggs, beaten separately
2 recipe quantities plain, orange or lemon Glacé Icing (see page 105)
DECORATION:
25 g/1 oz flaked almonds, toasted
25 g/1 oz glacé cherries, roughly chopped

**American**
2 cups all-purpose or bread flour
large pinch of salt
2 tablespoons butter or margarine
¼ cup sugar
½ cup mixed dried fruit
½ cake compressed yeast, or ¾ package active dry yeast and 1 teaspoon sugar
⅓ cup warm milk (110°F)
2 eggs, beaten separately
2 recipe quantities plain, orange or lemon Glacé Icing (see page 105)
DECORATION:
¼ cup flaked almonds, toasted
¼ cup roughly chopped candied cherries

Grease a baking sheet. Sift the flour and salt into a bowl. Rub in the fat, then mix in the sugar and dried fruit. Dissolve the fresh (compressed) yeast in the milk; or for dried (active dry) yeast dissolve the 1 teaspoon sugar in the milk, sprinkle the yeast on top and leave for about 10 minutes in a warm place until frothy. Add the yeast liquid and 1 beaten egg to the dry ingredients and mix to form a fairly soft dough.

Turn out onto a lightly floured surface and knead until smooth – about 10 minutes by hand or 3 to 4 minutes if using an electric mixer. Put into an oiled polythene (plastic) bag and leave to rise in a warm place for about 1 hour or until doubled in size.

Turn out, knock back (punch down) and knead for about 2 minutes or until smooth and firm. Divide the dough into three equal pieces and roll each into a long thin sausage. Place side by side in front of you and, starting in the middle, plait (braid) the three pieces together towards you. Secure the ends. Turn the dough right over away from you and plait (braid) the remainder of the three pieces to complete the loaf, securing the ends again. Place on the baking sheet, cover with oiled polythene (plastic wrap) and put to rise in a warm place for about 25 minutes or until doubled in size.

Remove the polythene (plastic wrap). Glaze the plait (braid) with beaten egg and bake in a hot oven (220°C/425°F, Gas Mark 7) for about 20 minutes or until golden brown and the bottom of the bread sounds hollow when tapped. Cool on a wire rack.

Pour the icing over the plait (braid). Sprinkle with the nuts and cherries and leave to set.

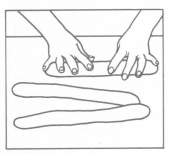

Roll into a long thin sausage

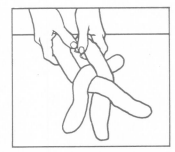

Plait (braid) from the middle

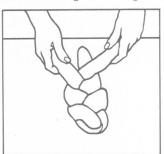

Turn the dough over to finish

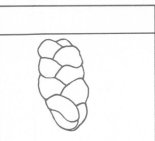

The plaited (braided) loaf

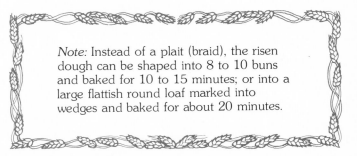

Note: Instead of a plait (braid), the risen dough can be shaped into 8 to 10 buns and baked for 10 to 15 minutes; or into a large flattish round loaf marked into wedges and baked for about 20 minutes.

# SPICED TEA RING

A tea ring with a spicy sugar filling, this can be iced or left plain.

**Metric/Imperial**

225 g/8 oz strong plain white flour

1 teaspoon caster sugar

15 g/½ oz fresh yeast, or 1½ teaspoons dried yeast

100 ml/4 fl oz warm milk (43°C/110°F)

½ teaspoon salt

50 g/2 oz butter or margarine

½ beaten egg

75 g/3 oz soft brown sugar

2–3 teaspoons ground cinnamon or mixed spice or 1½–2 teaspoons ground ginger

LEMON GLACÉ ICING:

½ teaspoon finely grated lemon rind

2–3 teaspoons lemon juice

100 g/4 oz icing sugar, sifted

DECORATION:

25 g/1 oz glacé cherries

25 g/1 oz nuts, chopped

**American**

2 cups all-purpose or bread flour

1 teaspoon sugar

½ cake compressed yeast, or ¾ package active dry yeast

½ cup warm milk (110°F)

½ teaspoon salt

¼ cup butter or margarine

½ beaten egg

½ cup dark brown sugar

2–3 teaspoons ground cinnamon or apple pie spice or 1½–2 teaspoons ground ginger

LEMON GLACÉ ICING:

½ teaspoon finely grated lemon rind

2–3 teaspoons lemon juice

1 cup confectioners' sugar, sifted

DECORATION:

¼ cup candied cherries

¼ cup chopped nuts

Grease a baking sheet. Put 65 g/2½ oz (½ cup plus 2 tablespoons) of the flour and the white sugar into a bowl with the yeast and milk. Mix lightly and leave in a warm place for about 20 minutes or until frothy. Sift the remaining flour with the salt and rub in 25 g/1 oz (2 tablespoons) of the fat. Add the egg and flour mixture to the yeast batter and mix to give a fairly soft dough which leaves the sides of the bowl clean.

Turn out onto a floured surface and knead until smooth – about 10 minutes by hand or 3 to 4 minutes in an electric mixer. Place in an oiled polythene (plastic) bag and put to rise in a warm place for about 1 hour or until doubled in size.

Remove from the bag. Knock back (punch down) and knead for about 2 minutes until smooth. Roll out to an oblong about 30 × 23 cm/12 × 9 inches. Melt the remaining fat and brush all over the dough. Sprinkle with the brown sugar, then with the spice. Starting from the long end, roll up tightly like a Swiss (jelly) roll and seal the ends together to make a ring. Place on the baking sheet. With a well-oiled pair of scissors, cut slashes about two-thirds of the way into the ring at 2.5 cm/1 inch intervals. Carefully twist these cut slices a little to open up the ring. Cover with oiled polythene (plastic wrap) and put to rise in a warm place for about 30 minutes or until well risen and puffy.

Remove the polythene (plastic wrap) and bake in a moderately hot oven (190°C/375°F, Gas Mark 5) for 30 to 35 minutes or until well risen and golden brown. Remove carefully to a wire rack to cool.

Make the glacé icing by adding the lemon rind and sufficient juice to the sugar to give a thick coating consistency. While the ring is still warm, spoon the icing over the top and allow it to run down the slices. Sprinkle with cherries and nuts.

# LARDY CAKE

This traditional British cake is made from a basic white bread dough, with the extra ingredients (lard, spices and dried fruit) rolled in after the first rising.

**Metric/Imperial**

100 g/4 oz lard

100 g/4 oz caster sugar

1 teaspoon ground cinnamon

pinch of grated nutmeg

100 g/4 oz sultanas, currants or mixed dried fruit

WHITE BREAD DOUGH:

450 g/1 lb strong plain white flour

1 teaspoon salt

15 g/½ oz lard

15 g/½ oz fresh yeast, or 1½ teaspoons dried yeast and 1 teaspoon caster sugar

about 250 ml/scant ½ pint warm water (43°C/110°F)

**American**

½ cup lard

½ cup sugar

1 teaspoon ground cinnamon

pinch of grated nutmeg

⅔ cup seedless white raisins, currants or mixed dried fruit

WHITE BREAD DOUGH:

4 cups all-purpose or bread flour

1 teaspoon salt

1 tablespoon shortening

½ cake compressed yeast, or ¾ package active dry yeast and 1 teaspoon sugar

about 1¼ cups warm water (110°F)

Grease a baking tin about 25 × 20 cm/10 × 8 inches. Make the white bread dough and let rise (see page 66).

Remove the dough from the polythene (plastic) bag. Knock back (punch down) and knead until smooth – about 2 minutes. Roll out on a floured surface to about 5 mm/¼ inch thick. Cover the surface with small flakes of half of the lard, then sprinkle with half of the sugar, cinnamon, nutmeg and dried fruit. Roll up loosely like a Swiss (jelly) roll, then roll out to an oblong the same size again. Repeat, covering with flakes of the remaining lard, most of the sugar and the remaining spices and fruit. Roll up loosely again and then roll out to fit the tin. Press well into it, especially at the corners, and cover with oiled polythene (plastic wrap). Put to rise in a warm place until doubled in size – 30 to 45 minutes.

Remove the polythene (plastic wrap). Brush the top with oil and, using a sharp knife, score the top into a criss-cross pattern. Sprinkle with the remaining sugar and bake in a hot oven (220°C/425°F, Gas Mark 7) for about 30 minutes or until well risen and golden brown. Turn out onto a wire rack and leave to cool. Serve in slices, plain or buttered.

# DANISH PASTRIES

These soft-textured flaky pastries are made with ordinary household flour – not the strong bread flour usually required for yeast cooking. The fillings and toppings can be varied according to taste.

### Metric/Imperial
25 g/1 oz fresh yeast, or 1 tablespoon dried yeast and 1 teaspoon caster sugar
about 150 ml/¼ pint warm water (43°C/110°F)
450 g/1 lb plain flour (not strong)
1 teaspoon salt
50 g/2 oz lard
25 g/1 oz caster sugar
2 eggs, beaten
275 g/10 oz butter
beaten egg to glaze

### American
1 cake compressed yeast, or 1½ packages active dry yeast and 1 teaspoon sugar
about ⅔ cup warm water (110°F)
4 cups all-purpose flour
1 teaspoon salt
¼ cup lard
2 tablespoons sugar
2 eggs, beaten
1¼ cups butter
beaten egg to glaze

*Danish Pastries*

Lightly grease three baking sheets. Dissolve the fresh (compressed) yeast in the water; or for dried (active dry) yeast, dissolve 1 teaspoon sugar in the water, sprinkle the yeast on top and leave in a warm place for about 10 minutes until frothy. Sift the flour and salt into a bowl, rub in the lard, then mix in the sugar. Add the yeast liquid and eggs to the dry ingredients and mix to form a soft, elastic dough, adding a little more water, if necessary.

Turn out onto a lightly floured surface and knead lightly by hand until smooth – 3 to 4 minutes. Put into an oiled polythene (plastic) bag and chill in the refrigerator for 10 minutes. Soften the butter and shape into an oblong about 25 × 10 cm/10 × 4 inches.

Roll out the dough to a 28 cm/11 inch square and spread the butter down the centre third of the dough. Enclose the butter by folding over the two flaps of dough just to overlap in the middle and seal the top and bottom with the rolling pin. Roll out into a strip three times as long as it is wide, then fold the bottom third of the dough up and the top third down. Seal the edges. Put into the polythene (plastic) bag and chill for 10 minutes.

Repeat the rolling, folding and resting twice more, leaving the dough to chill for at least 30 minutes after the last folding. The dough is now ready for shaping.

*Crescents:* Roll out one-quarter of the dough to a 23 cm/9 inch circle and cut into 8 even-sized wedges. Put 1 teaspoon Marzipan (see page 104), Confectioners' Custard (see page 105) or stewed apple at the wide base of each wedge and roll up towards the point. Curve into a crescent shape and place on a baking sheet. Cover with oiled polythene (plastic wrap) and put to rise in a warm place for 20 to 30 minutes or until puffy.

Brush with beaten egg and bake in a hot oven (220°C/425°F, Gas Mark 7) for 10 to 15 minutes or until a light golden brown. Remove to a wire rack and while warm brush with a little Glacé Icing (see page 105) and sprinkle with chopped nuts. Leave until cold.

MAKES 8

*Windmills and Imperial Stars:* Roll out one-quarter of the dough thinly and cut into 7.5 cm/3 inch squares. Make diagonal cuts from each corner to within 1 cm/½ inch of the centre. Put a small piece of Marzipan (see page 104) in the centre. Fold one corner of each cut section to the centre of the square and seal with beaten egg. Put onto a baking sheet and cover with polythene (plastic wrap). Leave to rise, glaze and bake, as above, for about 20 minutes.

While still warm; brush with Glacé Icing (see page 105) or clear honey. For windmills, sprinkle with toasted nuts and/or chopped glacé (candied) cherries. For Imperial Stars, brush the star projections with Glacé Icing and put a spoonful of Confectioners' Custard (see page 105) and half a glacé (candied) cherry in the centre. Leave to set.

MAKES 6 TO 8

*Cocks' Combs:* Roll out one-quarter of the dough thinly and cut into strips 11 × 12 cm/4½ × 5 inches. Spread half the width of each strip with a little Marzipan (see page 104), Confectioners' Custard (see page 105) or stewed apple sprinkled with cinnamon and currants. Fold over the other half to enclose the filling and seal with beaten egg. Make four or five cuts into the folded edge and put onto greased baking sheets, curving a little to open out the comb. Leave to rise, glaze and bake, as above, for about 20 minutes. Cool on a wire rack, spreading with Glacé Icing (see page 105) and sprinkling with nuts while still warm.

MAKES 6 TO 8

*Fruit Pinwheels:* Roll out one-quarter of the dough thinly and cut into an oblong 30 × 20 cm/12 × 8 inches. Spread all over with a mixture of 25 g/1 oz (2 tablespoons) butter, 25 g/1 oz (2½ tablespoons) soft brown (light brown) sugar and 1 teaspoon ground cinnamon and sprinkle with a few currants and a little chopped mixed candied peel. Roll up like a Swiss (jelly) roll, starting at the narrow end, and seal with beaten egg. Cut into 2.5 cm/1 inch slices and place on a baking sheet. Flatten slightly. Put to rise, glaze and bake, as above, for 15 to 20 minutes. Remove to a wire rack and ice and sprinkle with nuts and glacé (candied) cherries, as above.

MAKES 8

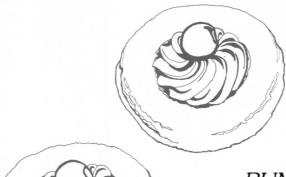

# RUM BABAS

Teatime treats or an elegant dessert, these rum-soaked yeasted rings are filled with currants and topped with whipped cream.

**Metric/Imperial**

15 g/½ oz fresh yeast, or 1½ teaspoons dried yeast and 1 teaspoon sugar

3 tablespoons warm milk (43°C/110°F)

100 g/4 oz strong plain white flour

pinch of salt

15 g/½ oz caster sugar

2 eggs, beaten

50 g/2 oz butter, softened

50 g/2 oz currants

RUM SYRUP:

2 tablespoons water

2 tablespoons clear honey

1–2 tablespoons rum

FILLING:

150–300 ml/¼–½ pint double cream

8 glacé cherries

**American**

½ cake compressed yeast, or ¾ package active dry yeast and 1 teaspoon sugar

3 tablespoons warm milk (110°F)

1 cup all-purpose flour

pinch of salt

1 tablespoon sugar

2 eggs, beaten

¼ cup butter, softened

⅓ cup currants

RUM SYRUP:

2 tablespoons water

2 tablespoons clear honey

1–2 tablespoons rum

FILLING:

1–1¼ cups heavy cream

8 candied cherries

Grease about eight small ring tins (molds) or two 600 ml/1 pint (2½ cup) ring moulds (tube pans) with lard. Mix the yeast (and 1 teaspoon sugar if using dried [active dry] yeast), milk and 25 g/ 1 oz (¼ cup) of the flour together. Put in a warm place for 20 to 30 minutes or until frothy. Sift the remaining flour and salt together and stir into the yeast batter with the sugar, eggs, butter and currants. Beat together for 3 to 4 minutes or until smooth.

Half fill the tins (molds) with the mixture. Cover with oiled polythene (plastic wrap) and put to rise in a warm place until the tins are two-thirds full.

Bake towards the top of a moderately hot oven (200°C/400°F, Gas Mark 6) for 15 to 20 minutes for small babas and 25 to 30 minutes for larger ones, or until well risen and firm to the touch. Turn out onto a wire rack.

Put the water, honey and rum into a saucepan and bring to the boil. Spoon over the babas while still warm and leave until cold. Whip the cream until stiff. Pipe a large whirl into each small baba and top it with a glacé (candied) cherry. Fill the large babas in a similar way.

MAKES ABOUT 8 INDIVIDUAL OR 2 LARGE BABAS

# DOUGH CAKE

**Metric/Imperial**

50 g/2 oz butter or margarine

50 g/2 oz caster sugar or soft brown sugar

100 g/4 oz mixed dried fruit

50 g/2 oz blanched almonds or walnuts, chopped

1 teaspoon mixed spice

honey or golden syrup to glaze

WHITE BREAD DOUGH:

225 g/8 oz strong plain white flour

½ teaspoon salt

10 g/¼ oz lard

10 g/¼ oz fresh yeast, or ¾ teaspoon dried yeast and ½ teaspoon caster sugar

about 125 ml/scant ¼ pint warm water (43°C/110°F)

**American**

¼ cup butter or margarine

¼ cup granulated or ⅓ cup dark brown sugar

⅔ cup mixed dried fruit

½ cup chopped blanched almonds or walnuts

1 teaspoon apple pie spice

honey or light corn syrup to glaze

WHITE BREAD DOUGH:

2 cups all-purpose or bread flour

½ teaspoon salt

1½ teaspoons shortening

¼ cake compressed yeast, or ½ package active dry yeast and ½ teaspoon sugar

about ⅔ cup warm water (110°F)

Grease a 450 g/1 lb loaf tin. Make the white bread dough and let rise (see page 66).

Remove the risen dough from the polythene (plastic) bag and put into a bowl. Add all the other ingredients, except the honey or syrup, and squeeze and knead until evenly mixed and smooth. Shape to fit the tin and put to rise in a large oiled polythene (plastic) bag in a warm place, until the dough reaches the top of the tin.

Remove the bag and bake in a very hot oven (230°C/450°F, Gas Mark 8) for about 30 minutes or until the bottom of the loaf sounds hollow when tapped. Remove from the tin to a wire rack and while still warm brush the top with honey or syrup. Cool.

# CROISSANTS

These classic crisp and flaky rolls, served for breakfast in Europe, are best warm and fresh. They freeze well so can be made in batches and thawed as required.

**Metric/Imperial**
25 g/1 oz fresh yeast, or 1 tablespoon dried yeast and 1 teaspoon caster sugar
225 ml/7 fl oz warm water (43°C/110°F)
450 g/1 lb strong plain white flour
2 teaspoons salt
25 g/1 oz lard
1 egg, beaten
150 g/6 oz hard butter or margarine
beaten egg to glaze

**American**
1 cake compressed yeast, or 1½ packages active dry yeast and 1 teaspoon sugar
⅞ cup warm water (110°F)
4 cups all-purpose flour
2 teaspoons salt
2 tablespoons lard
1 egg, beaten
¾ cup hard butter or margarine
beaten egg to glaze

Dissolve the fresh (compressed) yeast in the water; or for dried (active dry) yeast dissolve the sugar in the water, sprinkle the yeast on top and leave in a warm place for about 10 minutes or until frothy. Sift the flour and salt into a bowl and rub in the lard. Add the yeast liquid and beaten egg and mix to form a pliable dough.

Turn out onto a lightly floured surface and knead until smooth – 10 to 15 minutes by hand or 5 minutes in an electric mixer. Roll out to a rectangle about 50 × 20 cm/20 × 8 inches, keeping the edges neat and straight. Divide the butter or margarine into three even portions, then soften each portion with the back of a knife. Dot one portion over the top two-thirds of the dough, leaving a small margin clear all round. Fold into three bringing the plain third up and then the top third down over it. Turn the dough so the fold is on the right-hand side and seal the edges with the rolling pin. Repeat this process with the other two portions of fat. Put to rest in a lightly oiled polythene (plastic) bag in the refrigerator for 30 minutes.

Remove from the bag and repeat the rolling and folding process three times more. Replace in the bag and chill for at least 1 hour. (At this stage the dough can be left in the refrigerator for up to 3 days ready for shaping and cooking.)

Roll out the dough to a rectangle about 58 × 35 cm/23 × 14 inches. Cover with oiled polythene (plastic wrap) and leave to rest for 10 minutes. Trim the dough to 52 × 30 cm/21 × 12 inches, then cut in half lengthways. Cut each strip into 6 triangles 15 cm/6 inches high and with a 15 cm/6 inch base (see illustration). Brush all over with egg glaze and roll up each triangle loosely beginning at the base. Bend into a crescent shape and place on baking sheets, keeping the tip of each croissant underneath. Brush again with egg, cover with oiled polythene (plastic wrap) and put to rise in a warm place until puffy – about 30 minutes. Uncover, glaze again and bake in a hot oven (220°C/425°F, Gas Mark 7) for about 20 minutes or until well risen and golden brown.

MAKES 12

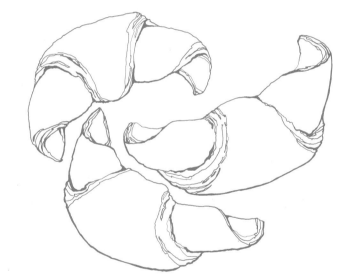

Fold the dough into three and seal the edges

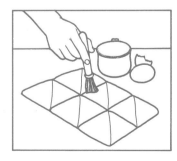
Cut into triangles and brush all over with egg glaze

Roll up each triangle, beginning at the base

Bend into a crescent shape and place on baking sheets

# BISCUITS AND COOKIES

## SUGAR BISCUITS (COOKIES)

These crunchy biscuits (cookies) are a favourite with children. Chopped nuts or coconut can be added for variety.

**Metric/Imperial**
175 g/7 oz self-raising flour
pinch of salt
25 g/1 oz cornflour
100 g/4 oz butter or
  margarine
100 g/4 oz caster sugar
1 egg or 2 egg yolks
¼ teaspoon vanilla essence
little milk
caster sugar or desiccated
  coconut for dredging

**American**
1¾ cups self-rising flour
pinch of salt
¼ cup cornstarch
½ cup butter or margarine
½ cup sugar
1 egg or 2 egg yolks
¼ teaspoon vanilla extract
little milk
sugar or shredded coconut
  for dredging

Grease two or three baking sheets. Sift the flour, salt and cornflour (cornstarch) into a bowl. Add the fat and rub in until the mixture resembles fine breadcrumbs. Stir in the sugar. Beat the egg or egg yolks and vanilla essence (extract) together. Add to the dry ingredients and mix to form a fairly soft dough (adding a little milk if necessary). Knead lightly, then wrap in foil and chill for about 30 minutes, if possible, before proceeding.

Turn the dough onto a lightly floured surface and roll out to about 5 mm/¼ inch thick. Cut into rounds or other biscuit (cookie) shapes (about 5 cm/2 inches in diameter) and place on the baking sheets. Bake in a moderately hot oven (200°C/400°F, Gas Mark 6) for 8 to 10 minutes or until light golden brown. Remove to a wire rack and dredge with sugar or coconut while still warm.

MAKES 30 TO 40

*Variations*
*Nutty:* add 25–40 g/1–1½ oz (¼ cup) very finely chopped nuts (walnuts, hazelnuts, almonds) to the dry ingredients and about 1 teaspoon milk.
*Coconut:* add 25 g/1 oz (⅓ cup) desiccated (shredded) coconut to the dry ingredients and about 1 teaspoon milk.

## ORANGE CREAMS

Soft-textured but crisp, these orange-flavoured biscuits (cookies) are sandwiched together with orange butter cream.

**Metric/Imperial**
100 g/4 oz margarine
100 g/4 oz caster sugar
2 teaspoons golden syrup
finely grated rind of 1 small
  orange
1 egg yolk
150 g/6 oz plain flour
25 g/1 oz custard powder
¼ teaspoon salt
½ teaspoon cream of tartar
½ teaspoon bicarbonate of
  soda
FILLING:
40 g/1½ oz butter
75 g/3 oz icing sugar, sifted
little grated orange rind
about 1 teaspoon orange
  juice

**American**
½ cup margarine
½ cup sugar
2 teaspoons light corn syrup
finely grated rind of 1 small
  orange
1 egg yolk
1½ cups all-purpose flour
¼ cup custard powder
¼ teaspoon salt
½ teaspoon cream of tartar
½ teaspoon baking soda
FILLING:
3 tablespoons butter
⅔ cup confectioners' sugar,
  sifted
little grated orange rind
about 1 teaspoon orange
  juice

Grease two or three baking sheets. Cream the margarine and sugar together until very light and fluffy. Beat in the syrup, orange rind and egg yolk. Sift the flour, custard powder, salt, cream of tartar and soda together and work into the creamed mixture. Roll into balls the size of a small walnut and put onto the baking sheets allowing room for spreading. Bake in a moderately hot oven (190°C/375°F, Gas Mark 5) for about 20 minutes until golden brown. Remove carefully to a wire rack to cool.

For the filling, cream the butter and sugar together, then beat in the orange rind and sufficient orange juice to give a thick spreading consistency. Use the orange butter cream to sandwich the biscuits (cookies) together.

MAKES ABOUT 12 PAIRS

Sugar Biscuits; Orange Creams; Bourbon Biscuits

# BOURBON BISCUITS (COOKIES)

These chocolate-flavoured biscuits (cookies) are delicious sandwiched together with a coffee and chocolate butter cream.

**Metric/Imperial**
100 g/4 oz butter or
    margarine
100 g/4 oz caster sugar
150 g/6 oz plain flour
50 g/2 oz custard powder
2 tablespoons cocoa powder
½ teaspoon baking powder
1 small egg
caster sugar for dredging
FILLING:
50 g/2 oz butter
65 g/2½ oz icing sugar, sifted
4 teaspoons drinking
    chocolate powder
1 teaspoon coffee essense

**American**
½ cup butter or margarine
½ cup sugar
1½ cups all-purpose flour
½ cup custard powder
2 tablespoons unsweetened
    cocoa
½ teaspoon baking powder
1 egg
sugar for dredging
FILLING:
¼ cup butter
½ cup plus 2 tablespoons
    confectioners' sugar, sifted
4 teaspoons hot chocolate
    powder
1 teaspoon strong black
    coffee

Lightly grease two baking sheets. Cream the butter or margarine and sugar together until very light and fluffy. Sift the flour with the custard powder, cocoa and baking powder. Beat the egg into the creamed mixture, then work in the flour mixture to give a fairly stiff dough. Roll out on a lightly floured surface to about 3 mm/⅛ inch thick and cut into 7.5 × 2.5 cm/3 × 1 inch fingers (bars). Prick all over. Dredge with sugar and transfer to the baking sheets. Bake in a moderate oven (180°C/350°F, Gas Mark 4) for 15 to 20 minutes or until just firm. Remove carefully to a wire rack to cool.

For the filling, beat the butter until soft, then gradually beat in the sugar, chocolate powder and coffee essence (strong black coffee). Sandwich the biscuits (cookies) together with the filling.

MAKES 22 TO 24

# HAZELNUT CINNAMON SHORTIES

Short-textured cinnamon-flavoured biscuits (cookies), these are rolled in chopped hazelnuts before baking.

| Metric/Imperial | American |
|---|---|
| 100 g/4 oz butter or margarine | $\frac{1}{2}$ cup butter or margarine |
| 75 g/3 oz caster sugar | 6 tablespoons sugar |
| 1 egg yolk | 1 egg yolk |
| 1 teaspoon ground cinnamon | 1 teaspoon ground cinnamon |
| 125 g/5 oz self-raising flour, sifted | 1$\frac{1}{4}$ cups self-rising flour, sifted |
| 50 g/2 oz hazelnuts, toasted and chopped | $\frac{1}{2}$ cup toasted and chopped hazelnuts |

Lightly grease two or three baking sheets. Cream the butter or margarine and sugar together until light and fluffy. Beat in the egg yolk and cinnamon. Add the sifted flour and mix to a smooth dough. Shape into a neat roll and cut into 24 slices. Flatten each slice slightly and coat in chopped hazelnuts. Place on the baking sheets a little apart to allow for spreading. Bake in a moderately hot oven (190°C/375°F, Gas Mark 5) for 15 to 20 minutes or until lightly browned. Cool on a wire rack.

MAKES 24

*Variation*
Omit the hazelnuts, top half the biscuits (cookies) with a walnut half and bake as above. When cold, sandwich together with Butter Cream (see page 104) flavoured with $\frac{1}{2}$ teaspoon ground cinnamon.

MAKES 12

# 1-2-3 BISCUITS (COOKIES)

This is an ideal mix to make for large numbers; simply double or treble the ingredients.

| Metric/Imperial | American |
|---|---|
| 50 g/2 oz butter | $\frac{1}{4}$ cup butter |
| 25 g/1 oz caster sugar | 2 tablespoons sugar |
| 75 g/3 oz plain flour, sifted | $\frac{3}{4}$ cup all-purpose flour, sifted |
| sugar for dredging | sugar for dredging |

Lightly grease one or two baking sheets. Cream the butter and sugar together until light and fluffy. Gradually work in the flour and knead until smooth. Chill if possible. Roll out thinly on a lightly floured surface and either cut into fingers (bars) and mark a pattern along the top with a fork; or into plain or fluted rounds 4 to 7.5 cm/1$\frac{1}{2}$ to 3 inches in diameter; or any other fancy biscuit (cookie) shape. Place on the baking sheets and bake in a cool oven (150°C/300°F, Gas Mark 2) for about 25 minutes until just tinged a pale brown. Cool on a wire rack and dredge with sugar. Store in an airtight container.

MAKES 10 TO 12

# SHORTBREAD

Famous in Scotland but well loved all the world over, shortbread is surprisingly simple to make.

| Metric/Imperial | American |
|---|---|
| 150 g/6 oz plain flour, or 100 g/4 oz plain flour and 50 g/2 oz ground rice or rice flour | 1$\frac{1}{2}$ cups all-purpose flour, or 1 cup all-purpose flour and $\frac{1}{3}$ cup ground rice or rice flour |
| pinch of salt | pinch of salt |
| 100 g/4 oz butter | $\frac{1}{2}$ cup butter |
| 50 g/2 oz caster sugar | $\frac{1}{4}$ cup sugar |
| extra sugar for dredging | extra sugar for dredging |

Line a 17 to 20 cm/7 to 8 inch sandwich tin (layer cake pan) with greaseproof (waxed) paper or line a baking sheet with the same. Sift the flour (or flour and rice) and salt into a bowl and rub in the butter with the fingertips until the mixture resembles breadcrumbs. Mix in the sugar, then knead the mixture until it forms a pliable dough. Either press into the tin or roll out to a 20 cm/8 inch round and place on the baking sheet. Prick the top, crimp the edges and mark into eight wedges.

Bake in a moderate oven (180°C/350°F, Gas Mark 4) for 40 to 50 minutes or until a very pale brown. If baked on a baking sheet, sprinkle with sugar and leave until cold before removing. If baked in a tin, turn out onto a wire rack immediately, sprinkle with sugar and leave to cool. Break into pieces when cold.

MAKES 8

# COCONUT RINGS

These crisp, coconut-flavoured rings have a jam filling.

| Metric/Imperial | American |
|---|---|
| 100 g/4 oz plain flour | 1 cup all-purpose flour |
| 100 g/4 oz caster sugar | $\frac{1}{2}$ cup sugar |
| 100 g/4 oz butter | $\frac{1}{2}$ cup butter |
| 100 g/4 oz desiccated coconut | 1$\frac{1}{3}$ cups shredded coconut |
| 1 egg, beaten | 1 egg, beaten |
| raspberry jam or bramble jelly | raspberry jam or blackberry jelly |

Lightly grease two baking sheets. Sift the flour into a bowl and mix in the sugar. Add the butter and rub in until the mixture resembles breadcrumbs. Stir in the coconut and bind to a fairly soft but manageable dough with the egg. Knead lightly and roll out thinly on a floured surface. Cut into rounds using a 6 cm/2$\frac{1}{2}$ inch plain or fluted cutter, then stamp out the centres using a 2.5 cm/1 inch cutter. Put the rings on the baking sheets.

Bake in a moderately hot oven (190°C/375°F, Gas Mark 5) for about 15 minutes or until lightly tinged brown. Cool on a wire rack and sandwich together with jam or jelly.

MAKES 16 TO 18

# EASTER BISCUITS (COOKIES)

These traditional Easter cookies are filled with currants and have a special sugar-glazed topping.

**Metric/Imperial**
100 g/4 oz butter or
    margarine
100 g/4 oz caster sugar
2 egg yolks
50 g/2 oz currants
150 g/6 oz plain flour
50 g/2 oz rice flour or
    ground rice
1 teaspoon mixed spice
1–2 tablespoons milk
TOPPING:
little egg white
caster sugar for dredging

**American**
$\frac{1}{2}$ cup butter or margarine
$\frac{1}{2}$ cup sugar
2 egg yolks
$\frac{1}{3}$ cup currants
$1\frac{1}{2}$ cups all-purpose flour
$\frac{1}{3}$ cup rice flour or ground
    rice
1 teaspoon apple pie spice
1–2 tablespoons milk
TOPPING:
little egg white
sugar for dredging

Line three or four baking sheets with greaseproof (waxed) paper or non-stick parchment. Cream the butter or margarine and sugar together until light and fluffy. Beat in the egg yolks followed by the currants. Sift the flour, rice flour or ground rice and spice together. Add to the creamed mixture and mix to a soft but manageable dough with a little milk, if necessary. Knead lightly and turn onto a floured surface.

Roll out to about 5 mm/$\frac{1}{4}$ inch thick and cut into 6 cm/$2\frac{1}{2}$ inch fluted rounds. (They can be made larger if preferred.) Place carefully on the baking sheets and score narrow lines on top with the back of a knife. Bake in a moderate oven (180°C/350°F, Gas Mark 4) for 10 minutes.

Brush with egg white and dredge with sugar. Return to the oven and bake for a further 5 to 10 minutes or until firm and lightly browned. Cool on a wire rack.

MAKES 20 TO 25

*Variations*
Finely grated lemon or orange rind can also be added to the mixture and the spice can be replaced by ground cinnamon or ginger or left out completely.

# VIENNESE BISCUITS (COOKIES)

These piped biscuits (cookies) can be baked in paper cases or on a baking sheet. The various shapes are then sprinkled with icing (confectioners') sugar and finished with a dot of red jam.

**Metric/Imperial**
200 g/8 oz plain flour
pinch of salt
200 g/8 oz butter or
    margarine
50 g/2 oz caster sugar
vanilla essence
icing sugar for dredging
1–2 tablespoons seedless
    raspberry jam

**American**
2 cups all-purpose flour
pinch of salt
1 cup butter or margarine
$\frac{1}{4}$ cup sugar
vanilla extract
confectioners' sugar for
    dredging
1–2 tablespoons raspberry
    jelly

Put 16 paper (cup) cake cases into patty (shallow muffin) tins, or grease two baking sheets. Sift the flour and salt together. Cream the butter or margarine and sugar together until very light and fluffy. Work in the flour and a few drops of vanilla essence (extract). Put into a piping bag fitted with a star vegetable tube and pipe a whirl of the mixture into each paper case, starting at the centre. Alternatively, pipe straight onto a greased baking sheet in a whirl, a star, figure of eight or fingers.

Bake in a moderate oven (180°C/350°F, Gas Mark 4) for 15 to 25 minutes or until pale golden brown and firm. The biscuits (cookies) in paper cases take the longest. Cool on a wire rack.

When cold, sprinkle with icing (confectioners') sugar and put a dot of jam (jelly) in the centre. This can be done with a spoon or in a paper piping bag with just the point cut off.

MAKES 16

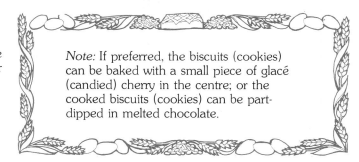

*Note:* If preferred, the biscuits (cookies) can be baked with a small piece of glacé (candied) cherry in the centre; or the cooked biscuits (cookies) can be part-dipped in melted chocolate.

Put paper cases into patty (muffin) tins

Pipe a whirl of the mixture into each paper case

Alternatively, pipe straight onto a greased baking sheet

To finish, sprinkle with icing (confectioners') sugar

# PEANUT BUTTER COOKIES

Children enjoy these delicious peanut-flavoured cookies.

**Metric/Imperial**
50 g/2 oz peanut butter
50 g/2 oz butter or
  margarine
grated rind of ½ orange
50 g/2 oz caster sugar
40 g/1½ oz light soft brown
  sugar
½ egg, beaten
40 g/1½ oz raisins or
  sultanas, chopped
100 g/4 oz self-raising flour,
  sifted

**American**
¼ cup peanut butter
¼ cup butter or margarine
grated rind of ½ orange
¼ cup sugar
¼ cup light brown sugar
½ egg, beaten
¼ cup chopped raisins or
  seedless white raisins
1 cup self-rising flour, sifted

Put the peanut butter, butter or margarine, orange rind and sugars into a bowl and beat until light and fluffy. Beat in the egg, then add the dried fruit and flour and mix to a fairly firm dough. Roll into balls about the size of a walnut and place well apart on ungreased baking sheets. Slightly flatten each one using a fork or blunt knife and mark with a criss-cross pattern.

Bake in a moderate oven (180°C/350°F, Gas Mark 4) for about 25 minutes or until well risen and golden brown. Remove to a wire rack to cool. Store in an airtight container.

MAKES 16 TO 20

*Above: Peanut Butter Cookies*
*Opposite: Flapjacks; Oat Crisps*

# FLAPJACKS

These oaty bars are deliciously crunchy, sweet and sticky.

| **Metric/Imperial** | **American** |
| --- | --- |
| 100 g/4 oz margarine | ½ cup margarine |
| 25 g/1 oz caster sugar | 2 tablespoons sugar |
| 2 tablespoons golden syrup | 2 tablespoons light corn |
| 200 g/8 oz rolled oats | syrup |
| pinch of salt | 2¼ cups rolled oats |
| | pinch of salt |

Grease a 20 cm/8 inch square shallow cake tin. Cream the margarine and sugar together until creamy and soft. Melt the syrup in a heatproof bowl over a saucepan of hot water, then beat into the creamed mixture, followed by the rolled oats and salt. Mix thoroughly. Spoon into the tin, pressing the mixture well down, especially in the corners.

Bake in a moderately hot oven (190°C/375°F, Gas Mark 5) for 30 to 40 minutes or until firm and golden brown. Cool in the tin for a few minutes, then cut into bars. Leave until quite cold before removing from the tin and breaking into bars.

MAKES 12

# OAT CRISPS

| **Metric/Imperial** | **American** |
| --- | --- |
| 150 g/5 oz butter | ½ cup plus 2 tablespoons |
| 50 g/2 oz golden syrup | butter |
| 100 g/4 oz demerara sugar | 3 tablespoons light corn |
| 75 g/3 oz rolled oats | syrup |
| 50 g/2 oz desiccated | ⅔ cup light brown sugar |
| coconut | 1 cup rolled oats |
| 100 g/4 oz plain flour, sifted | ⅔ cup shredded coconut |
| 1 teaspoon bicarbonate of | 1 cup all-purpose flour, |
| soda | sifted |
| 1 teaspoon hot water | 1 teaspoon baking soda |
| | 1 teaspoon hot water |

Grease two baking sheets. Put the butter, syrup and sugar into a small saucepan and heat gently until melted and the sugar has dissolved. Mix together the oats, coconut and flour, then stir into the melted mixture. Dissolve the soda in the hot water and stir into the oat mixture. Allow to cool slightly, then form into 20 to 25 small balls. Place well apart on the baking sheets.

Bake in a moderate oven (160°C/325°F, Gas Mark 3) for 15 to 20 minutes or until evenly browned. Leave to cool slightly before removing to a wire rack with a palette knife. When cold, store in an airtight container.

MAKES 20 TO 25

# MELTING MOMENTS

As the name implies, these cookies just melt in the mouth. They have a cornflake coating topped with a glacé (candied) cherry.

| Metric/Imperial | American |
|---|---|
| 75 g/3 oz butter or margarine | 6 tablespoons butter or margarine |
| 75 g/3 oz lard or white fat | 6 tablespoons lard or shortening |
| 125 g/5 oz caster sugar | ½ cup plus 2 tablespoons sugar |
| 1 egg, beaten | 1 egg, beaten |
| 250 g/10 oz self-raising flour, sifted | 2½ cups self-rising flour, sifted |
| 1 teaspoon vanilla essence | 1 teaspoon vanilla extract |
| about 50 g/2 oz cornflakes, crushed | about 2 cups crushed cornflakes |
| 8 glacé cherries, quartered | 8 candied cherries, quartered |

Grease two baking sheets. Beat the butter or margarine and lard or fat (shortening) together until soft. Add the sugar and cream until light and fluffy. Beat in the egg, then work in the flour and vanilla essence (extract) to give a fairly stiff dough. Divide the mixture into 30 pieces and roll into balls. Roll each ball in crushed cornflakes and place fairly well apart on the baking sheets. Flatten them slightly and press a quarter of a glacé (candied) cherry into the top of each one.

Bake in a moderate oven (180 C/350 F, Gas Mark 4) for 15 to 20 minutes or until golden brown. Cool on a wire rack and store in an airtight container.

MAKES 30

# JUMBLES

These crisp almond-flavoured cookies are baked in the shape of a figure 'S'.

| Metric/Imperial | American |
|---|---|
| 100 g/4 oz butter or margarine | ½ cup butter or margarine |
| 100 g/4 oz caster sugar | ½ cup sugar |
| 1 egg, beaten | 1 egg, beaten |
| almond essence (optional) | almond extract (optional) |
| 150 g/6 oz plain flour, sifted | 1½ cups all-purpose flour, sifted |
| 50 g/2 oz ground almonds | ½ cup ground almonds |

Grease two baking sheets. Cream the butter or margarine and sugar together until light and fluffy. Beat in the egg and a few drops of almond essence (extract), if used. Gradually work in the flour and ground almonds to give a firm but pliable dough and knead lightly.

Divide the dough into two pieces and roll each into a long sausage 1 to 2 cm/½ to ¾ inch in diameter. Cut into 10 cm/4 inch lengths and put onto the baking sheets in 'S' shapes. Bake in a moderate oven (180 C/350 F, Gas Mark 4) for 15 to 20 minutes or until a pale golden brown. Cool on a wire rack.

MAKES 16 TO 20

# PINWHEELS

Two colours and flavours of dough are pressed on top of each other and rolled up like a Swiss (jelly) roll. The roll is then sliced and baked to give the pinwheel effect.

| Metric/Imperial | American |
|---|---|
| 100 g/4 oz butter or margarine | ½ cup butter or margarine |
| 100 g/4 oz caster sugar | ½ cup sugar |
| 1 egg, beaten | 1 egg, beaten |
| 200 g/8 oz plain flour, sifted | 2 cups all-purpose flour, sifted |
| 15 g/½ oz cocoa powder | 2 tablespoons unsweetened cocoa |

Grease two baking sheets. Cream the butter or margarine and sugar together until light and fluffy, then beat in the egg. Gradually work in the flour to give a firm but pliable dough. Divide the mixture in half and work the sifted cocoa into one portion. Roll out each piece on a lightly floured surface to equal-sized rectangles. Carefully put the chocolate piece on top of the plain one. Roll up like a Swiss (jelly) roll. Wrap in waxed paper or polythene (plastic) and chill for about 30 minutes.

Cut carefully into slices about 5 mm/¼ inch thick, using a sharp knife. Arrange the slices on the baking sheets. Bake in a moderate oven (180 C/350 F, Gas Mark 4) for 15 to 20 minutes or until lightly browned. Cool on a wire rack.

MAKES 20 TO 24

*Variations*
The plain portion of the dough can be flavoured with 1 teaspoon finely grated lemon or orange rind or 50 g/2 oz (¼ cup) chopped glacé (candied) cherries, or 50 g/2 oz (½ cup) chopped nuts. The chocolate portion can have 25 g/1 oz (1 square) coarsely grated plain (semisweet) chocolate worked into it, or the cocoa powder replaced with 1 tablespoon instant coffee powder.

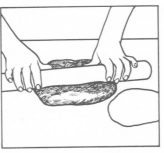
*Roll out the dough rectangles*

*Place chocolate dough on top*

*Roll up Swiss (jelly) roll style*

*Cut into even slices*

# SWEETMEAL BISCUITS (COOKIES)

These coarse-textured semisweet biscuits (cookies) can be eaten plain or sandwiched with butter cream.

| Metric/Imperial | American |
|---|---|
| 75 g/3 oz wholemeal flour | $\frac{3}{4}$ cup wholewheat flour |
| 15 g/$\frac{1}{2}$ oz plain flour | 2 tablespoons all-purpose |
| pinch of salt | flour |
| $\frac{1}{2}$ teaspoon baking powder | pinch of salt |
| 15 g/$\frac{1}{2}$ oz fine oatmeal | $\frac{1}{2}$ teaspoon baking powder |
| 40 g/1$\frac{1}{2}$ oz butter | 1 tablespoon fine oatmeal |
| 40 g/1$\frac{1}{2}$ oz caster sugar | 3 tablespoons butter |
| about 2 tablespoons milk | 3 tablespoons sugar |
| | about 2 tablespoons milk |

Grease two baking sheets. Sift the flours, salt and baking powder into a bowl and mix in the oatmeal. Add the butter and rub in until the mixture resembles fine breadcrumbs. Stir in the sugar. Add sufficient milk to mix to a stiff paste and knead well.

Roll out thinly on a lightly floured surface and cut into rounds using a plain or fluted 5 to 6 cm/2 to 2$\frac{1}{2}$ inch cutter. Transfer to the baking sheets and prick well all over.

Bake in the centre of a moderately hot oven (190°C/375°F, Gas Mark 5) for 15 to 20 minutes or until a light golden brown. Cool on a wire rack and store in an airtight container.

MAKES 16 TO 18

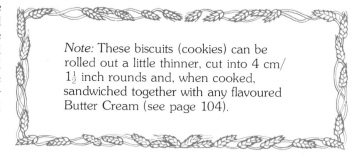

*Note:* These biscuits (cookies) can be rolled out a little thinner, cut into 4 cm/1$\frac{1}{2}$ inch rounds and, when cooked, sandwiched together with any flavoured Butter Cream (see page 104).

# GRANTHAM GINGERBREADS

These lightly ginger-flavoured biscuits (cookies) are surprisingly hollow in the centre when baked.

| Metric/Imperial | American |
|---|---|
| 100 g/4 oz butter or | $\frac{1}{2}$ cup butter or margarine |
| margarine | 1$\frac{1}{2}$ cups sugar |
| 300 g/12 oz caster sugar | 1 egg, beaten |
| 1 large egg, beaten | 2$\frac{1}{4}$ cups self-rising flour |
| 250 g/9 oz self-raising flour | 1–1$\frac{1}{2}$ teaspoons ground |
| 1–1$\frac{1}{2}$ teaspoons ground | ginger |
| ginger | little sugar |
| little granulated sugar | |

Grease two or three baking sheets. Cream the butter or margarine thoroughly, then beat in the sugar a little at a time until well incorporated, followed by the egg. Sift the flour and ginger together and add to the mixture. Knead until a pliable dough is formed. Roll into balls about the size of a walnut and place on the baking sheets, fairly well apart as they spread during cooking. Sprinkle each with a little sugar and bake towards the top of a cool oven (150°C/300°F, Gas Mark 2) for about 40 minutes or until puffed up and lightly browned. Cool on a wire rack.

MAKES 25 TO 30

*Variations*
A little finely grated lemon or orange rind can be added to the mixture; or, if preferred, use cinnamon or mixed spice (apple pie spice) in place of the ginger.

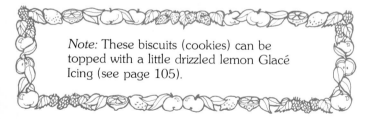

*Note:* These biscuits (cookies) can be topped with a little drizzled lemon Glacé Icing (see page 105).

# ALMOND COOKIES

Moist almond-flavoured squares, these have an apricot-glazed flaked almond topping.

| Metric/Imperial | American |
|---|---|
| 200 g/8 oz soft margarine | 1 cup soft margarine |
| 100 g/4 oz caster sugar | ½ cup sugar |
| 50 g/2 oz ground almonds | ½ cup ground almonds |
| 150 g/6 oz self-raising flour, sifted | 1½ cups self-rising flour, sifted |
| almond essence | almond extract |
| 50 g/2 oz sultanas | ⅓ cup seedless white raisins |
| 40–50 g/1½–2 oz flaked almonds | ½ cup flaked almonds |
| GLAZE: | GLAZE: |
| 3 tablespoons apricot jam | 3 tablespoons apricot jam |
| 1 tablespoon water | 1 tablespoon water |

Grease an oblong tin about 28 × 18 × 4 cm/11 × 7 × 1½ inches. Cream the margarine and sugar together until light and fluffy. Work in the ground almonds, flour, a few drops of almond essence (extract) and the sultanas (white raisins). Put into the tin and spread out evenly. Sprinkle with the flaked almonds and press in gently. Bake in a moderate oven (160°C/325°F, Gas Mark 3) for 50 to 60 minutes or until lightly browned and just firm.

Heat the apricot jam and water together in a saucepan until melted, then boil for 1 minute. Rub through a sieve (strainer) and brush over the almonds while still warm. Leave in the tin until cold, then cut into squares.

MAKES 15 TO 18

# BRANDY SNAPS

These crisp syrupy wafer rolls are flavoured with ginger and may be filled with whipped cream.

| Metric/Imperial | American |
|---|---|
| 50 g/2 oz butter or blended white vegetable fat | ¼ cup butter or shortening |
| 50 g/2 oz golden syrup | 3 tablespoons light corn syrup |
| 50 g/2 oz caster sugar | ¼ cup sugar |
| 50 g/2 oz plain flour | ½ cup all-purpose flour |
| large pinch of ground ginger | large pinch of ground ginger |
| FILLING (OPTIONAL): | FILLING (OPTIONAL): |
| whipped cream | whipped cream |
| few pieces of stem ginger | few pieces of preserved ginger |

Line two baking sheets with non-stick parchment. Grease several wooden spoon handles.

Melt the butter or fat (shortening) in a saucepan with the syrup and sugar, then remove from the heat. Sift the flour and ginger and stir into the melted mixture. Put teaspoons of the mixture well apart on the baking sheets. Bake in a moderate oven (160°C/325°F, Gas Mark 3) for 8 to 10 minutes or until golden brown. Cool until just firm enough to remove with a palette knife, then wind quickly round the spoon handles. Cool on a wire rack until firm, then slide off the handles.

If the wafers become too cool and brittle before winding round the handles, return to the oven for a minute or two to soften up again. Serve as they are or fill with whipped cream and top with a piece of stem (preserved) ginger.

MAKES 12 TO 16

# HAZEL NUTTIES

These are a little difficult to make but worth the effort.

| Metric/Imperial | American |
|---|---|
| 100 g/4 oz hazelnuts | ¾ cup hazelnuts |
| 100 g/4 oz demerara sugar | ⅔ cup light brown sugar |
| about ½ egg, beaten | about ½ egg, beaten |

Line one or two baking sheets with non-stick parchment. Toast the hazelnuts under a moderate grill (broiler) until the skins split and the nuts brown. Cool slightly, then rub off the skins. Grind the nuts and put into a bowl with the sugar. Mix well and bind to a pliable dough with the egg.

Turn onto a sheet of non-stick parchment or an oiled board. Using an oiled rolling pin, roll out to about 3 mm/⅛ inch thick. Cut into 4 cm/1½ inch plain rounds and transfer carefully to the lined baking sheets. Bake in a moderate oven (180°C/350°F, Gas Mark 4) for 10 to 12 minutes or until golden brown. Cool slightly, then remove carefully to a wire rack to cool.

MAKES 20 TO 24

*Left: Hazel Nutties*
*Opposite: Almond Cookies; Florentines*

# FLORENTINES

Almonds, raisins, candied peel and cherries are combined with a buttery syrup to make these delicious chocolate-coated wafers.

**Metric/Imperial**
75 g/3 oz butter
100 g/4 oz caster sugar
100 g/4 oz flaked almonds, roughly chopped
25 g/1 oz raisins, chopped
40 g/1½ oz mixed candied peel, chopped
40 g/1½ oz glacé cherries, chopped
finely grated rind of ¼ lemon
150–175 g/5–6 oz plain chocolate

**American**
6 tablespoons butter
½ cup sugar
1 cup roughly chopped almonds
3 tablespoons chopped raisins
¼ cup chopped mixed candied peel
¼ cup chopped candied cherries
finely grated rind of ¼ lemon
5–6 squares semisweet chocolate

Line two or three baking sheets with non-stick parchment. Melt the butter and sugar in a saucepan and boil for 1 minute. Remove from the heat and stir in all the remaining ingredients, except the chocolate. Leave to cool. Put teaspoons of the mixture in heaps on the baking sheets well apart – four or five per sheet. Bake in the centre of a moderate oven (180°C/350°F, Gas Mark 4) for 10 to 12 minutes or until golden brown. Cool until just firm, pressing the edges back to a neat shape. Remove carefully to a wire rack and leave until cold.

Melt the chocolate in a heatproof bowl over a saucepan of hot water. Spread over the smooth side of each florentine. As it sets, mark into wavy lines with a fork. Leave to harden. The florentines can be stored (without the chocolate) for about a week in an airtight container with waxed paper or non-stick parchment separating them.

MAKES 24 TO 30

# WALNUT BARS

These thin nutty bars are baked with a coffee glaze.

| Metric/Imperial | American |
|---|---|
| 200 g/8 oz plain flour | 2 cups all-purpose flour |
| 150 g/6 oz butter | $\frac{3}{4}$ cup butter |
| 100 g/4 oz icing sugar | 1 cup confectioners' sugar |
| 100 g/4 oz walnuts, finely chopped | 1 cup finely chopped walnuts |
| 1 egg white | 1 egg white |
| 2 teaspoons coffee essence | 2 teaspoons strong black coffee |

Sift the flour onto a working surface and make a well in the centre. Cut the butter into pieces and put into the well with the sugar. Work the butter and sugar together with the fingertips, then gradually work in the flour. Finally work in the walnuts and knead to a smooth dough. Wrap the dough in greaseproof (waxed) paper and chill for 20 minutes if possible.

Using half the dough at a time, roll out to a rectangle about 5 mm/$\frac{1}{4}$ inch thick. Mark into a criss-cross pattern with a sharp knife. Mix the egg white and coffee essence (strong black coffee) together and brush all over the surface. Cut the dough into bars about 7.5 × 4 cm/3 × $1\frac{1}{2}$ inches and transfer carefully to the baking sheets. Repeat with the remaining dough.

Bake in a moderately hot oven (190°C/375°F, Gas Mark 5) for about 15 minutes or until lightly coloured. Cool on a wire rack and store in an airtight container.

MAKES ABOUT 30

# MACAROONS

These traditional, slightly sticky, almond biscuits (cookies) are best baked on rice paper.

| Metric/Imperial | American |
|---|---|
| 1 standard egg white | 1 egg white |
| 75 g/3 oz ground almonds | $\frac{3}{4}$ cup ground almonds |
| 100 g/3$\frac{1}{2}$ oz caster sugar | 7 tablespoons sugar |
| $\frac{1}{4}$–$\frac{1}{2}$ teaspoon almond essence | $\frac{1}{4}$–$\frac{1}{2}$ teaspoon almond extract |
| few split blanched almonds (optional) | few split blanched almonds (optional) |

Line two baking sheets with rice paper. Beat the egg white until stiff, then fold in the ground almonds, sugar and almond essence (extract) to taste. Put into a piping bag fitted with a large plain vegetable tube and pipe small dots of the mixture onto the prepared baking sheets, keeping them fairly well apart. Top each with a piece of almond, if liked. Bake in a moderate oven (180°C/350°F, Gas Mark 4) for 20 to 25 minutes or until lightly coloured. Cool on a wire rack, then tear off the surplus rice paper before serving.

MAKES ABOUT 15

# ALMOND BUTTER WAFERS

These curled wafers are an excellent accompaniment to soft fruit or ice cream.

| Metric/Imperial | American |
|---|---|
| 1 egg white | 1 egg white |
| 50 g/2 oz caster sugar | $\frac{1}{4}$ cup sugar |
| 25 g/1 oz plain flour, sifted | $\frac{1}{4}$ cup all-purpose flour, sifted |
| 25 g/1 oz flaked almonds | $\frac{1}{4}$ cup flaked almonds |
| 25 g/1 oz butter, melted | 2 tablespoons butter, melted |

Line two baking sheets with non-stick parchment. Lightly grease a rolling pin and stand on a wire rack. Beat the egg white until very stiff. Fold in the sugar, well-sifted flour and almonds and mix gently but thoroughly. Finally fold in the cooled melted butter. Put teaspoons of the mixture onto the baking sheet and spread out thinly. Bake in a moderately hot oven (190°C/375°F, Gas Mark 5) for about 8 minutes or until browned round the edges and a pale brown in the centre.

Cool slightly on the sheet, then remove with a palette knife and curl around the rolling pin. Leave until cool and firm, then transfer to a wire rack until cold. Store in an airtight container.

MAKES ABOUT 20

*Variations*
Nibbed almonds or ground almonds can be used in place of flaked almonds and a little finely grated orange or lemon rind can be added with the nuts.

*Note:* For petit fours put coffee spoons of the mixture onto the baking sheet and curl around wooden spoon handles.

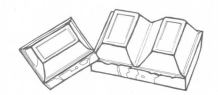

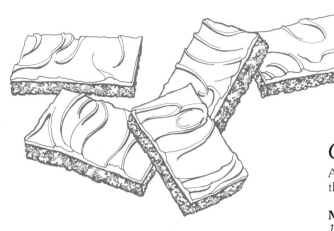

# CHOCOLATE CARAMELS

A chocolate topping, caramel centre and shortbread base make these mouth-watering munchy squares.

| Metric/Imperial | American |
|---|---|
| 125 g/5 oz plain flour | 1¼ cups all-purpose flour |
| ½ teaspoon salt | ½ teaspoon salt |
| 50 g/2 oz caster sugar | ¼ cup sugar |
| 100 g/4 oz butter | ½ cup butter |
| FILLING: | FILLING: |
| 100 g/4 oz margarine | ½ cup margarine |
| 100 g/4 oz soft brown sugar | ⅔ cup dark brown sugar |
| 2 tablespoons golden syrup | 2 tablespoons light corn syrup |
| 1 small or ½ large can condensed milk | 1 small or ½ large can condensed milk |
| vanilla essence | vanilla extract |
| 100 g/4 oz plain chocolate, broken up | 4 squares semisweet chocolate, broken up |

Grease an 18 cm/7 inch square shallow cake tin. Sift the flour and salt into a bowl. Add the sugar and butter. Rub in until the mixture resembles breadcrumbs, then knead it into a smooth ball. Press evenly into the prepared tin. Bake in a moderate oven (180 C/350 F, Gas Mark 4) for about 25 minutes or until pale golden brown and just firm. Leave to cool in the tin.

For the filling, put the margarine, sugar, syrup and condensed milk into a saucepan and heat gently until melted. Bring to the boil and boil gently for 7 to 8 minutes, stirring occasionally. Add a few drops of vanilla essence (extract) and beat well until smooth and beginning to thicken. Pour over the shortbread base in the tin. Cool and then chill.

Melt the chocolate in a heatproof bowl over a saucepan of hot water. Beat until smooth and pour over the caramel. Spread out evenly. As it begins to set, make swirling patterns in the chocolate with a round-bladed knife. When completely set, cut into 16 squares and remove from the tin.

MAKES 16

# CHOCOLATE QUICKIES

Children love to make – and eat – these uncooked chocolatey biscuits (cookies).

| Metric/Imperial | American |
|---|---|
| 100 g/4 oz butter or margarine | ½ cup butter or margarine |
| 2 tablespoons cocoa powder | 2 tablespoons unsweetened cocoa |
| 1 tablespoon demerara sugar | 1 tablespoon light brown sugar |
| 2 tablespoons golden syrup | 2 tablespoons light corn syrup |
| 200 g/8 oz semisweet biscuits, crushed | 2 cups crushed semisweet cookies |
| 100 g/4 oz plain or milk chocolate, broken up | 4 squares plain or milk chocolate, broken up |

Grease an 18 cm/7 inch square shallow cake tin. Melt the butter or margarine in a small pan. Add the cocoa, sugar and syrup and when melted bring to the boil. Boil for 1 minute. Remove from the heat and stir in the biscuit (cookie) crumbs. Turn into the tin and press in well to give a smooth top.

Melt the chocolate in a heatproof bowl over hot water. Beat until smooth, then pour over the biscuit (cookie) mixture. As the chocolate sets mark it into swirls with a round-bladed knife. Chill until set firm, then cut into squares or bars.

MAKES 12 TO 16

*Variations*
Add 25 g/1 oz of any of the following to the mixture with the crushed biscuits (cookies): chopped nuts, chopped glacé (candied) cherries, sultanas (seedless white raisins), currants or chopped raisins, or desiccated (shredded) coconut. Alternatively, sprinkle the setting chocolate with chopped or flaked almonds or coconut.

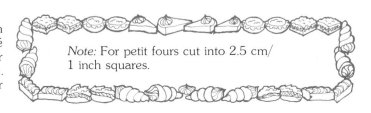

*Note:* For petit fours cut into 2.5 cm/ 1 inch squares.

# GÂTEAUX AND CHEESECAKES

## BUTTERSCOTCH CARAMEL GÂTEAU

| Metric/Imperial | American |
|---|---|
| 150 g/6 oz butter or margarine | ¾ cup butter or margarine |
| 150 g/6 oz soft brown sugar | 1 cup dark brown sugar |
| 3 eggs, beaten | 3 eggs, beaten |
| 150 g/6 oz self-raising flour | 1½ cups self-rising flour |
| 1 teaspoon vanilla essence | 1 teaspoon vanilla extract |
| 1 tablespoon black treacle | 1 tablespoon molasses |
| 1 recipe quantity Confectioners' Custar (see page 105) | 1 recipe quantity Confectioners' Custard (see page 105) |
| BUTTER CREAM: | BUTTER CREAM: |
| 75 g/3 oz butter | 6 tablespoons butter |
| 1½ tablespoons black treacle | 1½ tablespoons molasses |
| 2 teaspoons lemon juice | 2 teaspoons lemon juice |
| 200 g/8 oz icing sugar, sifted | 2 cups confectioners' sugar, sifted |
| CARAMEL: | CARAMEL: |
| 100 g/4 oz caster sugar | ½ cup sugar |
| 4 tablespoons water | ¼ cup water |

Grease a 20 cm/8 inch round deep cake tin or, if possible, a moule-à-manqué (slope-sided) cake tin, and line the bottom with greased greaseproof (waxed) paper. Cream the fat and sugar together until light and fluffy and very pale in colour. Beat in the eggs one at a time, following each one with a spoonful of flour. Sift the remaining flour and fold into the mixture, followed by the vanilla essence (extract) and treacle (molasses). Turn into the prepared tin and bake in a moderately hot oven (190°C/375°F, Gas Mark 5) for 40 to 50 minutes or until well risen and firm to the touch. Turn out onto a wire rack and leave to cool.

Split the cake into three layers and sandwich back together with the confectioners' custard.

For the butter cream, beat the butter and treacle (molasses) together until soft. Add the lemon juice and gradually beat in the sugar and a little water, if necessary, to give a spreading consistency. Use most of the butter cream to mask the cake, decorating into swirls with a round-bladed knife. Use the remainder to pipe a border around the top and base of the cake using a star tube.

For the caramel, put the sugar and water into a pan and boil until a dark caramel colour. Pour onto a greased baking sheet and leave until hard. Break into pieces and use to decorate the top of the gâteau.

SERVES 8

## PINEAPPLE CREAM GÂTEAU

| Metric/Imperial | American |
|---|---|
| 3 large eggs | 3 eggs |
| 100 g/4 oz caster sugar | ½ cup sugar |
| 100 g/4 oz self-raising flour | 1 cup self-rising flour |
| 376 g/13½ oz can crushed pineapple | 13½ oz can crushed pineapple |
| 2 teaspoons arrowroot | 2 teaspoons arrowroot |
| 4 teaspoons cold water | 4 teaspoons cold water |
| little Kirsch or sherry | little Kirsch or sherry |
| 300 ml/½ pint double cream | 1¼ cups heavy cream |
| 50 g/2 oz flaked almonds, toasted | ½ cup flaked almonds, toasted |
| few Chocolate Squares (see page 118) or chocolate drops for decoration | few Chocolate Squares (see page 118) or chocolate chips for decoration |

Grease a shallow oblong tin about 28 × 18 cm/11 × 7 inches and line the bottom and sides with greased greaseproof (waxed) paper. Whisk the eggs and sugar together until very thick and the beater leaves a trail when lifted. Sift the flour twice and fold quickly and evenly through the mixture. Turn into the prepared tin and level the top. Bake in a moderately hot oven (190°C/375°F, Gas Mark 5) for 20 to 25 minutes or until well risen, firm and lightly browned. Turn onto a wire rack and leave to cool.

Put the undrained pineapple in a saucepan and heat gently. Dissolve the arrowroot in the water. Add to the pan and bring to the boil, stirring continuously. Simmer until thickened and clear. Cool.

Cut the cake in half lengthways and place one half on a serving plate. Sprinkle with Kirsch or sherry. Whip the cream until stiff and mix about one-quarter of it with half of the pineapple mixture. Spread this over the sponge base and cover with the second layer. Spread all round the sides of the cake lightly with cream and cover with nuts. Pipe the remaining cream in a wide band around the top of the cake and down each corner, then fill the centre of the top with the remaining pineapple mixture. Decorate with chocolate squares or drops (chips) and chill for at least 30 minutes before serving.

SERVES 8

*Black Forest Gâteau*

# BLACK FOREST GÂTEAU

| Metric/Imperial | American |
|---|---|
| 3 large eggs | 3 eggs |
| 125 g/4½ oz caster sugar | ½ cup plus 1 tablespoon sugar |
| 75 g/3 oz plain flour | ¾ cup all-purpose flour |
| 15 g/½ oz cocoa powder | 2 tablespoons unsweetened cocoa |
| 425 g/15 oz can black cherries | 15 oz can black cherries |
| 2 teaspoons arrowroot | 2 teaspoons arrowroot |
| 450 ml/¾ pint double cream | 2 cups heavy cream |
| 2–3 tablespoons Kirsch, Cointreau or brandy | 2–3 tablespoons Kirsch, Cointreau or brandy |
| 3 flaked chocolate bars for decoration | 3 flaked chocolate bars for decoration |

Grease a 23 to 24 cm/9 to 9½ inch round deep cake tin and line the bottom and sides with greased greaseproof (waxed) paper. Whisk the eggs and sugar together until the mixture is thick and pale and the beater leaves a trail when lifted. Sift the flour and cocoa together twice and fold evenly and lightly through the mixture. Pour into the prepared tin and bake in the centre of a moderately hot oven (190°C/375°F, Gas Mark 5) for about 30 minutes or until firm to the touch. Turn out and cool.

Cut the cake into three equal layers. Drain the cherries and mix 150 ml/¼ pint (⅔ cup) of the juice (adding water if necessary) with the arrowroot. Bring slowly to the boil, stirring continuously, and boil until clear. Halve the cherries, remove the stones (pits) and stir into the sauce, reserving a few for decoration. Leave to cool. Whip the cream until stiff.

Place the bottom cake layer on a serving plate and spread with half the cherry mixture and a layer of cream. Cover with the second cake layer. Sprinkle with liqueur, then cover with the remaining cherry mixture, another layer of cream and the top of the cake. Reserve a little cream for piping and use the remainder to mask the whole cake, making a decorative pattern on the top.

Cut 8 to 10 pieces off the chocolate bars for decoration and chop the remainder. Use the chopped chocolate to coat the sides of the cake. Using a large star tube, pipe 8 to 10 whirls of cream on top of the cake and decorate with pieces of chocolate and the reserved cherries. Leave for 2 to 3 hours before serving.

SERVES 8 TO 10

# HAZELNUT GÂTEAU

| Metric/Imperial | American |
|---|---|
| 150 g/6 oz butter or margarine | $\frac{3}{4}$ cup butter or margarine |
| 100 g/4 oz caster sugar | $\frac{1}{2}$ cup sugar |
| 50 g/2 oz light soft brown sugar | $\frac{1}{3}$ cup light brown sugar |
| 3 large eggs | 3 eggs |
| 150 g/6 oz self-raising flour, sifted | $1\frac{1}{2}$ cups self-rising flour, sifted |
| 50 g/2 oz toasted hazelnuts, chopped | $\frac{1}{2}$ cup chopped toasted hazelnuts |
| 300 ml/$\frac{1}{2}$ pint double cream | $1\frac{1}{4}$ cups heavy cream |
| 225 g/8 oz raspberries or strawberries | $\frac{1}{2}$ lb raspberries or strawberries |

Grease a 20 cm/8 inch loose-bottomed round cake tin (springform pan) and line the bottom with greased greaseproof (waxed) paper. Cream the fat and sugars together until light and fluffy, then beat in the eggs one at a time, following each with a spoonful of flour. Fold in the remaining flour, followed by half the hazelnuts. Turn into the prepared tin and level the top. Bake in a moderate oven (180°C/350°F, Gas Mark 4) for about 1 hour or until well risen and firm to the touch. Turn carefully onto a wire rack and leave to cool.

Cut the cake into 3 equal layers. Whip the cream until stiff. Slice the raspberries or strawberries, reserving 8 small or 4 large ones for decoration. Use most of the cream and the sliced fruit to sandwich the cake layers back together. Spread cream over the top of the gâteau. Use the remaining cream to pipe eight whirls around the edge of the cake and top each with a whole or halved berry. Sprinkle the remaining nuts over the centre of the gâteau.

SERVES 8 TO 10

# CHOCOLATE CREAM GÂTEAU

| Metric/Imperial | American |
|---|---|
| 150 g/5 oz plain flour | $1\frac{1}{4}$ cups all-purpose flour |
| 25 g/1 oz cornflour | $\frac{1}{4}$ cup cornstarch |
| 25 g/1 oz cocoa powder | $\frac{1}{4}$ cup unsweetened cocoa |
| 6 large eggs | 6 eggs |
| 225 g/8 oz caster sugar | 1 cup sugar |
| 75 g/3 oz butter, melted and cooled | 6 tablespoons butter, melted and cooled |
| 4 tablespoons orange or coffee liqueur or cherry brandy | $\frac{1}{4}$ cup orange or coffee liqueur or cherry brandy |
| 600 ml/1 pint double cream | $2\frac{1}{2}$ cups heavy cream |
| 225 g/8 oz plain chocolate | 8 squares semisweet chocolate |
| little icing sugar (optional) | little confectioners' sugar (optional) |

Grease two 25 cm/10 inch straight-sided deep sandwich tins (layer cake pans) and line the bottoms and sides with greased greaseproof (waxed) paper. Sift the flour, cornflour (cornstarch) and cocoa together. Put the eggs and sugar into an electric mixer bowl or a large heatproof bowl over a saucepan of gently simmering water. Beat until thick and pale and the beater leaves a thick trail when lifted. Remove from the heat (if necessary) and beat until cool. Gradually fold in the flour mixture alternating with the cooled melted butter until evenly mixed. Divide between the tins and bake in a moderately hot oven (190°C/375°F, Gas Mark 5) for about 30 minutes or until firm. Turn out and cool.

Split each cake into two layers and sprinkle three layers (not the top one) with liqueur. Whip the cream until stiff and use three-quarters of it to sandwich the cake layers together.

Melt the chocolate in a heatproof bowl over a pan of hot water. Use about one-quarter of it to make chocolate squares (see page 118). Pour the remaining chocolate over the cake and allow it to run down the sides. As it sets, use a palette knife to make a pattern on the top. Chill until set.

Using the remaining cream in a piping bag fitted with a large star tube, pipe large rosettes around the top of the cake. Decorate with chocolate squares. Leave for at least 1 hour in a cool place before serving. Just before serving, if liked, sprinkle a little icing (confectioners') sugar over the centre of the chocolate.

SERVES 10 TO 12

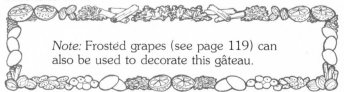

*Note:* Frosted grapes (see page 119) can also be used to decorate this gâteau.

# CHOCOLATE MERINGUE GÂTEAU

| Metric/Imperial | American |
|---|---|
| 4 egg whites | 4 egg whites |
| 225 g/8 oz caster sugar | 1 cup sugar |
| FILLING: | FILLING: |
| 150 ml/¼ pint milk | ⅔ cup milk |
| 50 g/2 oz caster sugar | ¼ cup sugar |
| 50 g/2 oz plain chocolate, broken up | 2 squares semisweet chocolate, broken up |
| 3 egg yolks | 3 egg yolks |
| 175 g/6 oz unsalted butter | ¾ cup unsalted butter |
| 1 tablespoon rum (optional) | 1 tablespoon rum (optional) |
| TOPPING: | TOPPING: |
| 150 ml/¼ pint double cream | ⅔ cup heavy cream |
| 2 tablespoons milk | 2 tablespoons milk |
| 6 marrons glacés, halved, or 12 raspberries | 6 marrons glacés, halved, or 12 raspberries |
| 25 g/1 oz plain chocolate, coarsely grated | 1 square semisweet chocolate, coarsely grated |

Line three baking sheets with non-stick parchment and draw a 20 cm/8 inch circle on each. Beat the egg whites until very stiff, then beat in the sugar a little at a time, making sure the meringue is stiff again before adding more sugar. Divide into three and spread the meringue evenly over each circle on the baking sheets. Bake in a cool oven (150°C/300°F, Gas Mark 2) for about 1 hour. Turn off the heat and leave in the oven until cold.

To make the filling, put the milk, sugar and chocolate into a heatproof bowl over a saucepan of hot water and heat until the chocolate melts. Stir until well mixed. Stir a little of the chocolate mixture into the egg yolks, then return to the bowl and cook gently, stirring continuously, until the mixture thickens sufficiently to coat the back of a spoon. Remove from the heat, cover and leave until cold (but do not chill).

Cream the butter until soft and gradually beat in the chocolate custard. Flavour with rum, if liked, and use to sandwich the meringue circles together.

Whip the cream and milk together until stiff and spread half over the top layer of meringue. Use the remainder to pipe 12 rosettes around the edge. Top each one with a piece of marron glacé or a raspberry and sprinkle chocolate over the centre. Leave at room temperature for 2 to 3 hours before serving.

SERVES 8

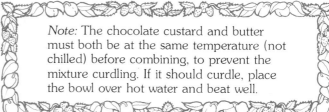

*Note:* The chocolate custard and butter must both be at the same temperature (not chilled) before combining, to prevent the mixture curdling. If it should curdle, place the bowl over hot water and beat well.

# STRAWBERRY SHORTCAKE

| Metric/Imperial | American |
|---|---|
| 225 g/8 oz self-raising flour | 2 cups self-rising flour |
| ½ teaspoon baking powder | ½ teaspoon baking powder |
| large pinch of salt | large pinch of salt |
| 75 g/3 oz butter or margarine | 6 tablespoons butter or margarine |
| 125 g/5 oz caster sugar | ½ cup plus 2 tablespoons sugar |
| 1 egg, beaten | 1 egg, beaten |
| 3–4 tablespoons milk | 3–4 tablespoons milk |
| 225 g/8 oz strawberries (or raspberries) | ½ lb strawberries (or raspberries) |
| 300 ml/½ pint double cream | 1¼ cups heavy cream |

Grease a 20 cm/8 inch deep sandwich tin (layer cake pan) and line the bottom with greased greaseproof (waxed) paper. Sift the flour, baking powder and salt into a bowl. Add the fat and rub in until the mixture resembles fine breadcrumbs. Stir in 100 g/4 oz (½ cup) of the sugar, then add the egg and 1 to 2 tablespoons milk to mix to a soft dough. Knead or mix lightly until smooth, then press the dough evenly into the tin. Bake in a moderately hot oven (190°C/375°F, Gas Mark 5) for 25 to 30 minutes or until firm to the touch and a light golden brown. Turn out onto a wire rack and leave to cool.

Reserve eight strawberries for decoration; slice the remainder and sprinkle with the rest of the sugar. Whip the cream with 2 tablespoons milk until stiff.

Split the shortcake into two layers and use half the cream to spread over both cut surfaces of the cake. Spoon the strawberries over one half and sandwich back together with the other half of the cake. Use the remaining cream to spread over the top of the cake. Use the reserved whole (or sliced) strawberries to decorate. Chill before serving.

SERVES 6 TO 8

# CHESTNUT GÂTEAU

**Metric/Imperial**
65 g/2½ oz plain flour
15 g/½ oz cornflour
3 large eggs
75 g/3 oz caster sugar
40 g/1½ oz butter, melted
3–4 tablespoons sherry
226 g/8 oz can sweetened
 chestnut purée
300 ml/½ pint whipping
 cream
50 g/2 oz flaked almonds,
 toasted
few pieces of marron glacé
 for decoration (optional)

**American**
½ cup plus 2 tablespoons all-
 purpose flour
2 tablespoons cornstarch
3 eggs
6 tablespoons sugar
3 tablespoons butter, melted
3–4 tablespoons sherry
8 oz can sweetened chestnut
 purée
1¼ cups whipping cream
½ cup flaked almonds,
 toasted
few pieces of marron glacé
 for decoration (optional)

Grease a 20 cm/8 inch square deep cake tin, or a deep oblong tin about 20 × 30 cm/8 × 12 inches, and line the bottom and sides with greased greaseproof (waxed) paper. Sift the flour and cornflour (cornstarch) together. Put the eggs and sugar into an electric mixer bowl or a large heatproof bowl over a saucepan of gently simmering water. Beat until very thick and pale and the beater leaves a trail when lifted. Remove from the heat (if necessary) and beat until cool. Using a metal spoon fold in half of the sifted flour, then the cooled melted butter. Finally fold in the remaining flour and turn into the prepared tin. Bake towards the top of a moderately hot oven (190°C/375°F, Gas Mark 5) for 25 to 30 minutes or until well risen and just firm to the touch. Turn out onto a wire rack and leave to cool.

Cut the square or oblong cake in half and sprinkle with the sherry. Beat the chestnut purée until very smooth and put just over half of it into a piping bag fitted with a star tube. Whip the cream until stiff and fold about one-quarter into the remaining chestnut purée. Use to sandwich the two cakes together. Completely mask the whole cake with the remaining cream and press the almonds around the edge. Pipe a trellis design of chestnut purée over the top of the gâteau and a row of stars all around the edge. Decorate with pieces of marron glacé, if liked.

SERVES 6 TO 8

# PEACH SHORTBREAD GÂTEAU

| Metric/Imperial | American |
|---|---|
| 225 g/9 oz plain flour | 2¼ cups all-purpose flour |
| 75 g/3 oz butter | 6 tablespoons butter |
| 150 g/6 oz soft brown sugar | 1 cup dark brown sugar |
| 300 ml/½ pint double cream | 1¼ cups heavy cream |
| 2 tablespoons top-of-the-milk | 2 tablespoons half-and-half |
| 538 g/1 lb 3 oz can peach halves, drained | 1 lb 3 oz can peach halves, drained |
| blanched pistachio nuts for decoration | blanched pistachio nuts for decoration |

Lightly grease a baking sheet. Sift the flour into a bowl. Add the butter cut into pieces and rub in until the mixture resembles breadcrumbs. Mix in the sugar and knead the mixture to a pliable dough. Divide the mixture into three. Roll out two portions thinly on sheets of greaseproof (waxed) paper to oblongs about 28 × 10 cm/11 × 4 inches. Crimp the edges and place on ungreased baking sheets, still on the paper. Prick all over. Roll out the third portion thinly and cut into six fluted 7.5 cm/3 inch rounds. Cut each one in half and place on the greased baking sheet. Mark with a sharp knife to look like a fan.

Bake all the shortbread in a moderate oven (180°C/350°F, Gas Mark 4), allowing 25 to 30 minutes for the oblongs and 15 to 20 minutes for the fans or until just firm. Transfer to a wire rack and leave until cold.

Whip the cream and milk (half-and-half) together until stiff and put half into a piping bag fitted with a star vegetable tube. Spread half the remaining cream over one layer of shortbread. Slice half the peaches, lay over the cream and cover with the remaining cream. Place the second layer of shortbread on top. Pipe cream over the top of the gâteau and decorate with the shortbread fans, placing them at an angle along the top with halved or quartered peaches in between. Decorate with pistachio nuts.

SERVES 8

# HIGH PEAK GÂTEAU

| Metric/Imperial | American |
|---|---|
| 1½ recipe quantities Choux Paste (see page 111) | 1½ recipe quantities Choux Paste (see page 111) |
| FILLING: | FILLING: |
| 600 ml/1 pint double cream | 2½ cups heavy cream |
| 2 tablespoons icing sugar | 2 tablespoons confectioners' sugar |
| 50 g/2 oz plain chocolate, coarsely grated | 2 squares semisweet chocolate, coarsely grated |
| 1 tablespoon rum | 1 tablespoon rum |
| CARAMEL: | CARAMEL: |
| 200 g/8 oz granulated sugar | 1 cup sugar |
| 150 ml/¼ pint water | ⅔ cup water |

Grease two baking sheets. Put the choux paste into a piping bag fitted with a 1 cm/½ inch plain tube. Pipe 40 to 45 walnut-sized choux balls on the baking sheets. Bake in a hot oven

Opposite: Chestnut Gâteau. Above: High Peak Gâteau

(220°C/425°F, Gas Mark 7) for about 25 minutes or until a pale golden brown and firm. Pierce each bun to release the steam and cool on a wire rack.

Whip the cream until stiff and fold in the sugar. Use about one-third of the cream to fill the choux buns. Fold the chocolate and rum into the remaining cream. Arrange a layer of buns on a serving dish about 18 cm/7 inches in diameter. Spoon the chocolate cream onto these buns and pile it up into a pyramid. Stick the buns in circles all around the cream pyramid, finishing with one at the top.

For the caramel, dissolve the sugar in the water in a heavy-based saucepan and boil until straw-coloured (127°C/260°F). Cool slightly until the caramel begins to thicken, then drizzle all over the pyramid. Leave to set.

SERVES 8 TO 10

# FRESH FRUIT CHEESECAKE

**Metric/Imperial**
PASTRY:
*100 g/4 oz self-raising flour, sifted*
*75 g/3 oz butter*
*50 g/2 oz icing sugar, sifted*
*1 standard egg*
FILLING:
*2 tablespoons cornflour*
*2 tablespoons natural yogurt*
*50 g/2 oz butter, softened*
*2 eggs, separated*
*225 g/8 oz cream cheese*
*225 g/8 oz cottage cheese*
*50 g/2 oz caster sugar*
*½ teaspoon vanilla essence*
*100–150 g/4–6 oz fresh soft fruit for decoration*

**American**
PASTRY:
*1 cup self-rising flour, sifted*
*6 tablespoons butter*
*½ cup confectioners' sugar, sifted*
*1 egg*
FILLING:
*2 tablespoons cornstarch*
*2 tablespoons unflavored yogurt*
*¼ cup butter, softened*
*2 eggs, separated*
*1 cup cream cheese*
*1 cup cottage cheese*
*¼ cup sugar*
*½ teaspoon vanilla extract*
*¼–½ lb fresh soft fruit for decoration*

Grease a 23 cm/9 inch loose-bottomed round deep cake tin. Put the flour, butter, icing (confectioners') sugar and egg into a bowl and beat together until smooth. Spread into the bottom of the tin and bake in a moderately hot oven (190°C/375°F, Gas Mark 5) for 15 minutes. Remove from the oven and leave to cool.

Mix the cornflour (cornstarch) and yogurt together, then add the butter, egg yolks, cheeses, sugar and vanilla essence (extract) and beat until smooth. Beat the egg whites until stiff and fold evenly through the cheese mixture. Spread over the cooked pastry base and return to the oven to bake for about 25 minutes or until just firm. Leave to cool.

Remove from the tin and decorate the top with fresh soft fruit, e.g., raspberries, sliced strawberries, grapes, currants, etc.

SERVES 8 TO 10

*Variation*
*For a citrus-flavoured cheesecake:* the vanilla flavour can be omitted and the finely grated rind of 1 lemon or 1 small orange used in its place.

# NO-COOK ORANGE CHEESECAKE

**Metric/Imperial**
*1 tablespoon powdered gelatine*
*75 g/3 oz caster sugar*
*2 eggs, separated*
*200 ml/7 fl oz milk*
*grated rind and juice of 1 orange*
*2 teaspoons lemon juice*
*350 g/12 oz cottage cheese or curd cheese*
*50 g/2 oz butter*
*100 g/4 oz digestive biscuits or gingernuts, crushed*
DECORATION:
*6 tablespoons double cream, whipped*
*orange jelly slices*

**American**
*1 tablespoon powdered unflavored gelatine*
*6 tablespoons sugar*
*2 eggs, separated*
*⅞ cup milk*
*grated rind and juice of 1 orange*
*2 teaspoons lemon juice*
*1½ cups cottage cheese*
*¼ cup butter*
*1 cup crushed graham crackers or gingersnaps*
DECORATION:
*6 tablespoons heavy cream, whipped*
*orange candy slices*

Grease an 18 cm/7 inch loose-bottomed round deep cake tin. Mix the gelatine, sugar, egg yolks and milk in a small saucepan and bring just to the boil, stirring continuously to make sure the gelatine is dissolved. Add the orange rind and juice and the lemon juice and leave to cool.

Sieve (strain) the cottage cheese and stir into the cooled gelatine mixture. Leave until on the point of setting. Beat the egg whites until stiff and fold through the cheese mixture. Pour into the prepared tin.

Melt the butter and stir in the biscuit (cracker or cookie) crumbs. Spoon in an even layer over the setting cheesecake and chill until firm. Remove carefully from the tin and invert onto a plate. Decorate the top with whirls of cream and orange jelly (candy) slices.

SERVES 6

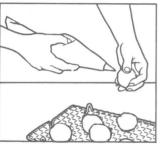
*Fill the choux buns with cream*

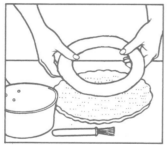
*Place the ring on the pastry*

*Arrange the buns on the ring*

*Decorate with whipped cream*

# GÂTEAU ST. HONORÉ

| Metric/Imperial | American |
|---|---|
| 1 recipe quantity Flan Pastry (see page 111) | 1 recipe quantity Flan Pastry (see page 111) |
| 1 recipe quantity Choux Paste (see page 111) | 1 recipe quantity Choux Paste (see page 111) |
| beaten egg to glaze | beaten egg to glaze |
| 300 ml/½ pint double cream, whipped | 1¼ cups heavy cream, whipped |
| CARAMEL. | CARAMEL: |
| 200 g/8 oz granulated sugar | 1 cup sugar |
| 150 ml/¼ pint water | ⅔ cup water |
| FILLING: | FILLING: |
| 425 g/15 oz can apricot halves, drained | 15 oz can apricot halves, drained |
| 2 recipe quantities Confectioners' Custard (see page 105) | 2 recipe quantities Confectioners' Custard (see page 105) |

Grease three baking sheets. Roll out the flan pastry dough to a 20 cm/8 inch round. Place on one baking sheet and crimp the edges. Prick all over and bake in a moderate oven (180°C/350°F, Gas Mark 4) for about 20 minutes or until lightly coloured. Cool until firm, then remove to a wire rack.

Put the choux paste into a piping bag fitted with a 1 cm/½ inch plain tube. Pipe a 20 cm/8 inch circle on another baking sheet. Use the remaining paste to pipe 16 to 20 walnut-sized choux balls on the third baking sheet. Glaze all the choux paste with beaten egg and bake in a hot oven (220°C/425°F, Gas Mark 7) for about 25 minutes or until golden brown and firm. Remove to a wire rack and pierce each ball and the ring to allow the steam to escape. When cold, fill the choux balls with whipped cream, reserving a little for decoration.

For the caramel, dissolve the sugar in the water in a heavy-based pan and boil rapidly until it just turns a pale straw colour (127°C/260°F). Spread a little caramel around the edge of the pastry round and position the choux ring on top. Dip the tops of the choux buns into the caramel, holding them with tongs. Put a dot of caramel on the bottom of each bun and stick them around the top of the choux ring. Pour any extra caramel over the caramelled buns.

Reserve six apricots for decoration and roughly chop the remainder. Spread half of the slightly warm confectioners' custard in the choux ring. Cover with the chopped apricots, then the remaining custard. Brush the custard with apricot can juice (to prevent a skin forming) and decorate with the remaining apricots, whipped cream and angelica, if liked.

SERVES 8

# CRUMB CHEESECAKE

| Metric/Imperial | American |
|---|---|
| CRUMB BASE: | CRUMB CRUST: |
| 50 g/2 oz butter | ¼ cup butter |
| 100 g/4 oz digestive biscuits, crushed | 1 cup crushed graham crackers |
| ½ teaspoon ground cinnamon | ½ teaspoon ground cinnamon |
| FILLING: | FILLING: |
| 350 g/12 oz cottage cheese or curd cheese | 1½ cups cottage cheese |
| 3 eggs, separated | 3 eggs, separated |
| 100 g/4 oz caster sugar | ½ cup sugar |
| 1 tablespoon cornflour | 1 tablespoon cornstarch |
| 1 tablespoon custard powder | 1 tablespoon custard powder |
| finely grated rind of 2 lemons | finely grated rind of 2 lemons |
| 4 tablespoons soured cream or natural yogurt | ¼ cup sour cream or unflavored yogurt |
| fresh lemon and orange slices for decoration | fresh lemon and orange slices for decoration |

Grease an 18 cm/7 inch loose-bottomed round deep cake tin. Melt the butter in a pan and stir in the biscuit (cracker) crumbs and cinnamon. Press the mixture into the bottom of the tin.

Rub the cottage cheese through a sieve (strainer) or blend in a liquidizer until smooth. (Curd cheese is used as it is.) Add the egg yolks to the cheese with 75 g/3 oz (6 tablespoons) of the sugar, the cornflour (cornstarch), custard powder, lemon rind and cream or yogurt and mix well until smooth. Beat the egg whites until stiff and fold in the remaining sugar. Fold evenly through the cheese mixture and pour into the tin over the crumb base.

Bake in a cool oven (150°C/300°F, Gas Mark 2) for 1 hour. Turn off the heat, open the door a little and leave the cheesecake in the oven for a further 30 minutes. Remove from the oven and leave to get cold. Carefully remove the cake tin and decorate the top of the cheesecake with slices of lemon and orange.

SERVES 8 TO 10

*Variation*
*For an orange-flavoured cheesecake:* use grated orange rind instead of lemon rind.

# CELEBRATION CAKES

## CHRISTMAS CAKE

A rich fruit cake, this may be coated with marzipan and royal icing for Christmas or left plain.

**Metric/Imperial**
200 g/8 oz raisins
200 g/8 oz currants
200 g/8 oz sultanas
100 g/4 oz mixed candied peel, chopped
50 g/2 oz almonds, ground or finely chopped
50 g/2 oz glacé cherries, quartered, rinsed and dried
200 g/8 oz butter
150 g/6 oz light soft brown sugar
4 large eggs
200 g/8 oz plain flour
pinch of salt
1 teaspoon mixed spice
1 tablespoon brandy, sherry or lemon juice

**American**
1⅓ cups raisins
1⅓ cups currants
1⅓ cups seedless white raisins
⅔ cup chopped mixed candied peel
½ cup ground or finely chopped almonds
⅓ cup quartered candied cherries, rinsed and dried
1 cup butter
1 cup light brown sugar
4 eggs
2 cups all-purpose flour
pinch of salt
1 teaspoon apple pie spice
1 tablespoon brandy, sherry or lemon juice

*[handwritten notes: place bowl of water in the oven to keep the cake moist]*

*[handwritten: ground almond]* *[handwritten: square]*

Grease a 20 cm/8 inch round deep cake tin and line the bottom and sides with greased greaseproof (waxed) paper. Mix the dried fruits, peel, almonds and cherries together. Cream the butter until soft, then add the sugar and continue creaming until very light and fluffy and pale in colour. Beat in the eggs one at a time, following each with a spoonful of flour. Sift the remaining flour with the salt and spice and fold into the creamed mixture, followed by the brandy and fruit mixture. Turn into the prepared tin and level the top. *[handwritten: 145 min]*

Bake in a cool oven (150°C/300°F, Gas Mark 2) for 3½ to 3¾ hours or until a skewer inserted into the centre comes out clean. Cool in the tin for 10 minutes before turning onto a wire rack. Store wrapped in foil until required.

*[handwritten: 1 tablespoon sour cream]*
*[handwritten: 1 tsp baking powder]*
*[handwritten: 2 tablespoon molasses]*
*[handwritten: caraway seed — 1 teaspoon]*

96

# YULE LOG

**Metric/Imperial**
3 eggs
75 g/3 oz caster sugar
65 g/2½ oz self-raising flour
1 tablespoon cocoa powder
150 ml/¼ pint double cream, whipped, or vanilla Butter Cream (see page 104)
1 recipe quantity Chocolate Icing (see page 106)
little icing sugar

**American**
3 eggs
6 tablespoons sugar
½ cup plus 2 tablespoons self-rising flour
1 tablespoon unsweetened cocoa
⅔ cup heavy cream, whipped, or vanilla Butter Cream (see page 104)
1 recipe quantity Chocolate Icing (see page 106)
little confectioners' sugar

Grease and line a Swiss roll tin (jelly roll pan), about 30 × 23 cm/12 × 9 inches. Beat the eggs and sugar together in a heatproof bowl over a pan of simmering water, or in a large electric mixer, until very thick and the beater leaves a trail when lifted. Remove from the heat and continue to beat until cool. Sift the flour and cocoa together twice and fold lightly and evenly into the mixture. Turn into the prepared tin, spreading right into the corners. Bake in a moderately hot oven (200°C/400°F, Gas Mark 6) for 10 to 15 minutes or until just firm.

Turn out onto a sheet of non-stick parchment; or onto greaseproof (waxed) paper sprinkled with caster sugar. Trim the edges of the sponge and roll up with the paper inside. Allow to cool on a wire rack.

Carefully unroll the cake and remove the paper. Spread all over with most of the whipped cream or vanilla butter cream, re-roll carefully and place on a foil-covered oblong board or plate. (The cake can be frozen at this stage if required.) Make up the chocolate icing (frosting), using a little more sugar than stated, and as it begins to thicken spread all over the roll including the ends. Mark with a fork along the length of the roll to resemble the 'bark', leaving the icing to thicken further if necessary. When set, use the remaining cream or butter cream to re-mark the filling on the ends.

When quite dry, sprinkle lightly with icing (confectioners') sugar to represent snow. Finish the cake with marzipan holly leaves and berries (see page 122) and add a model robin or a few Christmas roses (see page 130).

# SIMNEL CAKE

Traditionally made for Easter, this rich fruit cake has a layer of marzipan baked in the centre of the cake and a marzipan topping.

**Metric/Imperial**
150 g/6 oz butter
150 g/6 oz soft brown sugar
3 eggs
200 g/8 oz plain flour
pinch of salt
1 teaspoon baking powder
1 teaspoon mixed spice
large pinch of ground mace
2 tablespoons milk
100 g/4 oz raisins
150 g/6 oz currants
50 g/2 oz sultanas
50 g/2 oz mixed candied peel, chopped
50 g/2 oz glacé cherries, quartered, rinsed and dried
1 recipe quantity Marzipan (see page 104)
little apricot jam or egg white

**American**
¾ cup butter
1 cup dark brown sugar
3 eggs
2 cups all-purpose flour
pinch of salt
1 teaspoon baking powder
1 teaspoon apple pie spice
large pinch of ground mace
2 tablespoons milk
⅔ cup raisins
1 cup currants
⅓ cup seedless white raisins
⅓ cup chopped mixed candied peel
⅓ cup quartered candied cherries, rinsed and dried
1 recipe quantity Marzipan (see page 104)
little apricot jam or egg white

Grease an 18 cm/7 inch round deep cake tin and line the bottom and sides with greased greaseproof (waxed) paper. Cream the butter and sugar together until light and fluffy and pale in colour. Beat in the eggs, one at a time. Sift the flour, salt, baking powder and spices together and fold into the creamed mixture alternating with the milk. Finally fold in the dried fruit, peel and cherries. Put half of the mixture into the prepared tin and level the top.

Roll out one-third of the marzipan to an 18 cm/7 inch circle and lay on top of the cake mixture. Cover with the remaining cake mixture. Bake in a moderate oven (160°C/325°F, Gas Mark 3) for about 1½ hours or until cooked through. Cool in the tin for 10 minutes before turning out onto a wire rack.

For the traditional decoration, roll about half of the remaining marzipan into eleven small balls. Roll out the remainder to fit the top of the cake. Brush the top of the cake with apricot jam or egg white, place the marzipan circle in position and make a decorative edging. Put the marzipan balls round the top edge of the cake, fixing with a little jam or egg white. For an attractive finish tie a wide yellow ribbon around the cake.

# GLACÉ FRUIT CAKE

A white fruit cake full of chopped glacé (candied) cherries, pineapple, angelica, peel, etc., this can be prepared for a special occasion. It can be left plain or decorated with glacé (candied) fruit. Alternatively coat the whole cake in American (boiled) frosting or with marzipan and royal icing.

| Metric/Imperial | American |
|---|---|
| 100 g/4 oz glacé pineapple, chopped | ⅔ cup chopped candied pineapple |
| 150 g/6 oz glacé cherries, chopped, rinsed and dried | 1 cup chopped candied cherries, rinsed and dried |
| 25 g/1 oz crystallized ginger, chopped | ⅓ cup chopped candied ginger |
| 25 g/1 oz candied angelica, cut into 1 cm/½ inch strips | 3 tablespoons candied angelica, cut into ½ inch strips |
| 50 g/2 oz blanched almonds, chopped | ½ cup chopped blanched almonds |
| 100 g/4 oz mixed candied peel, chopped | ⅔ cup chopped mixed candied peel |
| 200 g/8 oz plain flour | 2 cups all-purpose flour |
| 200 g/8 oz butter or margarine | 1 cup butter or margarine |
| 150 g/6 oz caster sugar | ¾ cup sugar |
| 3 eggs | 3 eggs |
| 50 g/2 oz cornflour | ½ cup cornstarch |
| 1 teaspoon baking powder | 1 teaspoon baking powder |
| grated rind of 1 orange or lemon | grated rind of 1 orange or lemon |
| 3 tablespoons orange or lemon juice | 3 tablespoons orange or lemon juice |

Grease an 18 cm/7 inch square deep cake tin and line the bottom and sides with greased greaseproof (waxed) paper (or for a round cake use a 20 cm/8 inch tin). Mix together the pineapple, cherries, ginger, angelica, almonds, peel and 50 g/ 2 oz (½ cup) of the flour. Cream the fat and sugar together till light and fluffy, then beat in the eggs one at a time. Sift the remaining flour, cornflour (cornstarch) and baking powder together and fold into the creamed mixture, followed by the orange or lemon rind, fruit mixture and fruit juice.

Turn into the prepared tin and level the top. Bake in a moderate oven (160°C/325°F, Gas Mark 3) for about 2¼ hours or until firm to the touch and a skewer inserted into the centre of the cake comes out clean. Cool in the tin for 10 to 15 minutes before turning onto a wire rack.

*Note:* Sometimes you can buy packets of mixed glacé (candied) fruits in which case substitute these for all the different ones in the recipe.

# LIGHT FRUIT CAKE

This is an excellent alternative to the traditional heavily fruited Christmas cake for those who prefer a less rich cake. It can be left as it is or covered with marzipan and royal icing or covered with a frosting. It also makes a good birthday cake.

| Metric/Imperial | American | |
|---|---|---|
| 200 g/8 oz sultanas | 1⅓ cups seedless white raisins | Soak in rum |
| 50 g/2 oz currants | ⅓ cup currants | |
| 50 g/2 oz raisins | ⅓ cup raisins | |
| 50 g/2 oz mixed candied peel, chopped | ⅓ cup chopped mixed candied peel | |
| 50 g/2 oz glacé cherries, roughly chopped | ⅓ cup roughly chopped candied cherries | |
| grated rind of ½ lemon or orange | grated rind of ½ lemon or orange | |
| 200 g/8 oz butter or margarine | 1 cup butter or margarine | |
| 125 g/5 oz caster sugar | ½ cup plus 2 tablespoons sugar | |
| 100 g/4 oz light soft brown sugar | ⅔ cup light brown sugar | |
| 250 g/10 oz plain flour | 2½ cups all-purpose flour | |
| 50 g/2 oz self-raising flour | ½ cup self-rising flour | |
| 5 eggs | ~~5 eggs~~ 6 eggs | |
| 1–2 tablespoons lemon juice | 1–2 tablespoons lemon juice | |

Grease a 20 cm/8 inch round or square deep cake tin and line the bottom and sides with greased greaseproof (waxed) paper. Mix the dried fruits with the peel, cherries and lemon or orange rind. Cream the fat until soft, then add the sugars and cream until the mixture is very light and fluffy and pale in colour. Sift the flours together. Beat the eggs into the creamed mixture one at a time, following each with a spoonful of flour. Fold in the remaining flour, followed by the fruit. Add enough lemon juice to give a stiff dropping consistency.

Turn into the prepared tin and bake in a cool oven (150°C/300°F, Gas Mark 2) for 2½ to 2¾ hours until well risen and firm. Turn out onto a wire rack and leave to cool.

*Variation*
Spices can be sifted with the flour if liked – ½ teaspoon ground cinnamon, 1 teaspoon mixed spice (apple pie spice) and a good pinch of grated nutmeg.

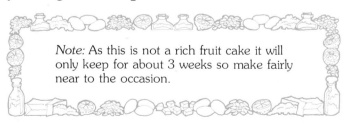

*Note:* As this is not a rich fruit cake it will only keep for about 3 weeks so make fairly near to the occasion.

# RUBY WEDDING CAKE

A rich chocolate sponge cake with chocolate butter cream, this is made in the shape of a 40 to celebrate a fortieth wedding anniversary.

**Metric/Imperial**
400 g/14 oz butter or
  margarine
400 g/14 oz caster sugar
7 large eggs
325 g/11 oz self-raising
  flour, sifted
75 g/3 oz cocoa powder
1 tablespoon coffee essence
1–2 tablespoons water
3 recipe quantities chocolate
  Butter Cream (see page
  104)
DECORATION:
100 g/4 oz flaked almonds,
  toasted
few glacé cherries, halved
silver balls

**American**
1¾ cups butter or margarine
1¾ cups sugar
7 eggs
2¾ cups self-rising flour,
  sifted
¾ cup unsweetened cocoa
1 tablespoon strong black
  coffee
1–2 tablespoons water
3 recipe quantities chocolate
  Butter Cream (see page
  104)
DECORATION:
1 cup flaked almonds,
  toasted
few candied cherries, halved
silver balls

Grease a 23 cm/9 inch round deep cake tin and a 23 cm/9 inch square deep cake tin and line the bottoms with greased greaseproof (waxed) paper. Cream the fat and sugar together until light and fluffy. Beat the eggs in one at a time, following each with a spoonful of flour. Sift the remaining flour with the cocoa and fold into the creamed mixture alternating with the coffee essence (strong black coffee) and sufficient water to give a dropping consistency. Divide between the prepared tins and level the tops.

Bake in a moderately hot oven (190°C/375°F, Gas Mark 5) allowing 40 to 50 minutes for the square tin and 35 to 40 minutes for the round one or until well risen and just firm to the touch. Turn out onto a wire rack and leave to cool.

Split each cake into two layers and sandwich back together with some of the butter cream. Cut the centre out of the round cake to make a zero and cut the square cake into the shape of a four. Place the numeral cakes on two 25 cm/10 inch square silver cake boards. Spread a very thin layer of butter cream all round the sides of the cakes and a thicker layer over the tops, then press the flaked almonds into the sides of the cakes.

Put most of the remaining butter cream into a piping bag fitted with a star tube. Pipe a shell edging around the top edge of the cakes and a border around the bases. Use the rest to write 'Happy Anniversary' or the two people's names with a thick writing tube. Decorate with pieces of glacé (candied) cherry and silver balls.

# GOLDEN WEDDING CAKE

This rich sponge cake, coated in golden American (boiled) frosting, is ideal for any celebration.

**Metric/Imperial**
350 g/12 oz butter or margarine
350 g/12 oz caster sugar
2 eggs, beaten
8 egg yolks
yellow food colouring
$\frac{1}{2}-\frac{3}{4}$ teaspoon vanilla essence
450 g/1 lb plain flour
2 teaspoons baking powder
large pinch of salt
lemon juice (optional)
1 recipe quantity lemon Butter Cream (see page 104)
1 recipe quantity American Frosting (see page 106)

**American**
1$\frac{1}{2}$ cups butter or margarine
1$\frac{1}{2}$ cups sugar
2 eggs, beaten
8 egg yolks
yellow food coloring
$\frac{1}{2}-\frac{3}{4}$ teaspoon vanilla extract
4 cups all-purpose flour
2 teaspoons baking powder
large pinch of salt
lemon juice (optional)
1 recipe quantity lemon Butter Cream (see page 104)
1 recipe quantity Boiled Frosting (see page 106)

Grease a 23 cm/9 inch and 15 cm/6 inch round deep cake tin and line the bottoms and sides with greased greaseproof (waxed) paper. Cream the fat and sugar together until very light and fluffy. Beat in the eggs and egg yolks, a few drops of yellow food colouring and the vanilla essence (extract). Sift the flour, baking powder and salt and fold into the mixture. If necessary add a little lemon juice to give a dropping consistency. Divide between the prepared tins and make a slight hollow in the centre of each. Bake in a moderate oven (180°C/350°F, Gas Mark 4) until firm to the touch, allowing about 50 minutes for the smaller cake and 1$\frac{1}{4}$ to 1$\frac{1}{2}$ hours for the large one. Turn out onto a wire rack and leave to cool.

Split each cake into two layers and sandwich together with three-quarters of the butter cream. Use the remaining butter cream to position the smaller cake on top of the large one. Place on a gold-coloured cake board.

Make up the American (boiled) frosting and colour gold with a few drops of yellow food colouring. Quickly use to mask the cakes completely, pulling the frosting into peaks. Decorate with golden leaves, horseshoes, golden coins etc. Leave to set.

# AMERICAN WEDDING CAKE

This sponge celebration cake comprises three tiers set directly on top of each other and is completely covered in butter cream before adding the decoration. It can be made round or square and could be covered with royal icing if preferred, after adding a layer of marzipan. The decoration can be kept fairly simple as described here or made very elaborate with the addition of twisting garlands of roses and leaves made from royal icing, sugar paste or marzipan.

**Metric/Imperial**
600 g/1½ lb butter or
   margarine
600 g/1½ lb caster or light
   soft brown sugar
12 eggs
600 g/1½ lb self-raising flour
2 teaspoons vanilla essence
1–2 tablespoons cold water
450–550 g/1–1¼ lb
   raspberry or apricot jam
Apricot Glaze (see page
   107)
3 recipe quantities vanilla
   Butter Cream (see page
   104)
pink food colouring
silver balls to decorate

**American**
3 cups butter or margarine
3 cups granulated sugar or
   4 cups light brown sugar
12 eggs
6 cups self-rising flour
2 teaspoons vanilla extract
1–2 tablespoons cold water
1–1¼ lb (1⅓–1⅔ cups)
   raspberry or apricot jam
Apricot Glaze (see page
   107)
3 recipe quantities vanilla
   Butter Cream (see page
   104)
pink food coloring
silver balls to decorate

Grease and line three round or square deep cake tins: 28 cm/11 inch, 20 cm/8 inch and 12.5 cm/5 inch. Make up the cake mixture by the method for Victoria Sandwich (layer) cake (see page 6). Divide between the prepared tins and bake in a moderate oven (180°C/350°F, Gas Mark 4), allowing about 40 minutes for the small tin, 1 hour 10 minutes for the middle size and about 1½ hours for the large tin, or until well risen and firm to the touch. Turn out onto a wire rack and leave to cool.

Split each cake into three layers and sandwich back together with jam. Stand the smaller cakes on thin silver boards the same size as the cake and the bottom tier on a larger silver cake drum. Brush off any loose crumbs from the cakes and, if liked, coat lightly in apricot glaze.

Use part of the butter cream to cover each cake. Position the cakes on top of each other and smooth the butter cream as much as possible using a hot wet palette knife, if necessary. Leave to set a little.

Tint the remaining butter cream a pale pink (or other colour) and put into a piping bag fitted with a medium star tube. Mark each cake tier into 8 parts on the side and work a star of butter cream towards the top of the cake at each point. Then fill in a curved loop of stars all round the cakes. Next work a pillar shape at the join of each curve finishing each with a larger star. Work a shell border round the base of each cake and then another shell edging to just overlap the edges of each cake tier. Finish off with silver balls.

Extra pink decoration can be worked around the top of each tier or a pattern of sugar roses. The top of the cake is traditionally topped with a silver horseshoe and ribbon decoration.

# WEDDING CAKE (RICH FRUIT CAKE)

The quantities given in the chart opposite will produce a fairly deep cake when cooked. Grease and line the cake tin, using double greaseproof (waxed) paper. Tie two or three thicknesses of brown paper or newspaper around the outside of the tin.

Mix together the prepared dried fruits. Cut the cherries into quarters, rinse and dry thoroughly, then add to the fruits with the peel, almonds and grated lemon rind. Sift the flour and spices together. Cream the butter until soft, then add the sugar and continue creaming until very pale and fluffy. Add the eggs one at a time, adding a spoonful of flour after each one. Fold in the remaining flour, followed by the dry fruit mixture. At this stage a tablespoon of black treacle (molasses) can be added to the mixture for extra flavour (add 1 teaspoon for cakes 15 cm/ 6 inches or less in size).

Spread the mixture evenly into the prepared tin, making a slight hollow in the centre. Place the tin on a folded newspaper in a cool oven (150°C/300°F, Gas Mark 2). Bake for the time suggested in the chart, covering with greaseproof (waxed) paper or foil when sufficiently browned. With the large cakes it is best to turn the oven down to 140°C/275°F, Gas Mark 1 after about two-thirds of the cooking time has elapsed. To test if the cake is cooked, insert a skewer in the centre; it should come out clean. Leave to cool in the tin.

Turn out and make holes with a skewer in the top of the cake. Spoon over brandy or other spirits. It will quickly seep in. This process can be repeated at monthly intervals while maturing. Store the cake wrapped in greaseproof (waxed) paper and foil in a cool place. If possible, allow 2 to 3 months for maturing.

*Note:* For the smaller cakes it is often a good idea to add a little gravy browning to the mixture so that when baked it will be the same good dark colour as the larger cakes.

# WEDDING CAKE INGREDIENTS

| | | | | | | | | | |
|---|---|---|---|---|---|---|---|---|---|
| SQUARE | | 12.5 cm/ 5 in | 15 cm/ 6 in | 18 cm/ 7 in | 20 cm/ 8 in | 23 cm/ 9 in | 25 cm/ 10 in | 28 cm/ 11 in | 30 cm/ 12 in |
| ROUND | 12.5 cm/ 5 in | 15 cm/ 6 in | 18 cm/ 7 in | 20 cm/ 8 in | 23 cm/ 9 in | 25 cm/ 10 in | 28 cm/ 11 in | 30 cm/ 12 in | |
| CURRANTS | 150 g/5 oz (1 cup) | 225 g/8 oz ($1\frac{1}{3}$ cups) | 350 g/12 oz (2 cups) | 450 g/1 lb ($2\frac{2}{3}$ cups) | 625 g/ 1 lb 6 oz ($3\frac{2}{3}$ cups) | 775 g/ 1 lb 12 oz ($4\frac{2}{3}$ cups) | 1.2 kg/ 2 lb 8 oz ($6\frac{2}{3}$ cups) | 1.4 kg/ 3 lb (8 cups) | 1.6 kg/ 3 lb 8 oz ($9\frac{1}{3}$ cups) |
| SULTANAS (seedless white raisins) | 50 g/2 oz ($\frac{1}{3}$ cup) | 100 g/$3\frac{1}{2}$ oz ($\frac{1}{2}$ cup) | 125 g/$4\frac{1}{2}$ oz ($\frac{2}{3}$ cup) | 200 g/ 7 oz (1 cup) | 225 g/8 oz ($1\frac{1}{3}$ cups) | 375 g/13 oz (2 cups) | 400 g/14 oz ($2\frac{1}{3}$ cups) | 500 g/ 1 lb 2 oz (3 cups) | 550 g/ 1 lb 4 oz ($3\frac{1}{3}$ cups) |
| RAISINS | 50 g/2 oz ($\frac{1}{3}$ cup) | 100 g/$3\frac{1}{2}$ oz ($\frac{1}{2}$ cup) | 125 g/$4\frac{1}{2}$ oz ($\frac{2}{3}$ cup) | 200 g/7 oz (1 cup) | 225 g/8 oz ($1\frac{1}{3}$ cups) | 375 g/13 oz (2 cups) | 400 g/14 oz ($2\frac{1}{3}$ cups) | 500 g/ 1 lb 2 oz (3 cups) | 550 g/ 1 lb 4 oz ($3\frac{1}{3}$ cups) |
| GLACÉ (candied) CHERRIES | 40 g/$1\frac{1}{2}$ oz ($\frac{1}{4}$ cup) | 65 g/$2\frac{1}{2}$ oz ($\frac{1}{3}$ cup) | 75 g/3 oz ($\frac{1}{2}$ cup) | 100 g/4 oz ($\frac{2}{3}$ cup) | 150 g/6 oz (1 cup) | 225 g/8 oz ($1\frac{1}{3}$ cups) | 300 g/10 oz ($1\frac{2}{3}$ cups) | 350 g/12 oz (2 cups) | 400 g/14 oz ($2\frac{1}{3}$ cups) |
| CHOPPED MIXED CANDIED PEEL | 25 g/1 oz (3 tbsp) | 50 g/2 oz ($\frac{1}{3}$ cup) | 50 g/2 oz ($\frac{1}{3}$ cup) | 75 g/3 oz ($\frac{1}{2}$ cup) | 100 g/4 oz ($\frac{2}{3}$ cup) | 150 g/5 oz ($\frac{5}{6}$ cup) | 200 g/7 oz ($1\frac{1}{4}$ cups) | 250 g/9 oz ($1\frac{1}{2}$ cups) | 275 g/10 oz ($1\frac{3}{4}$ cups) |
| BLANCHED ALMONDS, CHOPPED | 25 g/1 oz ($\frac{1}{4}$ cup) | 50 g/2 oz ($\frac{1}{2}$ cup) | 50 g/2 oz ($\frac{1}{2}$ cup) | 75 g/3 oz ($\frac{3}{4}$ cup) | 100 g/4 oz (1 cup) | 150 g/5 oz ($1\frac{1}{4}$ cups) | 200 g/7 oz ($1\frac{3}{4}$ cups) | 250 g/9 oz ($2\frac{1}{4}$ cups) | 275 g/10 oz ($2\frac{1}{2}$ cups) |
| GRATED LEMON RIND | a little | $\frac{1}{2}$ lemon | $\frac{3}{4}$ lemon | 1 lemon | 1 lemon | 1 lemon | $1\frac{1}{2}$ lemons | 2 lemons | 2 lemons |
| PLAIN (all-purpose) FLOUR | 100 g/$3\frac{1}{2}$ oz ($\frac{3}{4}$ cups plus 2 tbsp) | 175 g/6 oz ($1\frac{1}{2}$ cups) | 200 g/$7\frac{1}{2}$ oz ($1\frac{3}{4}$ cups plus 2 tbsp) | 350 g/12 oz (3 cups) | 400 g/14 oz ($3\frac{1}{2}$ cups) | 600 g/ 1 lb 5 oz ($5\frac{1}{4}$ cups) | 700 g/ 1 lb 8 oz (6 cups) | 825 g/ 1 lb 13 oz ($7\frac{1}{4}$ cups) | 1 kg/ 2 lb 4 oz (9 cups) |
| GROUND CINNAMON | $\frac{1}{2}$ tsp | $\frac{1}{2}$ tsp | $\frac{3}{4}$ tsp | 1 tsp | $1\frac{1}{2}$ tsp | 2 tsp | $2\frac{1}{2}$ tsp | $2\frac{3}{4}$ tsp | 3 tsp |
| GROUND MIXED SPICE (apple pie spice) | $\frac{1}{4}$ tsp | $\frac{1}{4}$ tsp | $\frac{1}{2}$ tsp | $\frac{3}{4}$ tsp | 1 tsp | $1\frac{1}{4}$ tsp | $1\frac{1}{2}$ tsp | $1\frac{3}{4}$ tsp | 2 tsp |
| BUTTER | 75 g/3 oz (6 tbsp) | 150 g/5 oz ($\frac{2}{3}$ cup) | 175 g/6 oz ($\frac{3}{4}$ cup) | 275 g/10 oz ($1\frac{1}{4}$ cup) | 350 g/12 oz ($1\frac{1}{2}$ cups) | 500 g/ 1 lb 2 oz ($2\frac{1}{4}$ cups) | 600 g/ 1 lb 5 oz ($2\frac{2}{3}$ cups) | 800 g/ 1 lb 12 oz ($3\frac{1}{2}$ cups) | 900 g/ 2 lb (4 cups) |
| SOFT BROWN (light brown) SUGAR | 75 g/3 oz ($\frac{1}{2}$ cup) | 150 g/5 oz ($\frac{5}{6}$ cup) | 175 g/6 oz (1 cup) | 275 g/10 oz ($1\frac{2}{3}$ cups) | 350 g/12 oz (2 cups) | 500 g/ 1 lb 2 oz (3 cups) | 600 g/ 1 lb 5 oz ($3\frac{1}{2}$ cups) | 800 g/ 1 lb 12 oz ($4\frac{2}{3}$ cups) | 900 g/ 2 lb ($5\frac{1}{3}$ cups) |
| EGGS (large) | $1\frac{1}{2}$ | $2\frac{1}{2}$ | 3 | 5 | 6 | 9 | 11 | 14 | 16 |
| APPROX. BAKING TIME | 2–$2\frac{1}{2}$ hrs | $2\frac{3}{4}$ hrs | 3 hrs | $3\frac{1}{2}$ hrs | 4 hrs | $4\frac{1}{2}$–5 hrs | $5\frac{1}{2}$–6 hrs | $6\frac{1}{2}$–7 hrs | 7–$7\frac{1}{2}$ hrs |
| APPROX. COOKED WEIGHT | 800 g/ $1\frac{3}{4}$ lb | 1.1 kg/ $2\frac{1}{2}$ lb | 1.6 kg/ $3\frac{1}{4}$ lb | 2.2 kg/ $4\frac{3}{4}$ lb | 2.7 kg/ 6 lb | 4 kg/ 9 lb | 5 kg/ 11 lb | 6.6 kg/ $14\frac{1}{2}$ lb | 7.5 kg/ $16\frac{1}{2}$ lb |

# ICINGS AND FILLINGS

## BUTTER CREAM OR BUTTER ICING

This standard recipe can be coloured and flavoured as you like to complement the particular cake to be iced or filled.

| Metric/Imperial | American |
|---|---|
| 100 g/4 oz butter | ½ cup butter |
| 175–225 g/6–8 oz icing sugar, sifted | 1½–2 cups confectioners' sugar, sifted |
| vanilla essence | vanilla extract |
| 1–2 tablespoons milk, top-of-the-milk or evaporated milk | 1–2 tablespoons milk, half-and-half or evaporated milk |

Cream the butter until soft, then beat in the sugar a little at a time, adding a few drops of vanilla essence (extract) and sufficient milk to give the required consistency. It should be a fairly firm but spreading consistency.

This will make a sufficient quantity to coat the top and sides of an 18 cm/7 inch cake.

### Variations

*Coffee:* omit the vanilla and replace 1 tablespoon of the milk with coffee essence (strong black coffee) – or more if a really strong coffee flavour is required; or beat in 2–3 teaspoons instant coffee powder with the icing (confectioners') sugar.

*Chocolate:* either add 25–40 g/1–1½ oz (1–1½ squares) melted chocolate or 1–2 tablespoons cocoa powder (unsweetened cocoa) dissolved to a thin paste with a little hot water (cool before adding).

*Orange or lemon:* omit the vanilla and replace the milk with orange or lemon juice; add the finely grated rind of 1 orange or lemon.

*Mocha:* dissolve 1–2 teaspoons cocoa powder (unsweetened cocoa) in 1 tablespoon coffee essence (strong black coffee) and omit 1 tablespoon of the milk. For a stronger flavour increase the quantity.

*Liqueur:* omit the vanilla and replace 1–2 tablespoons of the milk with any liqueur, rum, brandy, whisky or sherry; add a few drops of an appropriate food colouring.

*Almond:* replace the vanilla with almond essence (extract) and beat in about 2 tablespoons toasted almonds which have been very finely chopped, or 2 tablespoons toasted ground almonds.

*Walnut:* beat in 25–50 g/1–2 oz (¼–½ cup) walnuts, very finely chopped.

*Minted:* replace the vanilla with peppermint essence (extract) and add a few drops of green food colouring.

*Apricot:* omit the vanilla and milk and beat in 3 tablespoons sieved (strained) apricot jam, a pinch of grated lemon rind and a squeeze of lemon juice.

## MARZIPAN OR ALMOND PASTE

This is used for covering all cakes to be coated with royal icing; for a decorative top to a plain or sandwich (layer) cake; or for moulding animals, flowers, leaves and other decorations.

| Metric/Imperial | American |
|---|---|
| 100 g/4 oz caster sugar | ½ cup sugar |
| 100 g/4 oz icing sugar, sifted | 1 cup confectioners' sugar, sifted |
| 200 g/8 oz ground almonds | 2 cups ground almonds |
| 1 teaspoon lemon juice | 1 teaspoon lemon juice |
| almond essence | almond extract |
| 1 egg or 2 egg yolks | 1 egg or 2 egg yolks |

Combine the sugars and ground almonds and make a well in the centre. Add the lemon juice, a few drops of almond essence (extract) and sufficient beaten egg or egg yolks to mix to a firm but manageable dough. Turn out onto a lightly sugared surface and knead until smooth. Keep wrapped in polythene (plastic wrap) or foil until required.

MAKES 450 g/1 lb

## CONFECTIONERS' CUSTARD OR CRÈME PÂTISSIÈRE

Widely used for filling cakes and gâteaux, this is a thick, sweet mock cream.

| Metric/Imperial | American |
| --- | --- |
| 300 ml/½ pint milk | 1¼ cups milk |
| 50 g/2 oz caster sugar | ¼ cup sugar |
| 20 g/¾ oz plain flour | 3 tablespoons all-purpose flour |
| 15 g/½ oz cornflour | 2 tablespoons cornstarch |
| 1 egg | 1 egg |
| 1 egg yolk | 1 egg yolk |
| vanilla essence | vanilla extract |
| knob of butter | pat of butter |

Heat the milk gently in a pan. Beat the sugar, flour, cornflour (cornstarch), egg and egg yolk together until smooth and creamy, then beat in a little of the hot milk. Beat into the rest of the milk and cook gently, stirring continuously, until the mixture thickens and just comes to the boil. Stir in a few drops of vanilla essence (extract) and the butter and heat for a few minutes more. Leave to cool with a piece of wet greaseproof (waxed) paper touching the surface of the custard to prevent a skin forming.

MAKES ABOUT 400 ml/⅔ PINT (1¾ CUPS)

## GLACÉ ICING

Glacé icing is a very quick and useful icing for sponge, sandwich (layer) and other cakes, as well as individual cakes and biscuits (cookies). Using warm water instead of cold makes the icing easier to handle.

| Metric/Imperial | American |
| --- | --- |
| 100 g/4 oz icing sugar | 1 cup confectioners' sugar |
| 1–2 tablespoons warm water | 1–2 tablespoons warm water |
| food colouring and/or flavouring (optional) | food coloring and/or flavoring (optional) |

Sift the icing (confectioners') sugar into a bowl. Gradually beat in sufficient water to give a smooth icing, thick enough to coat the back of a spoon. Extra water or sugar can be added to achieve the correct consistency. A few drops of food colouring or flavouring can be added at this stage. Use at once.

The icing can also be made by putting all the ingredients into a saucepan and heating gently, stirring, until well mixed and smooth. Take care not to overheat.

This will make a sufficient quantity to cover the top of an 18 cm/7 inch cake or 16 to 18 small buns. Double the quantities for a sandwich (layer) cake or if the sides are to be covered.

*Variations*
*Lemon or orange:* use strained fruit juice instead of the water, and a few drops of food colouring, if liked.
*Coffee:* use a little coffee essence (strong black coffee) or black coffee in place of part of the water.
*Chocolate:* dissolve 2 teaspoons cocoa powder (unsweetened cocoa) in the water.
*Mocha:* dissolve 1 teaspoon cocoa powder (unsweetened cocoa) and 2 teaspoons instant coffee powder in the water.

# AMERICAN (BOILED) FROSTING

This frosting has a crisp outer crust with a soft inside. It is suitable for most cakes and will keep for 1 to 2 weeks. A sugar thermometer is required to guarantee success and it is vital to beat until the frosting really does stand in peaks or it may slide off the cake.

| **Metric/Imperial** | **American** |
| --- | --- |
| 450 g/1 lb loaf or | 2 cups sugar |
| granulated sugar | ⅔ cup water |
| 150 ml/¼ pint water | pinch of cream of tartar |
| pinch of cream of tartar | 2 egg whites |
| 2 egg whites | food coloring (optional) |
| food colouring (optional) | |

Put the sugar and water into a large heavy-based saucepan and heat gently until the sugar has dissolved. Add the cream of tartar and the sugar thermometer and bring to the boil. Boil to a temperature of 115°C/240°F.

Meanwhile, beat the egg whites until very stiff. Pour the sugar syrup in a thin stream onto the beaten egg whites, continuing to beat briskly all the time. Continue to beat until the frosting is thick enough to stand in peaks with the tips just tipping over. Quickly spread over the cake, pulling the frosting into peaks all over the cake.

This will make a sufficient quantity to fill and cover a 20–23 cm/8–9 inch cake.

*Variations*
*Coffee:* add 1 teaspoon coffee essence (strong black coffee) to the mixture while beating.
*Chocolate:* add 1–2 teaspoons cocoa powder (unsweetened cocoa) dissolved in 1 teaspoon warm water while beating.

> *Note:* If adding food colouring to the frosting, do so following the sugar syrup remembering that with continued beating the frosting will become paler in colour.

# FONDANT ICING

A good icing to use for light-textured cakes and small fairy cakes, this needs a sugar thermometer to make it correctly.

| **Metric/Imperial** | **American** |
| --- | --- |
| 150 ml/¼ pint water | ⅔ cup water |
| 450 g/1 lb loaf or | 2 cups sugar |
| granulated sugar | 2 tablespoons glucose or 1 |
| 25 g/1 oz glucose or 1 | tablespoon liquid glucose |
| tablespoon liquid glucose | or a large pinch of cream |
| or a large pinch of cream | of tartar |
| of tartar | |

Use a large heavy-based saucepan for this icing. Put the water into the pan, add the sugar and heat gently, without stirring, until the sugar dissolves. Bring very slowly to the boil. Add the glucose or cream of tartar and continue to boil until the syrup reaches 115°C/240°F. Remove at once from the heat. Allow the bubbles to subside and pour in a thin stream into a heatproof bowl. Cool until a skin forms on the top.

Using a stainless steel spatula or wooden spoon, work the fondant from the outside to the middle and beat well until it thickens and becomes white. Then knead it until firm and smooth. Colourings or flavourings can be worked in at this stage or when heated for use. Put pieces into a screwtop jar and, when cold, screw down tightly.

To use, put the required amount of fondant into a heatproof bowl over a pan of hot water or the top of a double saucepan and heat gently until the fondant is the consistency of thick cream and will coat the back of a spoon. Add a little sugar syrup (see page 115) if too thick, but do not overheat the icing.

This will make a sufficient quantity to coat an 18 cm/7 inch cake.

# CHOCOLATE ICING (FROSTING)

This is a fudge type of chocolate icing (frosting). If preferred, a smooth icing can be made by adding less icing (confectioners') sugar.

| **Metric/Imperial** | **American** |
| --- | --- |
| 100 g/4 oz plain chocolate, | 4 squares semisweet |
| broken up | chocolate, broken up |
| 50 g/2 oz butter | ¼ cup butter |
| 2 egg yolks | 2 egg yolks |
| about 100 g/4 oz icing | about 1 cup confectioners' |
| sugar, sifted | sugar, sifted |

Put the chocolate and butter in the top of a double saucepan or heatproof bowl over a pan of gently simmering water. Heat until the chocolate melts, then remove from the heat and beat until smooth. Beat in the egg yolks and sufficient sugar to give a thick smooth spreading consistency. Cool slightly so the icing (frosting) will not run off the edge of the cake. Use to fill a sandwich (layer) cake and spread over the top, swirling it into small peaks with a palette knife. Leave to set.

This will make a sufficient quantity to fill and cover the top of an 18–20 cm/7–8 inch cake.

# RICH BUTTER CREAM

Richer than the usual butter cream, this has the addition of an egg yolk.

| Metric/Imperial | American |
| --- | --- |
| 75 g/3 oz butter | 6 tablespoons butter |
| 1 egg yolk | 1 egg yolk |
| 200 g/8 oz icing sugar, sifted | 2 cups confectioners' sugar, sifted |
| 1 tablespoon flavouring (orange or lemon juice, coffee essence etc.) or milk | 1 tablespoon flavoring (orange or lemon juice, strong black coffee etc.) or milk |

Melt the butter in a saucepan. Remove from the heat and beat in the egg yolk. Gradually beat in the icing (confectioners') sugar, alternating with the flavouring or milk until light and fluffy.

This will make a sufficient quantity to fill and coat the top of a 20 cm/8 inch sandwich (layer) cake.

# SEVEN MINUTE FROSTING

A quick and excellent substitute for American (boiled) frosting, this does not require a sugar thermometer and should take only 7 minutes to make. It sets quickly so once made it must be used immediately.

| Metric/Imperial | American |
| --- | --- |
| 1 egg white | 1 egg white |
| 150 g/6 oz caster sugar | $\frac{3}{4}$ cup sugar |
| pinch of salt | pinch of salt |
| 2 tablespoons water | 2 tablespoons water |
| pinch of cream of tartar | pinch of cream of tartar |

Put all the ingredients together in a heatproof mixing bowl and mix lightly. Place over a saucepan of gently simmering water and beat hard (preferably with a hand-held electric mixer) until thick and stiff and the mixture will stand up in peaks. Remove from the heat and pour over the cake. Spread all over and pull up into peaks. Add the decorations at once and leave to set.

This will make a sufficient quantity to fill and cover an 18 cm/7 inch sandwich (layer) cake.

*Variation*
*For a butterscotch frosting:* use soft brown sugar (light brown sugar) in place of caster sugar.

# APRICOT GLAZE

| Metric/Imperial | American |
| --- | --- |
| 225 g/8 oz apricot jam | $\frac{1}{2}$ lb ($1\frac{1}{3}$ cups) apricot jam |
| 2–3 tablespoons water | 2–3 tablespoons water |

Put the jam and water into a saucepan and heat gently until the jam is dissolved. Rub through a sieve (strainer) and return to a clean pan. Bring back to the boil and simmer until the required consistency is obtained. The cooled glaze can be kept in an airtight container as for jam and used as required.

# ROYAL ICING

Royal icing is used for wedding cakes and celebration cakes where a really white and firm icing is required. The glycerine should be omitted for the first coat on the top surface of the lower tiers of a wedding cake, because a hard surface is needed to take the weight of the cakes.

| Metric/Imperial | American |
| --- | --- |
| 3 egg whites | 3 egg whites |
| about 700 g/1$\frac{1}{2}$ lb icing sugar, sifted | about 6 cups confectioners' sugar, sifted |
| 1 tablespoon lemon juice, strained | 1 tablespoon lemon juice, strained |
| 1 teaspoon glycerine (optional) | 1 teaspoon glycerine (optional) |

Beat the egg whites until very frothy, then gradually beat in half the sugar using a wooden spoon. (A mixer can be used but it will incorporate a lot of air and the resulting bubbles will be difficult to disperse.) Add the lemon juice and glycerine (see note above) and half the remaining sugar, then beat very well until smooth and very white. Gradually beat in enough of the remaining sugar to give a consistency which will just stand in soft peaks. Put into an airtight container or cover the bowl with a damp cloth and leave for several hours, if possible, to allow most of the air bubbles to come to the surface and burst.

The icing is now ready for use and can be thickened, if necessary, with more sifted icing (confectioners') sugar or thinned down (for flooding) with lightly beaten egg white.

This will make a sufficient quantity to cover and add simple decorations to a 20 cm/8 inch round cake.

# SUGAR PASTE (COLD FONDANT)

Used for covering cakes and moulding flowers, sugar paste should not be used for tiered cakes as it does not set as firmly as royal icing. If to be used for moulding flowers, omit the glycerine.

| Metric/Imperial | American |
| --- | --- |
| about 450 g/1 lb icing sugar, sifted | about 4 cups confectioners' sugar, sifted |
| 3 tablespoons liquid glucose (glucose syrup) | 3 tablespoons liquid glucose or glucose syrup |
| 1 egg white, lightly beaten | 1 egg white, lightly beaten |
| 2–4 teaspoons lemon juice, strained | 2–4 teaspoons lemon juice, strained |
| 1 teaspoon glycerine | 1 teaspoon glycerine |
| food colouring (optional) | food coloring (optional) |

Put the sugar into a bowl and make a well in the centre. Add the liquid glucose, egg white, lemon juice and glycerine, if used, and mix thoroughly. With your hands dusted in a little cornflour (cornstarch), knead until smooth and even, adding extra sugar if necessary to give a stiff paste. Add any colouring to all or part of the paste during the kneading so it becomes evenly coloured with no streaks. It is now ready for use. This will make a sufficient quantity to cover a 20 cm/8 inch cake.

# BASIC PASTRIES

# SHORTCRUST (PIE) PASTRY

Made by the rubbing-in method, this standard pastry using half the weight of fat to flour can be made quickly and used for nearly every purpose, both sweet and savoury. The fat used is usually half margarine and half lard (shortening) or white vegetable fat, but all margarine or butter or all white fat (shortening) can be used. Each will give a slightly different flavour and you will soon find which combination of fats gives the preferred result. The dry rubbed-in mixture can be kept in an airtight container for up to 2 weeks in the refrigerator, and the finished dough will keep for a few days in the refrigerator or several months in the deep freeze.

**Metric/Imperial**
*200 g/8 oz plain flour*
*½ teaspoon salt*
*50 g/2 oz margarine or*
*   butter*
*50 g/2 oz lard or white*
*   vegetable fat*
*about 2 tablespoons cold*
*   water*

**American**
*2 cups all-purpose flour*
*½ teaspoon salt*
*¼ cup margarine or butter*
*¼ cup lard or shortening*
*about 2 tablespoons cold*
*   water*

Sift the flour and salt into a bowl. Add the fats cut into small pieces and rub in with the fingertips until the mixture resembles fine breadcrumbs. (The fats should be firm but not hard, and definitely not too soft.) Add sufficient water to mix to a pliable dough with a round-bladed knife. Knead very lightly until smooth, but do not knead more than necessary or the pastry will be tough. The dough is now ready for use; however, if possible, wrap in polythene (plastic wrap) or foil and chill for at least 15 minutes before use.

For pies, etc., the pastry should be baked in a moderately hot to hot oven (200–220°C/400–425°F, Gas Mark 6–7) and can be glazed with milk or beaten egg before baking. To bake 'blind' (unfilled), cover with greaseproof (waxed) paper and a layer of dried baking beans and bake in a moderately hot oven (200°C/400°F, Gas Mark 6) for 15 to 20 minutes or until just set. Remove the paper and beans, reduce the oven temperature to moderate (180°C/350°F, Gas Mark 4) and continue baking for about 10 minutes to dry out the bottom of the pastry case.

MAKES 200 g/8 oz (2 CUP) QUANTITY

# ONE-STAGE SHORT PASTRY

This pastry is very speedy but requires a special soft or 'luxury' margarine for it to work properly.

| Metric/Imperial | American |
|---|---|
| 100 g/4 oz soft (luxury) margarine | ½ cup soft margarine |
| 1 tablespoon water | 1 tablespoon water |
| 150 g/6 oz plain flour | 1½ cups all-purpose flour |
| large pinch of salt | large pinch of salt |

Cut the margarine into small pieces and put into a bowl with the water and 2 tablespoons flour. Beat together until smooth and creamy – about 30 seconds. Sift in the remaining flour and salt and mix to form a fairly soft dough. Turn out onto a lightly floured surface and knead lightly until smooth. Roll out fairly thinly ready for use; or wrap in polythene (plastic wrap) or foil and chill until required. One-stage pastry is usually baked in a moderately hot oven (190°C/375°F, Gas Mark 5).

MAKES 150 g/6 oz (1½ CUP) QUANTITY

# FLAKY PASTRY

Not so frequently used as puff pastry and made with not quite such a high proportion of butter to flour, flaky pastry has a very good flavour. It is used when a little less rise is required such as for sausage rolls, sweet and savoury pies, turnovers, etc.

| Metric/Imperial | American |
|---|---|
| 450 g/1 lb plain flour | 4 cups all-purpose flour |
| ½ teaspoon salt | ½ teaspoon salt |
| 350 g/12 oz butter or a mixture of butter and lard | 1½ cups butter or a mixture of butter and shortening |
| about 300 ml/½ pint cold water | about 1¼ cups cold water |
| 1 teaspoon lemon juice | 1 teaspoon lemon juice |

Sift the flour and salt into a bowl. Soften the fat a little and divide into four portions. Rub one quarter of the fat into the flour until the mixture resembles fine breadcrumbs. (Keep the rest of the fat cold but do not let it become too hard – it should be firm enough to cut into flakes.) Mix to a soft elastic dough with water and the lemon juice and knead lightly on a floured surface until smooth. Roll out to an oblong three times as long as it is wide. Dot the top two-thirds of the dough with a second quarter of the fat, cutting it into flakes. Fold the bottom third of the dough up and the top third down and seal the edges with the rolling pin. Wrap in lightly oiled polythene (plastic wrap) and chill for 15 minutes.

With the folded side of the dough at the side, roll out again to an oblong and repeat the dotting with fat, folding and chilling twice. Wrap lightly in polythene (plastic wrap) again and chill for 30 to 60 minutes before use.

Glaze with beaten egg before baking. Flaky pastry is usually baked in a hot oven (220°C/425°F, Gas Mark 7). Flaky pastry dough can be stored in the refrigerator for about 3 days before use or stored in a freezer for several months.

MAKES 450 g/1 lb (4 CUP) QUANTITY

# PUFF PASTRY

Homemade puff pastry takes time and trouble, but it can be made in quantity and frozen for later use. It will also keep wrapped in foil in the refrigerator for a few days. The rise of puff pastry is better than flaky pastry, and after the first rolling used for vol-au-vents (patty shells), cream slices, etc., the trimmings can be rerolled and used for recipes such as Cream Horns, Palmiers and Sacristans. It is the richest of all pastries.

| Metric/Imperial | American |
|---|---|
| 450 g/1 lb plain flour | 4 cups all-purpose flour |
| 1 teaspoon salt | 1 teaspoon salt |
| 450 g/1 lb butter, firm but not hard | 2 cups butter, firm but not hard |
| about 300 ml/½ pint iced water | about 1¼ cups iced water |

Sift the flour and salt into a bowl. Add 100 g/4 oz (½ cup) of the butter cut into small pieces and rub into the flour until the mixture resembles fine breadcrumbs. Add sufficient iced water to mix to a soft dough and knead lightly into a ball. Form the rest of the butter into an oblong. Roll out the dough into a square. Place the block of butter on one half of the dough and fold the other over to enclose it completely. Seal the edges with the rolling pin. Turn the dough so the fold is to the right hand side, then roll out into a strip three times as long as it is wide. Mark the dough into three and fold the lower third up and the top third down. Seal the edges with the rolling pin, wrap in lightly oiled polythene (plastic wrap) and chill in the refrigerator for 30 minutes.

Repeat this rolling, folding and chilling process 5 times more. If time allows, give three rollings on one day, chill overnight and complete the process on the following day. Leave for at least 30 minutes before rolling out for use after the last folding process.

Always glaze with beaten egg before baking to give the characteristic shine to the pastry. The usual baking temperature is a hot oven (230°C/450°F, Gas Mark 8).

MAKES 450 g/1 lb (4 CUP) QUANTITY

*Note:* Unsalted butter can give an even better flavour to the pastry, in which case increase the amount of salt to 2 teaspoons.

# CHOUX PASTE

More of a paste than a pastry, this is usually piped into shapes for éclairs, profiteroles, cream buns, aigrettes, Gâteau St. Honoré, etc. When cooked it is well puffed up with a crisp crust and a hollow centre. The success or failure depends entirely on the amount of air beaten in after the addition of the eggs.

| **Metric/Imperial** | **American** |
|---|---|
| 50 g/2 oz butter or margarine | $\frac{1}{4}$ cup butter or margarine |
| 150 ml/$\frac{1}{4}$ pint water | $\frac{2}{3}$ cup water |
| 65 g/2$\frac{1}{2}$ oz plain flour, sifted | $\frac{1}{2}$ cup plus 2 tablespoons all-purpose flour, sifted |
| pinch of salt | pinch of salt |
| 2 standard eggs, beaten | 2 eggs, beaten |

Melt the fat in the water and bring to the boil. Remove from the heat and tip all the flour into the pan at once. Beat with a wooden spoon until the paste is smooth and forms a ball, leaving the sides of the pan clean. Spread the mixture over the bottom of the pan and leave to cool for several minutes.

Add the salt to the eggs and beat into the paste a little at a time, as vigorously as possible, to give a glossy mixture and piping consistency. A hand-held electric mixer is ideal for this as it helps to incorporate as much air as possible. Continue beating until glossy and leave to cool. Choux pastry is usually baked in a moderately hot to hot oven (200–220°C/400–425°F, Gas Mark 6–7).

MAKES 65 g/2$\frac{1}{2}$ oz ($\frac{1}{2}$ CUP PLUS 2 TABLESPOON) QUANTITY

> *Note:* If beating the mixture by hand it will probably be necessary to omit some of the beaten egg or the mixture will become too slack, due to lack of air incorporated.

# RICH FLAN (TART) PASTRY

A very useful rich sweet pastry for sweet flans, tartlets etc., this is made with butter, sugar and egg yolks.

| **Metric/Imperial** | **American** |
|---|---|
| 125 g/5 oz plain flour | 1$\frac{1}{4}$ cups all-purpose flour |
| pinch of salt | pinch of salt |
| 75 g/3 oz butter | 6 tablespoons butter |
| 1$\frac{1}{2}$ teaspoons caster sugar | 1$\frac{1}{2}$ teaspoons sugar |
| 1 egg yolk | 1 egg yolk |
| about 4 teaspoons water | about 4 teaspoons water |

Sift the flour and salt into a bowl. Add the butter cut into pieces and rub in with the fingertips until the mixture resembles breadcrumbs. Stir in the sugar. Mix the egg yolk with 2 teaspoons of the water and add to the dry ingredients with enough of the remaining water to mix to a firm but pliable dough. Knead lightly and roll out ready for use; or wrap in foil or polythene (plastic wrap) and chill until required. This pastry is baked in a moderately hot oven (200°C/400°F, Gas Mark 6).

MAKES 125 g/5 oz (1$\frac{1}{4}$ CUP) QUANTITY

# THE ART OF CAKE DECORATION

Cake decorating is a skill in itself and can mean anything from a simple coating of glacé icing or piped decoration of butter cream to the ultimate of an elaborately royal-iced wedding cake. This book provides a selection of designs and techniques for all types of occasions. The beginner should practice different kinds of icing and decoration, gradually attempting the more difficult designs, and eventually making up designs of her own.

## *BASIC EQUIPMENT FOR SIMPLE CAKE DECORATING*

It is not necessary to have a vast selection of equipment at first, and probably most of what you require is already in the kitchen. However, once you become more ambitious, that is the time to add to the collection:

- selection of bowls
- 600 ml/1 pint (2 cup or 1 pint) and 300 ml/$\frac{1}{2}$ pint (1 cup) measuring jugs
- tablespoons and teaspoons
- nylon sieve (strainer)
- wooden spoons
- spatula
- kitchen scissors
- round-bladed knife or small palette knife/spreader
- icing ruler
- greaseproof (waxed) paper
- selection of basic icing tubes (see note below) including fine, medium and thick writing; small 8-point star; larger 10- or 12-point star; small petal.

Icing tubes are all sold by number, but the different manufacturers have different numbers for the same tube, so check on the chart shown with the tubes when buying. They are also obtainable with a plain base for use with homemade paper icing bags or with screw bands to use with plastic icing bags fitted with a special screw adaptor.

# SIMPLE CAKE DECORATING

### Filling the cake

Whatever type of filling is to be used – jam, butter cream, frosting, etc. – first place the cake on a wire rack or plate. Spread the filling evenly over one cake (or layer) using a round-bladed knife and taking it right out to the edge of the cake. Position the second cake (or layer) neatly on top and brush off any loose crumbs from around the cake.

### Decorations for sponge and sandwich (layer) cakes with sugar

Fill the cake and place it on a plate. Select a paper or plastic doily with a pretty open pattern and put on the top of the cake. Alternatively, arrange thin strips of paper in an attractive design over the top of the cake or cut your own pattern from paper. Dredge the top of the cake heavily with sifted icing (confectioners') sugar. Very carefully lift away the doily or paper to leave a pretty pattern of sugar on the cake. If you are short of time, simply dredge the top of the cake with caster or icing (confectioners') sugar.

### Decorating the sides of a cake

The sides can, of course, be left plain, but for a more professional finish, coat in chopped or flaked nuts, toasted or plain desiccated (shredded) coconut, grated chocolate, etc. Brush a little Apricot Glaze (see page 107) all round the sides of the cake or spread it on with a knife. Put the chosen coating on a sheet of greaseproof (waxed) paper and, holding the cake carefully on its side, roll in the coating until well covered. About 75 g/3 oz ($\frac{3}{4}$ cup) nuts will be required to coat the sides of an 18 to 20 cm/7 to 8 inch sandwich (layer) cake. If the top of the cake is to be covered in butter cream, a thin layer of the butter cream can be spread round the sides of the cake in place of jam.

### Glacé iced cakes

Before beginning to glacé ice a cake always prepare all the decorations you need first, because once on the cake the icing sets very quickly and will crack and be spoiled if it is disturbed. Either ice just the top, leaving the sides plain or coated (as above), or the whole cake. For the whole cake, place it on a wire rack over a plate or baking sheet so the icing can drip through.

Make up the icing (see page 105) and when at the correct coating consistency (thick enough to coat the back of a spoon) pour it all over the middle of the cake. Using a round-bladed knife spread it over the top of the cake almost to the edge. If the icing drips over the edge, quickly remove it with a knife or leave until set and then cut it off.

To cover the whole cake, pour almost all the icing over the centre and spread it out evenly, allowing it to run down the sides. Use a wet knife to help the icing cover the cake completely and fill in any gaps quickly with the icing left in the bowl.

Add the decorations before the icing sets and do not move until completely set or it may crack. If butter cream decorations are to be added, wait until the icing is set.

Butter cream can be used to pipe rosettes on top, using a star tube; or for a shell edge around the top of the cake and/or the base; or to pipe a trellis or other design using a medium writing tube. When using a writing tube the butter cream should be a little thinner than usual.

*Prepare the icing*

*Roll the cake in the coating*

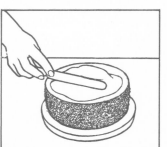

*Spread the icing over the top*

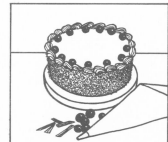

*When set, finish the decoration*

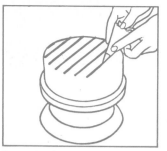

*Pipe straight lines*

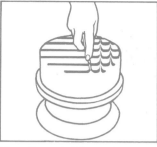

*Draw lines at right angles*

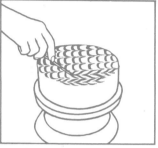

*Draw lines between first lines*

*A circular feather design*

Melted chocolate can also be used to decorate the top of the glacé icing. Put it into a paper icing bag (see page 126) with just the tip cut off.

Allow about 225 g/8 oz (2 cups) icing (confectioners') sugar for glacé icing for the top of a 20 cm/8 inch round cake.

## Feather icing

This gives a very professional and attractive finish and is most suitable for sandwich (layer) cakes, sponges and biscuits (cookies). It must be done very quickly before the glacé icing even begins to set or the effect will not be as good as it should. Prepare and ice or coat the sides of the cake first (if to be iced). Then make up the usual amount of white (or coloured) glacé icing for the top and a second amount using about 50 g/2 oz ($\frac{1}{2}$ cup) icing (confectioners') sugar in a bright contrasting colour (e.g. pink, green, chocolate, etc.). If the top is to be a dark colour use white icing for the feathering.

Ice the top of the cake as above, then quickly put the contrasting icing into a paper icing bag (see page 126). Cut off the tip of the bag and pipe straight lines across the cake at 1 to 2 cm/$\frac{1}{2}$ to $\frac{3}{4}$ inch intervals. Immediately draw a skewer or point of a knife across the lines at right angles about 2 cm/$\frac{3}{4}$ inch apart. Quickly turn the cake around and draw the skewer across again in between the first lines, but in the opposite direction to complete the feathered effect. Leave to set.

Another design is made by piping the contrasting colour in circles on top of the cake, beginning in the centre of the cake and again about 2 cm/$\frac{3}{4}$ inch apart. This time draw the skewer from the centre of the cake to the edge marking it into four quarters, then draw the skewer from the outer edge to the centre between the first lines to complete the pattern. Other feathered designs can also be made up with a little forethought.

## Butter icings for cakes

Butter cream is quick and easy to make (see recipe on page 104) and can be used for most types of cakes, particularly those for children. It can be spread or piped straight onto a cake, although a thin layer of marzipan can be added first if you wish.

## Simple toppings

Cover the top of the cake as evenly as possible with butter cream. If the cake is very crumbly brush it first with Apricot Glaze (see page 107) to prevent pulling crumbs up into the icing.

1. The easiest design of all is to draw a round-bladed knife backwards and forwards across the butter cream, slightly overlapping the previous line each time to give even spaces between each. Arrange nuts, sweets (candies) or pieces of chocolate around the edge; or pipe rosettes of butter cream around the edge and top with the decorations.

2. Spread a fairly thick layer of rather soft butter cream over the top and, using a round-bladed knife or spoon handle, pull the icing up into peaks.

3. On a perfectly smooth coating of butter cream, mark the cake into diamonds with a sharp knife, wiping it clean regularly, and put a small decoration into alternate diamonds.

4. Using a round-bladed knife, swirl the butter cream into circles, some one way and some the other to give a swirled effect all over the cake.

5. A serrated comb or scraper can be used to pull round the top of the cake either evenly to give the effect of the grooves on a

115

record or with indentations from time to time to give a scalloped pattern.

These designs can be left plain or decorated with a sprinkling of icing (confectioners') sugar, plain or toasted desiccated (shredded) coconut, grated chocolate or chocolate vermicelli before leaving to set in a cool place. The decorations can then be made more elaborate by adding piped butter cream either using a writing tube for straight lines, wavy patterns, writing or dots; or a star tube for borders, rosettes, shells and other decorations (see royal icing decorations).

For children's birthday cakes see the designs on pages 145–147.

### Fondant icing

This is a very sweet icing which keeps much better than glacé icing. It is the icing widely used professionally but can easily be made at home. To get the correct results a sugar thermometer is required. For the method of making the icing see page 106. Once made, fondant icing should be kept in a screwtop jar (screwing down only when cold). Colourings and/or flavourings can be added when the fondant is first made or when it is reheated ready for use.

Fondant icing is only suitable for sponge and Madeira types of cakes if they are not covered with Marzipan, but can be used for any other cake if it is first coated with Marzipan (see page 104). For the lighter cakes and small fancies place them on a wire rack and brush all over first with Apricot Glaze (see page 107). It is a good idea – although not necessary – to brush large cakes with Apricot Glaze before adding the icing.

Put the required amount of made fondant icing into a heatproof bowl over a saucepan of hot water. Heat gently until the icing becomes the consistency of thick cream and coats the back of a spoon. Take care not to overheat but add a few drops of sugar syrup (see below) if necessary.

*For coating small cakes:* either spoon it over until evenly covered or impale each cake on a fork or skewer and dip into the fondant. Add any decorations and leave to set on a wire rack.

*For large cakes:* place the wire rack over a plate and pour the icing all over the cake, letting it run down the sides. Do not touch the icing with a knife or the gloss will be spoiled but tilt it if necessary to help it coat evenly. Add any decorations (but not anything piped) while still wet, then leave to set. Trim off evenly at the base when set.

*For cake toppings:* first tie a band of lightly greased double greaseproof (waxed) paper or foil or non-stick parchment around the cake to come about 2.5 cm/1 inch above the top. Melt about 225 g/8 oz (1 cup) quantity fondant icing with a little sugar syrup (see below) and pour over the top of the cake. Leave until set, then carefully ease off the band of paper with the help of a hot wet knife if necessary. Decorate the top as the icing is setting or when set. This icing is not suitable for tiered wedding cakes.

*Piping fondant icing:* it is possible to do simple piping with fondant icing if heated, then carefully cooled to the correct consistency.

### Sugar syrup

Put 225 g/8 oz (1 cup) sugar into a saucepan with 200 ml/7 fl oz ($\frac{7}{8}$ cup) water and heat gently until dissolved. Bring to the boil and boil for 30 seconds. Cool and store in a screwtop jar.

*Opposite: Large and small cakes covered with fondant icing*
*Below: Coating small cakes with fondant icing*

# DECORATIONS FOR CAKES AND GÂTEAUX

Many homemade decorations can be made to give the finishing touch to a cake or gâteau. Flowers and models made from icing and marzipan are described later but here are some very effective decorations using chocolate, nuts, fruit and flowers.

## Chocolate

Apart from using coarsely grated chocolate to cover the sides and tops of cakes, try making squares and curls. Use a special chocolate cake covering or plain (semisweet) chocolate. Break into pieces and put in a heatproof bowl over a pan of hot (not boiling) water or the top of a double saucepan. Heat gently until the chocolate melts, taking care not to let any water get into the chocolate as this will spoil the texture. Remove from the heat and beat until smooth.

*Chocolate squares:* using a palette knife spread a thin, even layer of melted chocolate over a sheet of non-stick parchment but not quite to the edges. When set firm, but not hard, cut into squares of the required size using a sharp knife and a ruler. Leave until really hard (chill if liked), then either cut the squares apart or break over the edge of a table. They will peel off the paper easily.

*Chocolate curls:* spread a thin layer of melted chocolate on a marble (or similar) slab using a palette knife. Leave until just firm but not set hard, and then 'shave' off curls using a sharp thin-bladed knife. It is possible to make curls with a potato peeler on some softer varieties of special covering or blocks of chocolate without having to melt it.

*Chocolate leaves:* wash and dry the leaves. Using a fine paint brush, coat the underside of each leaf with melted chocolate cake covering. Place the leaves on a plate and chill in the refrigerator until set. When hard, peel the leaf away from the

chocolate. Store in a covered container in the refrigerator. Rose leaves are ideal for making these decorations.

## Nuts

Walnuts are perhaps the most popular nuts used for decoration; but there are many other types which can be used to add colour and flavour to the finished cake.

*Pistachios:* these elongated kernels turn green when blanched and make most effective decorations either left whole, split in half or chopped. Put into boiling water and leave for 3 to 5 minutes until the skins loosen. Drain and cover with cold water. The skins should split and slide off when pressed between the fingers.

*Almonds:* whole almonds need to be blanched as for pistachio nuts but for 2 to 3 minutes only. Once skinned either leave whole, split in half, chop or cut into slivers. While the nuts are still damp, split in half with a sharp knife, then cut each half into long narrow strips for slivers. Almonds can be toasted in any of these shapes on a piece of foil under a medium grill (broiler) for a few minutes; shake from time to time and watch continuously for the almonds will suddenly turn brown.

*Hazelnuts:* first remove the skins either by putting on a baking sheet in a moderately hot oven (200°C/400°F, Gas Mark 6) for a few minutes or under a moderately hot grill (broiler), shaking from time to time until the skins split and the nuts are lightly browned. Cool a little, then tip into a polythene (plastic) bag and rub the nuts together until the skins flake off. They can then be toasted further if so required. Use whole or chopped.

## Coconut

Both desiccated (shredded) and the long strands of coconut are used for decoration. The strands can be used to decorate animals and figures made of marzipan, for hair or whiskers etc. Both varieties of coconut can be toasted either under a medium grill (broiler) or in a moderate oven (180°C/350°F, Gas Mark

4). Stir frequently as the coconut colours, to get an even brown. It can also be tinted in many colours for use on cakes to depict grass, sea, sand, etc. To colour coconut, add a few drops of the required liquid food colouring to a bowl of water, stir in the coconut and leave to soak up the colour. Drain well and dry on absorbent kitchen paper before use. But remember to add only a drop or two of colour at first; more can be added if required.

## Frosted fruit

Black and green grapes, mandarin oranges, redcurrants, cherries, etc., all make pretty decorations for cakes and desserts when coated in caster sugar. First wash the fruit, if necessary, and dry it well. Either whip an egg white lightly or make a syrup using 50 g/2 oz ($\frac{1}{4}$ cup) sugar and 2 tablespoons water and boil for 2 to 3 minutes, then remove from the heat. Dip the fruit into syrup or egg white and then roll in caster sugar. Arrange the frosted fruit on wire racks and leave to dry. Either single pieces or small clusters of fruit can be frosted in this way.

## Crystallized flowers

These are so pretty and keep well if properly made. The advantage is that out-of-season flowers can suddenly appear on a special cake if they were crystallized when available. Use fairly small flowers which are not quite fully open and remove all leaves and bruised petals. Primroses, violets and rose petals are all excellent as are mint and all herb leaves. When completed, store the crystallized flowers in airtight containers between layers of tissue paper. There are two methods of crystallization.

*Method 1:* put 100 ml/4 fl oz ($\frac{1}{2}$ cup) triple-strength rose water into a screwtop jar with 50 g/2 oz gum arabic crystals and leave overnight, or longer, giving an occasional shake until dissolved. Hold the flower carefully by the stem (remove the stem when crystallized) and, using a fine paintbrush, paint all over the petals and centre of the flower both on the top and underside. Quickly dredge with or roll in caster sugar, making sure the flower is completely covered; shake off any surplus. Place on a wire rack or non-stick parchment or waxed paper and leave to dry in a

fairly warm place for 1 to 2 days, then pack away with care.

*Method 2:* melt 450 g/1 lb (2 cups) loaf or granulated sugar in a large heavy-based saucepan. Bring to the boil and strain through scalded muslin (cheesecloth) into a clean saucepan to remove any impurities. Now bring back to the boil and boil to 104 C/220 F on a sugar thermometer. Leave to cool to about blood heat. Arrange the flowers on a wire rack over a shallow tin and pour the syrup over each flower, using a fine paint brush to help reach all parts on the top and underside. Drain off excess syrup and leave the flowers undisturbed for 12 to 18 hours until crystals begin to form on the surface. This is a sign that crystallization is taking place; leave in a warm place until completed, then pack away with care.

## Chestnuts

Marrons glacés are a very popular decoration if you can afford to buy them. It is not possible to achieve under home conditions the same result as those commercially prepared, but these chestnuts in syrup are a good alternative. They can be used in the same way as the bought marrons glacés and are very much cheaper.

Cut a nick in the skins of 350 g/12 oz ($\frac{3}{4}$ lb) sweet chestnuts, put into a pan of water and bring to the boil. Boil for 2 minutes. Remove from the water a few at a time and peel off the outer and inner skins. Put 225 g/8 oz (1 cup) of both granulated sugar and powdered glucose or dextrose into a fairly large saucepan with 200 ml/7 fl oz ($\frac{7}{8}$ cup) water and beat gently until the sugar is dissolved. Bring to the boil. Remove from the heat, add the chestnuts and bring to the boil again. Remove from the heat, cover the pan and leave in a cool place overnight. The next day, bring to the boil as before and leave overnight again. On the third day add a few drops of vanilla essence (extract), bring to the boil and boil for 3 minutes. Warm some small bottling (canning) jars in the oven and fill with the chestnuts and syrup. If you want to keep the chestnuts for more than 2 weeks, seal the jars as for bottling (canning). Otherwise just cover with the tops and store.

119

# MARZIPAN OR ALMOND PASTE

This mixture of sugars and ground almonds bound together with egg is used to coat a cake before adding royal or other icing, to prevent the white icing being stained by rich cakes. It is also used for moulding decorations of all types and in a variety of colours.

## To cover a cake

Make up the required quantity (see chart on page 136) or use a commercial marzipan. The same method is used for both round and square cakes. A 20 cm/8 inch round cake requires approximately 575 g/1¼ lb marzipan.

1. Measure around the circumference of the cake with a piece of string and also the depth of the cake.
2. Roll out about two-thirds of the marzipan on a surface dredged with icing (confectioners') sugar, or between two sheets of polythene (plastic wrap), to a rectangle which is half the length of the string and twice the depth of the cake. Trim to the exact size and cut into two strips. Knead the trimmings into the remaining marzipan and roll out to a circle to fit the top.
3. Brush the sides of the cake with Apricot Glaze (see page 107) and then carefully put the strips of marzipan round the cake to cover it. Smooth the joins with a round-bladed knife and make sure the top and base edges are neat and even.
4. Brush the top of the cake with apricot glaze and carefully place the marzipan circle in position. Roll over very lightly with a rolling pin and smooth the join all round with a round-bladed knife. If the sides are at all uneven, roll a straight-sided jam jar around the sides of the cake. Remove the cake to a cake board and leave to dry at room temperature for 5 to 7 days before adding the royal icing. If icing is added too soon, the oils from the marzipan may seep through it.

## To make marzipan decorations

Most attractive 'cut-outs' and figures can be made from coloured marzipan to use for decorations on royal iced or butter cream coated cakes, particularly for Christmas cakes.

To colour marzipan, knead food colouring evenly into the marzipan a few drops at a time, until no longer streaky and the correct colour is obtained. In some cases you may need to mix two or three colours to obtain the required colour. Bought or homemade marzipan can be used for modelling, but if making your own mix with all icing ('confectioners') sugar to give a very smooth paste which is easier to shape.

Draw the chosen shape on stiff paper and cut out. If the design needs two colours then cut out each part separately

(more than two colours can look a bit fussy – extra colour can be added with piped icing). Try stars, leaves, Christmas trees, Father Christmas, Easter decorations and figures and shapes for birthday cakes. Roll out the marzipan thinly on a little icing (confectioners') sugar or between sheets of waxed paper, non-stick parchment or polythene (plastic wrap). Place the paper pattern on top and cut carefully round the outside with a sharp pointed knife. Remove the pattern and mark any design or detail on the cut-out using a cocktail stick or point of a knife. Leave the shape on a plate or sheet of paper to dry for several days if time allows. Attach to the cake with a dab of icing. If the marzipan is still wet the colour will seep from the figure to the white icing on the cake – so take care.

# SEASONAL MARZIPAN DECORATIONS

### Christmas trees

Draw a pattern for a simple Christmas tree of the required size then a smaller one to fit on top (see diagram). Cut out both in green marzipan and lay the smaller one on top of the larger one. Cut a small piece of red marzipan for the tub of the tree and attach. When dry, put dots of icing (white or coloured) at the ends of the branches and top of the tree and top these with silver balls or other coloured balls to represent baubles.

### Stars

Draw patterns of stars in the sizes required and cut out of yellow marzipan. When set, the points of the stars can be decorated with fine lines and/or dots of white or pale yellow icing.

### Holly leaves

You will need a dark green marzipan – adding a little brown colouring to obtain a good dark green colour for the leaves – and a deep red for the berries (made by rolling tiny amounts into balls). Roll out the green marzipan thinly to a strip and cut into rectangles about 2.5 to 4 cm/1 to 1¾ inches long and about 2 cm/½ inch wide. Using a tiny curved cutter or base of a piping tube take cuts out of the marzipan to form the leaves. Mark a vein down the centre and leave to dry, arranging some over a rolling pin or spoon handle to give curved shapes.

### Ivy leaves

Draw several different sizes of ivy leaves on a piece of paper (using real ivy leaves as a pattern if available) and cut out. Place on thinly rolled-out green marzipan and cut round the paper. Mark the veins with a sharp knife and leave to dry, laying some over a spoon handle to give variations in shape.

### Father Christmas

Draw the outline of a Father Christmas on a sheet of paper or trace the pattern in the diagram and cut out. Cut off his boots and sack and draw a circle for his face. Colour a little marzipan pink for the face, some red for the suit and some brown for his boots and sack. Roll out all the marzipan thinly and cut out the shapes. Put the face on the red suit and mark the eyes and nose. Attach the sack and boots. Mark the arms and jacket onto the figure and leave to set. When dry, using white icing and a writing

tube, pipe squiggly lines around his face for hair, to make a pointed beard and as a fur edging to the bottom of his coat and sleeve. Paint in the eyes and nose using a fine paint brush dipped in liquid food colouring. Carefully put on the cake.

### Poinsettia

Draw a leaf pattern, copying from a picture if possible, then cut out each leaf from deep red marzipan. Model with the fingers to join together in the centre and curve slightly to make the correct shape. Fill the centre with tiny balls of yellow marzipan. These make attractive decorations for a Christmas cake.

### Primroses

Carefully cut out small fluted circles on thinly rolled pale yellow marzipan. Using a sharp knife, make fine small cuts almost into the centre to form the petals. The edges of the petals can be pressed out slightly to give a thinner edge. Press the centre firmly to close up the flower slightly. Using pale orange marzipan, make minute balls and arrange three or five in the centre of each flower. Leave to dry. For the leaves, use a fairly dark green marzipan and cut long oval shapes, turning up the edges in places to give a natural shape. Mark the veins with a knife.

### Witches, broomsticks and cats (for halloween)

Colour the marzipan black, or dark brown or dark green; also yellow and orange. Draw the shapes on paper and cut out as described above. Add extra decorations with bright orange or yellow icing using a fine writing tube.

### Other marzipan leaves and flowers

Many types of leaves and flowers can be modelled or cut from coloured marzipan. With a little time and patience you will soon be able to make a great variety. When the marzipan is dry, features and designs can be painted onto them using a fine paint brush dipped into liquid food colourings.

A great assortment of leaves can be made by copying a real leaf and scaling it down to size.

### Marzipan roses

Roses have always been a very popular cake decoration and can be made in several types of icing – royal, pastillage and modelling fondant as well as marzipan.

Roll out the chosen coloured marzipan. Remember roses vary tremendously in colour so almost any shade of pink,

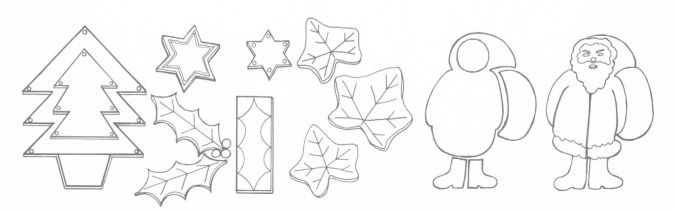

yellow, red or orange can be used and even the natural coloured marzipan. It is probably best to colour the marzipan lightly first and when a few roses have been made to deepen it and continue that way, unless, of course, you require them all the same colour.

For the basic shape of the rose make a solid cone of marzipan about 1 cm/$\frac{1}{2}$ inch overall. Roll out the remaining marzipan thinly and cut out a small circle about 1 cm/$\frac{1}{2}$ inch in diameter. Hold the base of the circle in one hand and with the other hand carefully press the rest of the circle out very thinly until almost transparent. Wrap carefully round the cone with the thick part at the base, attaching with a dab of water or egg white. Continue to make three more petals, attaching them carefully and curving them slightly to give a good shape. For a small rose, four petals should be sufficient but for larger ones add a few more petals, cutting the circles a little larger as and when necessary. Take care not to press the central cone too firmly or into a point or the rose will become too elongated, looking more like a cabbage than a rose. Dry carefully on waxed or non-stick parchment and store each separately in waxed paper in an uncovered container in a cool place.

# MODELLED ANIMALS AND FRUIT

The marzipan used for modelling must be supple enough to bend without breaking but not too soft or it will be too sticky to hold the shape and have an uneven surface. The finished results are a lovely decoration for children's birthday cakes.

## Cats and kittens
These can be made in orange, black or natural coloured marzipan. Begin with a pear-shaped piece for the body. Dust the fingers with cornflour (cornstarch) to prevent them sticking and roll the marzipan on a cool surface, not in the palms of the hand or it will become too sticky or oily. Split the narrow end of the 'pear' in half to form paws. Shape a round for the head, pinching up two pieces at the top to form ears. Use a blunt skewer to mark the eyes. Take a small piece of marzipan and roll into a thin sausage for the tail. Stick the head in position, folding one front paw over the other to help support it and attach the tail. Leave to dry on waxed paper and then add a dab of melted chocolate for the paws, eyes and nose. Pipe whiskers, eyebrows,

etc., with white icing using a fine writing tube or paint on with a dark coloured food colouring.

## Rabbits
Form the coloured marzipan into a roll about as thick as your finger. Cut off a piece to form an oval for the head and shape into a cone with a point at one end. Cut down this narrow end to make two ears and shape the head carefully. Bend under one end of the marzipan roll to make the body and back legs, cut the narrow end in half and shape into front paws. Carefully mould the rest of the piece to give a rounded back and two back legs. Position the head and add a tiny ball for the tail. Leave to set. Mark the eyes with white icing and a dot of chocolate icing in the centre. Mark the nose and whiskers with chocolate icing.

Make mice, pigs, chickens, birds, etc., in the same way.

## Bananas
Roll a little yellow marzipan to a banana shape with one end blunt and the other tapering off. Paint on brown stripes and markings using liquid food colouring.

## Oranges and lemons
Use orange and yellow marzipan for these fruits, shaping oranges round and lemons slightly elongated. To get the texture of the skin either prick all over with a pin head or roll on a grater. A small clove can be added for the calyx.

## Strawberries
Shape deep pink marzipan to the correct shape of a strawberry, then roll in granulated sugar to give the effect of seeds. Make a hull from a little green marzipan.

## Apples
Roll small balls of natural coloured or pale green marzipan, making slight indentations at the top and base. Cut the top off a clove and use for the calyx and the rest of it to represent the stem. If using green marzipan, paint part of the apple with red food colouring, blending it gradually into the green; or with natural marzipan first paint with red as above then complete with green food colouring.

## Pears
Use a little natural coloured marzipan and form into a pear shape. Add a stem and calyx as for apples, then paint with green and brown food colouring to give the desired effect.

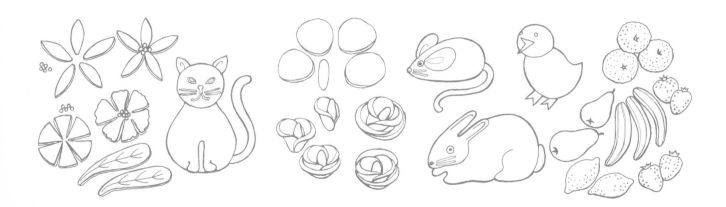

# ROYAL ICING

This icing is used for special occasion and formal cakes. It sets hard and can be used for all types of piping and elaborate and intricate designs as well as for making flowers, birds and many other decorations. It takes a little time to learn to use royal icing, but with practice and a lot of patience more ambitious designs will soon be achieved.

Use royal icing to produce a firm, smooth, absolutely white icing. To achieve this finish you must use spotlessly clean equipment and utensils – a spot of grease or fat left on the bowl may spoil the finished result. Also make sure the sugar is perfectly dry and well sifted – lumps will ruin all your efforts.

Royal icing used to be made from egg whites and icing (confectioners') sugar, but now it is possible to obtain special dried egg white or albumen powder prepared for royal icing and meringues. This solves the problem of all those leftover egg yolks. If using a substitute, follow the manufacturer's directions for reconstituting.

It is most important when making royal icing to beat it well at the beginning, preferably with a wooden spoon, to achieve a light icing that is easy to handle. If too much air is incorporated this will show on the surface, making it uneven with holes, and will cause air bubbles and breaks in piping. The correct consistency is reached when the icing will stand in soft peaks but the tops just flop over. If a mixer is used it must be at the slowest speed and for the minimum of time; when ready the icing should be beaten with a wooden spoon for a few minutes to remove some of the excess air.

The cake to be iced should be put on a board 5 cm/2 inches larger than the cake; for the bottom tier of a wedding cake it can be 7.5 to 10 cm/3 to 4 inches larger. Make the required amount of royal icing (see chart page 136 and method page 105). To prevent the icing becoming too hard on a cake, add $1\frac{1}{2}$ to 2 teaspoons glycerine during mixing.

A wedding cake will need three coats of icing all over and sometimes an extra coat on the top. Made-up royal icing will keep for several days in an airtight container, but beat until smooth before using after it has been standing for some time.

## Decorating equipment for royal icing

The following items are all helpful when you begin to use royal icing and want to experiment with different styles of piping and decorations. They are widely available in large department stores, hardware shops, speciality kitchenware shops and from various cake decorating schools and mail order sources.

● *An icing turntable*

● *Medium-sized palette knife*

● *Icing ruler:* plastic or stainless steel; some have one serrated edge

● *Icing comb or scraper:* ideal for smoothing the sides of a cake; plain and serrated edges.

● *A larger selection of piping tubes:* these are usually collected as and when required for something special or more ambitious icing.

● *Icing bags and screws:* these can be used for cake decorating but it is easier to manipulate paper icing bags fitted with the appropriate tube.

● *Cake marker:* this can be useful for making circles, dividing into sections and marking scroll shapes on a cake although this can also be done with a homemade template.

● *An icing nail:* for use when making sugar flowers.

*Opposite: Wedding Cake (Lace and Daisy design, page 138)*
*Left: Piping a rose*

# MAKING PAPER ICING BAGS

Use greaseproof or waxed paper for making icing bags. It is a good idea to make several bags at a time, especially if you are decorating a large cake.

1. Cut the paper into 25 cm/10 inch squares then fold each in half to make a triangle.

2. Fold in half again to make a smaller triangle and press the folds firmly.

3. Open out the triangle and fold the bottom half of the triangle up to the folded line, creasing firmly (B to C).

4. Continue to fold the bag round D to F and then C to A, still creasing firmly.

5. Either secure the join with a strip of sticky tape (scotch tape) or fold the top point (A) over twice to secure. Cut off the tip of the bag and open out before inserting a tube.

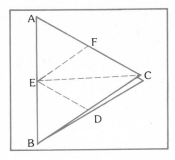
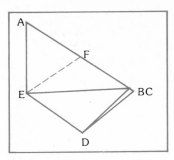
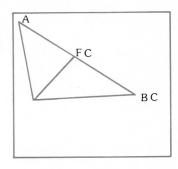

# ICING THE CAKE

Slightly different techniques are used for round and square cakes and several thin coats of icing will be required to obtain a perfectly smooth surface. Some people prefer to begin with the sides, others the top. It does not make a great deal of difference where you begin, but it is wise to apply the icing in sections rather than all in one go.

### For the sides

Place the cake (secured in the centre of a silver board with a little icing) on a turntable, if possible, or upturned plate. For a round cake, spread a thin but covering layer of icing all round the sides with a palette knife. Using a paddling action, push out as much air as possible and smooth as much as possible. Holding an icing comb or scraper (or a palette knife) at a 45° angle to the cake, at the back of the cake, with the left hand gradually rotate the turntable. Move the comb slowly and smoothly round the sides. Quickly remove the scraper and lift off any excess icing from the top and base of the cake using a palette knife. If not sufficiently smooth and even, wipe the scraper clean and repeat. Leave to set.

For a square cake, the simplest way of getting good straight corners is to ice two opposite sides first and then, when set, the other two. Spread some icing onto one side, then draw the comb or palette knife towards you to give a smooth side. Cut off surplus icing in a straight line down the corners and also along the top and base of the cake. Repeat with the opposite side and leave to dry. Repeat the process again with the two remaining sides, taking great care when cutting the surplus off the corners to give a good straight and even shape. Leave to dry.

For ribbed sides, put a plain coat of icing on first, then for the top coat use the serrated edge of the comb or scraper. Ribbed sides are suitable for round and square cakes.

### For the top

When the sides are dry, remove the cake from the turntable and place on a flat surface. Spoon a quantity of icing onto the top of the cake and smooth out with a paddling movement using a palette knife. Draw an icing ruler (or long palette knife) steadily across the top of the cake towards you, holding the ruler at a slight angle. Do not press too heavily. Remove surplus icing by running a knife round the edge of the cake. If it is not sufficiently smooth and even, cover with a little more icing and draw the ruler across the cake again. Leave to dry.

### Second and third coats

Use the same method for the top and sides when applying each coat of icing to the cake but make sure each is fully dry before adding another or you may disturb the icing already on the cake. This would give a very uneven surface which is difficult to cover up. Leave the cake to dry for at least 24 hours before adding the decoration.

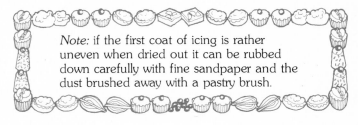

*Note:* if the first coat of icing is rather uneven when dried out it can be rubbed down carefully with fine sandpaper and the dust brushed away with a pastry brush.

### Rough icing

This is a popular way to ice Christmas cakes and ideal for snow scenes. An attractive cake can be made by rough icing all over (ideal if you are short of time) or, preferably, after putting two flat coats on the top of the cake and then rough icing the sides.

Use a slightly stiffer icing than usual, obtained by beating in a little more sifted icing (confectioners') sugar. Apply a fairly thick layer all over the cake or just to the sides. Using a round-bladed knife or handle of a spoon pull the icing up into peaks all over. With rough iced sides, you may like to let it tip over the edge onto the smooth top. Leave to set.

Various Christmas decorations such as animals, birds,

Christmas trees, etc., can be put onto the cake, or make decorations from Marzipan (see page 122) or Christmas roses from Royal Icing (see page 130). See page 140 for Christmas cake designs.

## SUGAR PASTE

This is another icing suitable for covering cakes either with or without a layer of marzipan, but it is not suitable for a tiered cake with pillars for it does not set hard enough to take the weight.

Sugar paste is also very good for moulding flowers. These are made in the same way as marzipan flowers (see page 122). Sugar paste takes the colour much better than marzipan and it dries out well.

Christmas cakes, birthday cakes and other celebration cakes can all be covered in sugar paste with the piped decoration added in royal icing, and the moulded decorations made with more sugar paste. Make up the paste (see page 107) and knead until very smooth and even. Prepare the cake, making sure it is completely flat and even all over for any indentations will show through. Dredge a flat surface with cornflour (cornstarch) and roll out the paste thinly. Brush the surface of the cake or the marzipan with Apricot Glaze (see page 107) and cover in the same way as for applying marzipan. With the fingers dipped in a little cornflour (cornstarch) rub the surface of the icing gently to give a smooth and shiny surface. Either leave to set as it is or mark indented patterns in the top of the cake using a pastry crimper or wheel or the edge of a serrated icing comb or scraper. Decorate with piped decorations of royal icing and sugar paste flowers and leaves, or other models.

## PIPED DECORATIONS

Royal icing is the best medium for piping decorations and can be used for simple designs through to the most elaborate. As with all icing, practice makes perfect, and it is always wise to practice an edging or border, lettering or writing on something other than the cake first. Once on the cake mistakes can be difficult to correct. All icing decorations should be made at least 24 hours in advance to allow time for drying out. Attach to the cake with a dab of icing.

### To prepare the icing bag

If using a paper icing bag (see page 126), cut about 1 cm/½ inch off the tip and insert the required tube. Half to two-thirds fill the bag with icing, fold over the top carefully and, pressing from the top, push icing right down to the tip of the tube. If using a commercial plastic icing bag first insert the screw adaptor

making sure it is in the right way round, then screw on the tube. Half fill with icing and proceed as above. The advantage of this type of bag is that it can be continually refilled and the tube can be easily replaced for another by just screwing on a different one; however, it is not so easy to manipulate.

Start by practising straight lines to get the 'feel' of the icing in a bag. Squeeze out just enough icing to touch the surface, then while continuing to squeeze gently lift the tube a little above the surface and pull it gently towards you. The icing should come out in a slightly sagging line which can then be manoeuvred to keep straight or guided as required. Dots of different sizes can also be made using fine, medium and thick writing tubes and these can be used for simple borders on cakes.

### Trellis

This attractive decoration can be worked in many different ways, from completely covering the top of a cake to small sections or shapes on part of the cake. It is made by piping straight lines close together using a fine or medium icing tube. When dry, more lines are piped across at a right angle to give a raised diamond or square effect. For the best effect pipe a third layer of trellis. (Some very fine trellis can be worked to five layers.) Carefully cut off any tails at the ends of the lines while still soft and always take care not to let the tube actually touch the cake or it will be impossible to obtain straight lines and will damage existing piped lines underneath.

### Stars

Hold the icing bag upright over the cake with the tip of the tube just above the surface. Pipe out sufficient icing and quickly pull away the tube with a quick down and up movement. All sizes of stars can be worked in this manner using different sized and shaped star tubes, e.g. 4, 6, 8, 10 or 12-point stars.

### Scrolls

Hold the icing bag as for a straight line. With the tube almost on the surface, work a question mark shape beginning with a fairly thick head and then gradually releasing the pressure while pulling into a long tail; break off. This whole curve is worked continuously. A second scroll can be worked in the same way to follow the first or can be reversed to make attractive designs or double scrolls. Other shaped scrolls can also be worked with a little practice, adding twists and graduating the width and size.

### Rosettes

Gradually press out the icing, moving the tube around in a circle towards the centre to completely enclose the middle. Finish off quickly to leave a slightly raised point right in the centre.

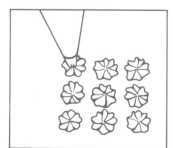

*Stars*

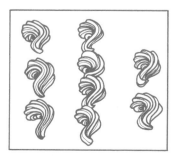

*Scrolls*

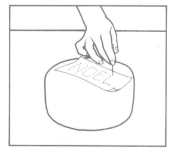

*Prick out letters with a pin*

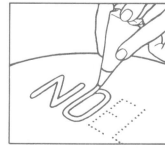

*Outline the dots with icing*

### Raised trellis (nets)

Raised trellis is worked in the same way as trellis (see page 127) but over lightly greased icing nails or moulds which are available in various shapes and sizes. These can be used to make net baskets, cribs, boat shapes, etc., and must be left 24 hours or so to become quite dry before removing from the mould. Attach carefully to the cake with a little icing and always make a few extra in case of accidents for they are very fragile. They are added to the tops, corners or sides of cakes for decoration. After the initial trellis is worked, decorate the edge and base with small dots or a very fine shell border.

As well as trellis work, a ribbon or large petal tube can be used to make a covering of wavy lines suitable for cribs and baskets. Also basket weave can be worked to give a real basket effect. This is done by first piping a vertical line down the nail using a thick writing tube. Then, using a ribbed tube, make short horizontal lines across the vertical line at intervals the width of the tube. Next pipe another vertical line covering the ends of the horizontal weave. Repeat with the ribbed tube this time filling in the spaces. Continue in this way until the nail is covered and the basket is complete.

### Shells

Begin by holding the piping bag on its side, press lightly and move the tube away from you a little and then towards you pressing out the icing and lifting it slightly. Pull it off sharply to finish in a point. Repeat, covering the finishing point each time with the next shell.

### Borders

Fairly bold designs are required to attach the bottom of the cake to the board and they can be any type of shell, rosette, large dot or other fancy design including a narrow strip of trellis stretching from the side of the cake to the board. For a top edging always use a more delicate design although it can be the same as the base but made using a finer tube.

### Writing

There are several sizes of writing tubes available, from very fine to thick. All writing needs practice for perfection and a trial of the writing should always be worked before actually putting it on the cake. Begin by using block capitals and then gradually try handwriting, etc. The words should be written on tracing paper first and then pricked out onto the cake to guarantee everything fits in and that it is correctly positioned. Use a pin or hat pin for pricking out. Use a fine or medium tube to outline the dots and make the letters. A second layer can be added for bolder writing. Another way to make the writing stand out is to cover the outline with tiny dots or stars. Decorative squiggles and dots can also be worked around the words, especially if it is a name on a birthday or Christening cake.

*Top: Piping trellis. Above: Piping a border*
*Opposite: Celebration cake (see pages 125–135 for decorations)*

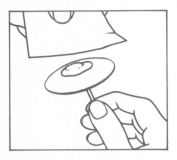

*Secure paper on icing nail*

*First pipe a tight coil*

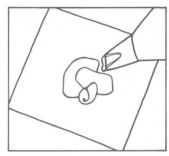

*Twist the nail while piping*

*Leave the finished rose to dry*

# PIPED FLOWERS

As with all icing decorations, flowers take a little practice, but once you feel confident there are numerous varieties which can be made. Roses are the most popular and can be used to decorate cakes for so many occasions.

To make flowers you need an icing nail or a cork impaled on a skewer, a quantity of non-stick parchment or waxed paper cut into 2.5 to 5 cm/1 to 2 inch squares, and a paper or plastic icing bag fitted with a large, medium or fine petal tube. Half fill the bag and fold down ready to begin. Secure a square of paper to the icing nail with a dab of icing.

### Rose
Hold the piping bag so the thin edge of the petal tube is upwards. Squeezing evenly and twisting the nail at the same time, pipe a tight coil for the centre of the rose. Continue to add five or six petals, one at a time, piping the icing and twisting at the same time, but taking each petal only about three-quarters of the way round the flower. Begin in a different part of the flower each time to keep the shape even. The petals can be kept tight to form a rosebud or left more open for full-blown flowers. One or two really open petals can be worked at the bottom of the flower, if liked. The larger flowers can have more petals and should be worked with the largest petal tube. Often a tiered wedding cake will have the sizes of roses graduated, with tiny ones on the top tier working down to large roses on the bottom. Leave all roses to dry before removing from the paper and store in an airtight container.

### Narcissus
These are flat flowers so begin with the thick edge of the petal tube to the centre. Keep the tube flat, and work each petal separately. Gently squeezing the icing, take the tip outwards to a point, still keeping it flat, then bring it back towards the centre, twisting slightly and gradually releasing the pressure; break off. This gives one petal. Make five more in the same way, each slightly underlapping its neighbour, by placing the tube just under the previous petal as you begin to pipe. Leave to dry, then add the centre using yellow or orange icing and a small petal tube. Pipe a cup right in the centre of the flower by making a

complete circle of icing while rotating the nail. Leave to dry, then using a fine paint brush dipped in orange colouring just tint the edges of the cup. Pipe dots of yellow in the centre of the cup for the stamens.

### Primrose
You will need a medium tube and pale yellow icing. This is a five-petalled flat flower made in a similar way to the narcissus, but the petals are almost heart-shaped. So when the tube is out from the centre, instead of bringing it straight back, dip it towards the centre and then take it out again before returning completely to the centre. This will give the required heart shape. Complete the flower with four more petals and leave to dry. Work a few tiny dots in the centre using a fine writing tube and either deep yellow or pale orange icing.

### Christmas rose
The Christmas rose is another flat flower made in a similar way to the narcissus but the petals are tilted slightly upwards at the edges and rounded to give the 'tea-rose' shape. The centre is filled with a lot of pale to deeper yellow dots for the stamens. For lenten lilies the stamen can be yellow or pale mauve and the centre of the petals can be tinted pale mauve using a fine paint brush and mauve and pink food colouring.

### Pansy
This again is a five-petalled flower, but worked in a different order and it is a little more complicated to obtain the correct colouring. If possible copy a real flower or a picture. Using a medium petal tube pipe two flat rounded petals, underlapping the second. Then work the next two petals slightly on top of the first two and a little larger (see illustration). Turn the flower around 180° and work another larger petal to complete the flower. Leave to dry. Pansies can be worked in yellow, mauve, deep red, etc., and some flowers can be a mixture with the first two petals in, say, yellow and the remainder mauve. When dry, paint deeper shades of mauve food colouring in the centre of the flower and finish with a few dots of yellow icing for stamens.

### Orange blossom
Using a small tube and white icing make this five-petalled flower

by holding the tube with the thin end upwards and then piping out a curled petal. Continue in this manner but start each petal with the tube just inside the previous one, to give a cup-shaped flower. Leave to dry, then pipe a few spiky deep yellow or pale orange dots in the centre of the cup. Make in different sizes.

## Violet
The most difficult part of this flower is to get a really deep mauve icing. Work in the same way as a pansy, but making the first four petals smaller and more pointed. Finally turn the flower around 180° and pipe a larger elongated petal. Add fine dots of green icing to the centre for stamens.

## Daisy
Probably the simplest of all icing flowers to pipe, the daisy is very effective. Using a medium petal tube, pipe five small rounded but fairly narrow petals, each just separate from its neighbour. Then using a medium writing tube pipe a large dot in the centre of the flower. These flowers can be made in a variety of colours with the centre yellow. However, for a wedding cake make the complete flower in white or, if you prefer, add just a pale yellow or pink centre.

## Leaves
There is a special piping tube, available in several sizes, for making leaves. They can either be made separately as for flowers or piped straight onto the cake. Leaves can be made in varying shades of green, but are very often made in white for use on a wedding or other special occasion cake where the addition of green would spoil the effect. A variety of shapes can be made and with practice you will soon find them easy.

It is easier to use a tube but if you don't have one, leaves can be made by just cutting the tip off a paper piping bag in a special way. First fill the bag as usual but without cutting off the tip. Press the end flat between the thumb and finger, then cut the point off in an inverted letter 'V' like the head of an arrow.

Begin with the tube or paper bag touching the paper (or cake) and the end turning up a fraction. Press gently and as the icing begins to come out of the bag, raise it slightly. When large enough, break the icing off quickly leaving a point. The tube can be gently twisted or moved up and down to give different shapes

and twists to the leaves and the size can be increased by extra pressure. Leave to dry. For a leaf edging to a cake, work each leaf separately, working backwards round the edge so the leaf tips overlap and are left showing. If some larger leaves are required, simply cut a larger V shape. To obtain a vein effect on the leaves, make a tiny cut into the centre of the V.

## Simple flowers
Small sprays of flowers and tiny individual flowers can be piped straight onto a cake (after first practising on a plate). Lily of the valley, forget-me-nots and ornamental flowers of no particular variety are suitable, with small leaves. A writing or fine star tube are the most useful for this job.

## Large royal icing flowers
Large shaped flowers, e.g. lilies, can be made using a special 'super' icing nail. This nail is cup-shaped and should be lightly greased before use.

If you do not have a super icing nail you can mould your own using two or three thicknesses of foil, non-stick parchment or waxed paper.

## Lily
Use a leaf tube and white icing for these large flowers. Start with the tube in the centre of the nail and pipe up the side of the nail and just over the edge. Break off carefully and mould the ends of the petal to a point. Work two more petals in this way evenly round the nail and then three more on top but in between the first ones to give a six-petalled flower. Leave to dry for 18 to 24 hours, then pipe a few dots in the centre for stamens using a pale yellow icing. Remove carefully from the nail and attach to the cake with icing. If not to be used at once, store carefully between layers of tissue paper.

## Carnation
Use a large petal tube and white or pink icing for carnations. Begin at the outer rim and working round in circles make small overlapping petals. Continue in circles until the centre is reached. To give the characteristic crinkled look to the edges of the petals, make small indentations with a pin all round the edges. Leave to dry.

# RUN-OUTS

Run-outs can be piped straight onto the cake or onto non-stick parchment or waxed paper and attached to the cake when dry. These raised designs are made using royal icing. The shape is first outlined by piping and then filled in with soft royal icing. They are suitable for small freehand or traced animals, bells, stars, emblems or other shapes; for initials, words or numbers; or plaques which can then have a further decoration on top.

First draw the outline on a piece of white card. Cut out pieces of non-stick parchment or waxed paper larger than the outline and place over the drawing, securing the corners with icing or a pin. Using a fine writing tube trace the outline of the drawing. Remove the paper to a flat surface and outline further shapes. Thin down a little royal icing with a little beaten egg white until it just flows. Spoon it into the centre of the outline if it is a large area to cover or put into a paper piping bag, cut off the end and pipe into the outline until filled. The latter method is easier if it is an awkward shape to fill. Prick any air bubbles which may rise to the surface and leave undisturbed for 2 to 3 days or until completely dry. Peel off the paper ready for use.

For a raised plaque in the centre of the lower tiers of a wedding cake, prick out the area to be covered, or use a template, taking into account the position of the pillars, then

outline it and flood with icing as above.

All types of things can be depicted in this way on a cake – e.g. Father Christmas, sledge and reindeer, racehorses or show jumpers, rabbits and dogs, tennis or cricket players, etc. A cake can thus be decorated to feature an event, favourite hobby or more or less anything. The run-out can be painted with food colourings – leave to dry before adding a different one – or decorated with further piping in a matching or contrasting colour.

Remember that run-outs are very fragile and it is wise to make a few extra in case of accidents. Attach to the cake with a small dab of icing at the corners.

An assortment of shaped, rather than flat, birds, butterflies and swans, etc., can be made using royal icing. Each design is made in several parts using the run-out method and is assembled just prior to attaching to the cake. The decoration and detail is piped either onto the run-out while on the paper or onto the actual design when on the cake.

### Birds

First decide whether it is to be a flying, perching or swimming bird. Draw a simple design of a bird with wings, tail and body, which can all be separated. Draw the separate parts on a sheet of non-stick parchment or waxed paper with the details to be marked. First work the wings and tail. Take a paper icing bag (see page 126) and fill with white royal icing. Fold down, then cut off the tip to give the equivalent of a fine to medium tube. Fill in the wings and tail shapes using long curving lines of icing which must touch to prevent breaking and with each line a little shorter than the previous one. This should represent feathers (see illustration). Leave to dry. Next outline the body and head and flood with icing as for a run-out (see opposite). As it begins to set insert the tail in the correct position, propping it up slightly with crumpled tissue or kitchen paper. Then attach the wings with a little icing, propping them up a little with paper if preferred. When quite dry attach very carefully to the cake with icing. Work a dot for each eye and the beak. Colours can be painted on to the birds when quite dry and before attaching to the cake, with liquid food colourings.

### Swans

First draw the body outline and two wings (one for each side if to stand upright, but only one if to attach to the side of a cake). Fill in the wings and body as for birds and leave to dry. Coat the underside of the body with more icing if it is to stand up. To assemble, pipe a thick squiggle of icing the length of the body in a straight line on non-stick parchment or in position on the cake. Place the body upright in this line propping it on each side with cotton wool (absorbent cotton) until dry. Pipe stars of icing onto the underside of the wings and carefully press into position. Leave to dry. Eyes can be marked with dots and the beak overpiped or painted with a touch of yellow or orange liquid food colouring.

### Butterflies

Draw the butterfly wings and body separately on non-stick parchment or waxed paper, tracing the shape from a picture. Outline and flood each separately (see run-outs opposite). Leave to dry. Then outline the shape of the wings and pipe a few dots on each wing using a fine writing tube. Overpipe lines across the body to give texture. Leave to dry, then pipe a little icing down each side of the body and attach the wings in the correct position, holding them in place with cotton wool (absorbent cotton) until dry. Attach to the cake with a dab of icing. Butterflies can also be worked in coloured icings or have liquid food colouring painted on the wings and body for decoration when dry.

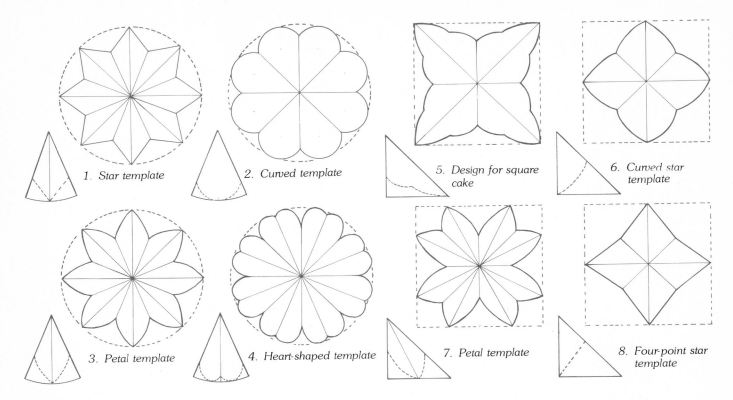

1. Star template

2. Curved template

5. Design for square cake

6. Curved star template

3. Petal template

4. Heart-shaped template

7. Petal template

8. Four-point star template

# DESIGNS FOR ROYAL ICED CAKES

Apart from run-outs for the tops of royal iced cakes, which are described on page 132, many cakes require a symmetrical design which needs to be carefully drawn to scale before marking on the cake. Cake markers can be bought to help simplify the making of patterns or you can make a set of templates yourself in various shapes and sizes for this purpose. A design or pattern on a cake which is not symmetrical when it should be will completely spoil the whole result, however good the rest of the icing may be.

Templates are first drawn on greaseproof (waxed) paper, then drawn onto thin cards or cardboard and cut out to be used many times.

### Round cakes

First draw a circle on greaseproof (waxed) paper about 2.5 cm/1 inch smaller than the top of the cake using the cake tin as a guide. Cut it out. Fold the circle in half, in half again and then in half again, each time from the centre point to give eight equal sections. This will give an 8-point decoration when the end of the paper is cut to make a pattern.

*Star template:* fold the paper in half yet again. Mark a point about 2.5 cm/1 inch down the open side of the paper and draw a straight line to the edge of the folded side. Cut across this line through all thicknesses and open out to give an 8-point star. The same design can be cut in different sizes for use on a tiered cake.

*Curved template:* fold into eight sections, then draw either a convex or concave curve across the end (diagram 2).

*Petal template:* fold into eight sections and then fold again just to mark the centre of each section at the edge. Open out to eight sections again and draw a deep petal shape coming to a point at the mark (diagram 3) or this can have a rounded edge if preferred.

*Heart-shaped template:* fold into eight sections, then in half again and mark a point about 2 cm/¾ inch from the edge of this fold. Open out and draw a heart shape (diagram 4).

For 6-point patterns fold the circle in half, then carefully fold it into three making sure each section is perfectly even before creasing the paper firmly, and that it is folded right from the middle each time. Draw patterns as above and cut out the templates. There are other designs which you can make up for yourself for different templates.

### Square cakes

First cut a square of paper the same size as the top of the cake. Fold in half diagonally, then in half again, and a third time, creasing the edges. With the folded edge to the left and the central point upwards, draw two curves as shown in diagram 5. Cut out.

*Curved star template:* fold as above and draw convex or concave curves (see diagram 6).

*Petal template:* fold as above and draw a petal shape (diagram 7).

*Four-point star template:* fold as above and draw one straight line across the section (diagram 8).

Once the basic patterns have been made and cut out they should be drawn on white card or thin cardboard which is absolutely flat. Then cut out a 'V' shape in the centre of the template so it is easily removed from the cake. Templates in graduated sizes should be cut for tiered wedding cakes.

The template can be interchanged using round patterns on square cakes and vice versa and can be altered and added to as the occasion demands. Six-point designs are not really suitable for square cakes; it is better to use 4- or 8-point.

## How to use a template

Templates can only be used on a hard icing such as royal icing or sugar paste. When the base icing has dried for 24 hours or more, place the template centrally on the cake. Using a medium or fine writing tube pipe round the template 2.5 mm/⅛ inch from the edge of the cardboard. With straight lines break the line of icing at each point and begin again to give a sharp angle. Make sure the curves are all even, holding the tube fairly high to ease the line of icing neatly round the curve. When complete remove the template carefully lifting by the 'V' in the centre. When the first line of icing is dry pipe a second on top either in white or coloured icing. Always pipe the first line in the same colour as the base icing to avoid leaving a mark if it has to be removed. The colour is added in the overpiping.

The template is only required to give the basic design to the cake; any further designs or outlines can be added freehand parallel to the original. The shapes and gaps left between the outlines can be filled in in several ways including small dots, lace work or trellis. It is wise to practise the design on something other than the cake first to prevent mistakes or adding a decoration which doesn't really fit in with the outline.

## Designs for the sides

An easy decoration is a wide band of ribbon, but although this is fine for most birthday, Christmas and Christening cakes, etc., it is not often used on wedding cakes. Garlands of fresh flowers can be arranged round the sides as can a variety of loops made in icing. Loops can be used by themselves or alternating with clusters or garlands of flowers. Dots and stars, simple or over-iced, can also be used to elaborate the loops.

Loops take a little practice, and can be added to the cake freehand or with the help of a template. Without a template the exact distance of each loop must be carefully measured, according to the pattern on the cake, with a dot of icing marked to ensure the finished loop is even.

To make a template for the sides of a cake, cut a strip of paper the same circumference as the cake and fold it to give the required size and number of loops. Draw a loop on the folded paper, cut along the line and open out. Put around the side of the cake and stick the ends with sticky tape (scotch tape) or tie a piece of thin string round to hold it in position.

Whether piping freehand or with a template, stand the cake on a turntable or tilt it onto the turntable. Using a medium writing tube, touch the cake at the beginning of a loop. Pipe out the icing allowing it to fall in a loop (away from the side of the cake) until it is the correct length, then attach to the cake again by simply touching the cake. This needs practice but it is soon easy to gauge the size and shape of the loop and less breakages will occur. If the cake is tilted on the turntable, pipe the loop 2.5 mm/⅛ inch from the template; then remove the template and over-pipe the loops.

Remember when piping loops that the tube must be held away from the cake to allow the icing to fall into an even shape; if held too close it becomes more difficult.

These are just a few ideas for loop-designed sides of a cake (see diagrams):
1. Single and double rows of overlapping loops with decorations of roses, horseshoes, leaves, etc.
2. Double line of double-iced loops with flowers at the joins and alternate decorations below the flowers of leaves and dots.
3. Double-iced loops with dots above and below the line and clusters of flowers at the joins.
4. Sets of three overlapping loops topped with flowers and a pillar piped between each set using a star tube.

*1.*

*3.*

*2.*

*4.*

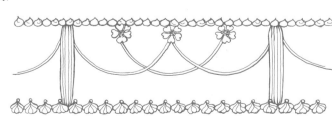

**Approximate quantities of icing (confectioners') sugar for round and square cakes**

| □ | □ | □ | □ | □ | □ | □ |
|---|---|---|---|---|---|---|
| 15 cm | 18 cm | 20 cm | 23 cm | 25 cm | 28 cm | 30 cm |
| 6 inch | 7 inch | 8 inch | 9 inch | 10 inch | 11 inch | 12 inch |
| ○ | ○ | ○ | ○ | ○ | ○ | ○ |
| 15 cm | 18 cm | 20 cm | 23 cm | 25 cm | 28 cm | 30 cm |
| 6 inch | 7 inch | 8 inch | 9 inch | 10 inch | 11 inch | 12 inch |
| 450 g | 575 g | 675 g | 900 g | 1 kg | 1.25 kg | 1.4 kg | 1.6 kg |
| 1 lb | 1¼ lb | 1½ lb | 2 lb | 2¼ lb | 2¾ lb | 3 lb | 3½ lb |

**Approximate quantities of marzipan for round and square cakes**

| □ | □ | □ | □ | □ | □ | □ |
|---|---|---|---|---|---|---|
| 15 cm | 18 cm | 20 cm | 23 cm | 25 cm | 28 cm | 30 cm |
| 6 inch | 7 inch | 8 inch | 9 inch | 10 inch | 11 inch | 12 inch |
| ○ | ○ | ○ | ○ | ○ | ○ | ○ |
| 15 cm | 18 cm | 20 cm | 23 cm | 25 cm | 28 cm | 30 cm |
| 6 inch | 7 inch | 8 inch | 9 inch | 10 inch | 11 inch | 12 inch |
| 350 g | 450 g | 575 g | 800 g | 900 g | 1 kg | 1.25 kg | 1.4 kg |
| ¾ lb | 1 lb | 1¼ lb | 1¾ lb | 2 lb | 2¼ lb | 2½ lb | 3 lb |

# DECORATING A CELEBRATION CAKE

This is the method for preparing and decorating a three-tier wedding cake. The same method is used for any celebration cake to be royal iced: the design can simply be altered to choice and to fit the occasion.

## Size

First decide the size of the cake: 450 g/1 lb cooked cake, weighed without marzipan and icing should cut into 8 to 10 portions, so for each 40 to 50 portions of cake required, you will need at least 2:25 kg/5 lb cake. If you want to keep the top tier, then remember to calculate the required weight from the lower tiers only.

## Shape

Round or square is a matter of preference. Square is the easier to cut, but takes a little longer to ice because only two sides can be iced at a time. Other shapes can also be made: octagonal – simply cut the corners off square cakes; horseshoe and heart – using special tins; or make up others as you wish.

If the cake is to be in tiers it is very important to get the correct proportions or the finished cake may look uneven or top-heavy. For three-tier cakes try:
30, 23 and 15 cm/12, 9 and 6 inches; or
28, 20 and 13 cm/11, 8 and 5 inches; or
25, 18 and 13 cm/10, 7 and 5 inches.
For two-tier cakes try:
30 and 20 or 18 cm/12 and 8 or 7 inches; or
28 and 18 cm/11 and 7 inches; or
25 and 15 or 13 cm/10 and 6 or 5 inches.

## Design

Plan this well in advance and have the cake completely finished if possible a week before the day. Any decorations to be attached such as roses, run-outs, etc., can be made quite a while beforehand, but must be given at least 2 days to dry before fixing to the cake. Begin to base ice the cake about 2 weeks before the wedding to give time for each coat to dry properly before adding the next.

## The cake

Make the cake well in advance (following the chart on page 103 for quantities) – at least 1 month and preferably 3 to 4 months. When the cake is cold prick all over with a skewer and pour 2 to 3 tablespoons of brandy over the surface. This will quickly sink in and is a good method of adding spirits to the cake. Wrap in greaseproof (waxed) paper and foil and store in a cool place. More brandy can be spooned over the cake at monthly intervals, if liked.

## Pillars and cake boards

Pillars are available in white or silver and are made round or square to correspond with the cake. They come in several heights, about 5 to 10 cm/2 to 4 inches. Use four pillars to support each tier (some smaller cakes may only need three), and preferably use taller pillars between the bottom and middle tiers and shorter ones between the middle and top tiers.

Cake boards are available in silver and gold with the thick ones usually called 'drums'. They can be round or square and occasionally other shapes. The board should be 5 cm/2 inches larger than the cake so that it projects 2.5 cm/1 inch all round the cake when covered with marzipan, icing and an icing border.

Thin cake boards, which are used for sponge-type or Christmas cakes, are also available. These can be placed in the centre of the lower tiers of a wedding cake, with pillars positioned on top, to take the weight of the other cake layers and prevent any sinking. The thin silver board can be flooded with icing and decorated around the edge with icing flowers to match the cake.

## Quantities

*Marzipan:* the chart on page 136 will help when calculating the amount required. For a very thick coating, however, you will need to increase the amounts. Cover the cake in marzipan (see method page 120) a week before beginning the royal icing to give plenty of time for the marzipan to dry. Lay sheets of greaseproof (waxed) paper over the cake but do not enclose in anything airtight.

After applying marzipan, put the cakes onto thick silver boards which are 5 cm/2 inches larger than the cake. The bottom tier will look better on a board 7.5 to 10 cm/3 to 4 inches larger than the cake.

*Royal icing:* the icing of the cake should be started about 2 weeks before the wedding or celebration, following the method on page 126 for flat icing cakes. During the icing process keep the bowl of icing covered with a damp cloth to prevent a crust forming, or keep it in an airtight plastic container. Put a little icing onto the cake board to attach the cake firmly.

The edge of the cake board can be 'flooded' with icing if liked, although some people prefer it to be left silver or gold. The cake will require at least two thin coats all over and the top will probably need a third. If possible leave for 12 to 24 hours before adding the next coat. Do not cover the wet or damp cakes – the top may be damaged – just keep it somewhere as clean and dust-free as possible.

Approximate amounts of icing (confectioners') sugar required for royal icing to give two coats and a few simple decorations are given in the chart on page 136. Elaborate or heavy decorations will require more icing.

Leave the flat iced cakes for 24 hours to harden before adding the decorations.

*Opposite: Butterfly and Rose Cake (page 139); Rose and Scroll Cake (page 138); Simple Christening Cake (page 142)*

# WEDDING CAKES

### Lace and daisy cake (two or three-tier round)

Make about 75 medium-sized white daisies and 40 smaller daisies (see page 131). The centres can be either white, or pale yellow or pale pink if you want to introduce colour. Leave to dry. Make 6-point deeply curved templates (see diagram on page 134) to fit the top of each cake tier with the outer curves about 2 cm/¾ inch from the edge of the cake. Place on the cakes and, using a medium writing tube, outline the template, then carefully remove it. Position the pillars, then pipe two more lines inside the first one leaving a good 5 mm/¼ inch between each one. Over-pipe the outer line, then pipe small dots all round between the two inner lines.

Make a template for the sides (see page 135). Fold the paper into six even sections and draw a curve to correspond with the one on the top of the cake but not quite so deep. Cut out and place around the cake a little above centre so that the tops of the curves come between those on the cake, i.e. at the centre of the outer curve.

Pipe a loop to follow the template using the same tube, then remove the template and pipe a second line just over 5 mm/¼ inch below the first one. Pipe a line of dots between the lines as on the top of the cake. Now take a fine writing tube and pipe a lacework pattern between the outline on the top of the cake, over the edge and down as far as the line on the side.

Lace is worked in a pattern that looks like a jigsaw puzzle. The tip of the tube is almost on the cake and wriggled about in a continuous line with no obvious pattern, no ends, and without touching another line, to give a neat even-spaced pattern.

When dry, stick a daisy to each point of the pattern worked on the top of the cake, and a cluster of three daisies on the plain side of the cake just under the joins of the curves. Finally, take a thick writing tube and pipe a border of large dots around the base of each cake tier and a much smaller dot on the board in between the large dots. Leave to dry.

To assemble, put the pillars in position and layer up the cake. Top with a silver vase filled with flowers to match the bride's, or if the icing flowers have coloured centres, to match these.

### Rose and scroll cake (two or three-tier round)

Make about 50 roses (see page 130) for each tier with those for the top tier significantly smaller. Make a straight-edged octagonal template for each tier about 2.5 cm/1 inch smaller than the top of the cake. Position on the top of the cakes and outline in icing using a medium writing tube. Remove the template and pipe two further lines fairly closely inside the first one. When dry, over-pipe the centre line. Position the pillars, then arrange 'V' shapes of seven or nine roses in between them (use a larger number of roses on the lower tiers). Stick on with dabs of icing.

Work eight plain or twisted scrolls (see page 127), using a medium star tube, around the top edge of the cake to correspond with the piped decoration on the top. When dry, using a medium tube, pipe a single or double line in an elongated 'S' shape on top of each scroll. Work a slightly heavier scroll border at the base of the cake adding the plain piped 'S' if liked. Mark the sides into eight sections to correspond with the joins of each scroll. Under four alternate joins arrange circles of roses and attach. Under the other four work a lily of the valley pattern using the medium writing tube. First pipe radiating stems for the flowers and leaves, then pipe small dots up and down alternate stems for the flowers.

When ready, place the pillars in position and assemble the cake. Top with a vase or low cluster of white roses and lily of the valley. Alternatively, make a pretty bouffant bow of white satin ribbon to sit on the top.

### Lattice rose cake (two or three-tier square)

It is difficult to estimate the number of roses required for this cake for it depends on the size of the tiers and the size of the

*Rose and Scroll Design*

roses; but make about 150 for a 25 to 28 cm/10 to 11 inch cake and less for smaller cakes.

Make square templates to fit diagonally on top of the cake and almost touching the edge of the cake. Use a fine writing tube to outline the template, then remove it carefully. Work a three layer trellis pattern to fill in the corners (see page 127), allowing each line to dry before adding the next. Work two lines inside the template, outline and over-pipe.

Arrange roses all round the top edge of the cake to cover the ends of the lattice, making sure there is a slightly larger rose at each corner. Fix a silver rose leaf or homemade icing leaf in each corner. Position two or three roses at each corner of the template outline and fix. On this cake the pillars fit in the corners of the trellis, not in the usual square arrangement.

Mark the centre of each side of the cake and on the bottom two tiers arrange two loops of roses with a leaf placed in the centre. On a small top tier one loop will be sufficient. On a very large bottom tier three loops may look better. Pipe a heavy shell border around the base of the cakes using a thick star tube and fix silver or run-out horseshoes to the corners.

### Butterfly and rose cake (two or three-tier square)

For each tier you will need four small and four medium butterflies (see page 133 for method but use a simple design). Do not stick the butterflies together until just before required and keep them all white. The wings can be covered with a very fine lace pattern instead of dots, if liked. Also make eight large and eight small roses for each tier.

Make templates to correspond to the design on the cake (similar to diagram 5 on page 134 but with a straight line from the right-hand curve to the folded edge). Position on the cakes and outline with a medium writing tube. When the line is dry, over-pipe. Position the pillars, then pipe two single layer lines inside the corners of the design, with a line of dots in graduated sizes towards the centre of the cake. Pipe three lines outside the

straight line in graduated lengths. Arrange clusters of one large and two small roses with two silver leaves in front of each row of straight lines. Pipe a continuous coiled edging to the top of the cake using a thick writing tube.

With a medium writing tube, pipe single layer loops around the side of the cake with the help of a template to give two single loops and one large double loop on each side. Decorate above and below the single loops and between the double row with graduated dots. Arrange one rose and two leaves centrally above the centre loops. Pipe a thick border of dots or a continuous coiled line round the base. Finally, carefully attach the completed small butterflies to the top corners of the cake and the larger ones to the base corners.

### Narcissus cake (two or three-tier, round or square)

For a two-tier cake make about 80 narcissi in various sizes; for a three-tier cake make a further 40 (see page 130). The flowers can be made completely white or just the very edge of the cup tinged pale yellow or orange with liquid food colouring.

Make a template by folding the circle in half and half again, then cut a V shape from just inside the curve towards the point (see templates for round cakes page 134). Outline with a medium writing tube. Remove the template and mark further rows inside the first one, taking them out to the edge of the cake at about 1 cm/$\frac{1}{2}$ inch intervals. Work a row of small dots using the same tube to outline the line of piping nearest the centre.

On the sides below the centre of each piped panel, arrange a cluster of five narcissi and then pipe in stems and leaves with the same tube. Next pipe a pattern of dots in the gaps between the flowers. Using a thick writing tube, pipe a twisted row of icing round the top edge and a similar but slightly heavier one round the base. Add two small dots in front of each twist on the cake board. Position the pillars and then arrange clusters of narcissi on top of the cake with spiky silver leaves to fill the gaps between the piped panels and pillars. Assemble the cake when required.

*Lattice Rose Design*

# CHRISTMAS CAKES

These designs have been worked on a 20 cm/8 inch round or square cake but can, in most cases, be adapted for smaller or larger cakes. First coat the cake in marzipan then either flat ice or rough ice as described and leave to set, if possible for 24 hours, before beginning the decorations.

## Holly and Christmas rose cake

For a traditional design, first flat ice the top and sides of a round cake and leave to dry. Draw an 18 cm/7 inch semi-circle on a piece of paper using a compass, then draw another semi-circle 2.5 cm/1 inch inside the first one and join the ends to give a curved plaque. Cut out and position on top of the cake. Prick out round the edge with a pin. Outline with a writing pipe and fill in (see run-outs page 132) and leave to dry. Then using a thick writing tube and either white or yellow icing write the words 'Merry Christmas' on top of the plaque. Using a star tube pipe individual stars round the top of the cake and larger individual stars round the base.

Make six to ten green marzipan ivy leaves in different sizes, five or six holly leaves (see page 122), a few red holly berries and several Christmas roses with yellow centres in royal icing (see page 130). Position the holly and berries above the writing and make two clusters of ivy leaves and Christmas roses, attaching them all with a dab of white icing. Finish with a red ribbon.

## Father Christmas cake

Flat ice the top of a round cake and give the sides a ribbed effect using a serrated comb or scraper; leave to dry.

Find the centre of the cake and pipe a straight line across the centre using a fairly thick writing tube, then pipe three lines on each side keeping them fairly close. Turn the cake round and pipe seven more lines to divide the cake into quarters. Using a large plain tube pipe large dots around the top edge of the cake and a second row around the top side between the first row so they just touch. Pipe large dots around the base of the cake with a smaller row of dots just above but between the first ones and another row on the board between the first row. Top some of the ones on the board with silver balls. Make two Christmas trees and two Father Christmas shapes from marzipan (see page 122) and put in the plain quarters on the cake, attaching with icing. Tie a green and red ribbon round the cake.

## Star cake

Flat ice the top of a round cake. Rough ice the sides, bringing the icing about 2 cm/$\frac{3}{4}$ inch over the top edge of the cake in peaks. When dry, draw a star on a sheet of paper about 10 cm/4 inches across and prick out on the top of the cake. Outline and flood with pale yellow or white icing (see run-outs page 132); leave to set. Pipe an outline to each point of the star.

Make three or four marzipan poinsettias and ten holly leaves with berries (see page 122). Arrange the poinsettias in the centre of the star and bunches of holly and berries in between each point of the star. If you want to tie a ribbon round the cake, a smooth border should be made through the centre of the rough icing using a wide palette knife before it sets.

## Red and white trellis cake

Flat ice the top and sides of a round cake and leave to dry. Draw a 10 to 11 cm/4 to 4$\frac{1}{2}$ inch square on a piece of paper and prick out in the centre of the cake with a pin. Fill icing bags fitted with fine writing tubes with white and red icing. Pipe a wide trellis pattern outside the square, using alternate lines of red and white icing and making sure the lines nearest the centre are red. Pipe a white line all round close inside the red square and then pipe 'corners' about 2.5 cm/1 inch long inside this line. Pipe 'Merry Christmas' in the centre of the plain square using red or white icing, piping a second line on top of the first. Using a medium star tube, pipe a shell edging round the top of the cake taking the ends of the shells slightly down the side of the cake. Pipe a heavy shell border round the base.

Make nine marzipan holly leaves and some red berries (see page 122) and, when set, place three leaves with a few berries in the square beneath the writing and pairs of leaves and berries at the three other corners on the trellis. Tie a wide red or green ribbon round the cake.

## Noel cake

Flat ice the top and sides of a square cake in white. Draw a 15 to 17 cm/6 to 6$\frac{1}{2}$ inch circle on paper, cut out and fold into eight. Cut the end into a semi-circle and open out to give an eight-scalloped circle. Place centrally on the cake and outline using a medium writing tube. Work a three-row trellis between the line and the edge of the cake. Then make two or three scalloped circles inside the first one with about 5 mm/$\frac{1}{4}$ inch between them. Work a second row on top of these.

Write the word 'Noel' on a piece of paper about 2 cm/$\frac{3}{4}$ inch in height and prick onto the cake in the centre. Outline and fill in these letters (see run-outs page 132) using white icing and leave to set. Place a candle above the writing; secure with icing.

Make about ten marzipan holly leaves and a few berries (see page 122) and two or three Christmas roses (see page 130). Pipe a looped border round the top edge of the cake using a fine star tube and a heavier border round the base. Position four holly leaves and a few berries round the candle and the remainder with the Christmas roses in a crescent below the writing. Tie a wide red or green ribbon round the cake.

## Christmas bells cake

Flat ice the top and sides of a square cake in white. The sides can have a ribbed effect made using a serrated comb or scraper, if liked. Leave to dry. Lay a very wide green ribbon across one corner of the cake and down the sides. A narrower royal blue or red ribbon can be placed over the green one. Draw three bells on paper, one larger than the others. Prick them out on the cake in a bunch with the largest facing downwards. Outline and fill in the main part of the bells with white or pale yellow icing (see run-outs page 132) but do not fill in the 'insides' of the bells, just outline. Leave to dry. Tint a little icing bright yellow and outline and flood the hammers. Make three or five marzipan holly leaves and a few berries, and position at the tops of the bells.

For the top edging, mark a square 2.5 cm/1 inch in from the edge of the cake. Using a medium writing tube, pipe slanting lines at 5 mm/$\frac{1}{4}$ inch intervals all round the cake; but not over the ribbon, or over the sides. Then repeat the lines in the opposite direction to form a lattice pattern. A line of small dots can be added at each edge of the trellis, if liked. Repeat the edging round the base of the cake, beginning the piping 1.5 cm/$\frac{1}{2}$ inch up the side and taking it out over the board.

*Star Cake; Noel Cake*

# OTHER CELEBRATION CAKES

### Simple Christening cake (for a boy or girl)

Flat ice the top and sides of a square cake in white and leave to dry. Work three squares on the top of the cake, about 2.5 cm/1 inch from the edge and 1 cm/½ inch apart, in white icing using a medium writing tube. When dry, outline the squares in pale blue or pink.

In the centre of the cake prick out the name of the child in fairly large block print and outline with white icing. When dry, pipe minute dots of blue or pink icing over the outline to give bold but even letters. Draw patterns for scrolls and prick out on the cake. These can be worked in white or a colour and can be piped in a double layer using the writing tube or in a simple layer using a small star tube.

Using a thick writing tube and white icing, pipe a row of large dots round the top edge of the cake followed by another row of the same size dots but on the side of the cake and in between the first ones. Pipe two rows around the base of the cake, again with one on the side of the cake and the second on the board in between the first ones. When dry, either top each dot with a spot of blue or pink icing or join up the dots in a coloured fine trellis. Finish the cake off with a wide satin ribbon to match the icing.

*Petal and Lace Christening Cake*

### Round Christening cake (petal and lace design for a girl)

Flat ice a round cake. Draw a petal-shaped eight-point template and position on the cake. Outline with a fine or medium writing tube in white. Write the name of the child and prick out on the cake positioned wherever you wish; outline this also in white. Next over-pipe both the name and design in pale pink icing. The name can have a third layer of piping, if liked.

If you want to add the lace, take a fine writing tube with white or pink icing and work between the outline and the edge of the cake (see page 138).

For the edging and border use a fairly small star tube and pink or white icing. Work a row of single shells beside each other around the very top of the sides but not tipping over onto the top of the cake. Then work two small shells under each other on the side of the cake under every other shell. Repeat round the base of the cake with the two shells worked on the board. Complete the cake with a pink or white satin ribbon round the sides and a model of a stork holding a cradle or a crib on the top.

### General celebration cake

Although the design for this lovely celebration cake is for a 25 cm/10 inch round cake, it can be made to fit any sized round cake by adjusting the size of the template, and can be used for any occasion, be it a birthday, golden wedding, Christening, retirement or other celebration. It is also a good design for a two- or three-tier wedding cake with the flowers in the centre of the cake omitted to make room for pillars.

Flat ice the cake in white. Colour some of the icing in three shades of the same colour, e.g. pale, medium and dark pink, yellow or green, etc. Make about 30 pale coloured icing roses (see page 130), 45 to 50 medium and 45 to 50 dark coloured roses; leave to dry.

Make a six-point template to produce a curve similar to the diagram of the cake and place on the cake. Outline in white icing using a medium writing tube. Fill in to the edge of the cake with a curved trellis pattern in white, then outline inside the trellis with two lines about 5 mm to 1 cm/¼ to ½ inch apart. Over-pipe the middle outline in the dark icing and the inner one with the medium coloured icing using a medium tube.

Mark the six points on the side of the cake directly under the points of the curves on top and position a dark rose at the top point of the curve to be worked. Mark an even curve from rose to rose either with a template or tiny dots of icing as a guide. Then fill in the curves with roses beginning with two dark ones

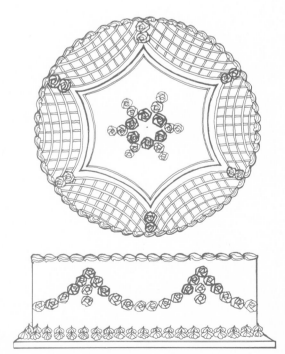

*General Celebration Cake*

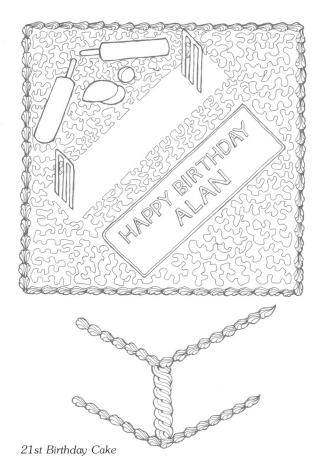

*21st Birthday Cake*

Then work scrolls to match the top edging, around the base in between the panels. Outline these on the board with arcs of plain piping.

On the top of the cake prick out the words 'Happy Birthday' and the name, leaving spaces for the flooded 18 and two keys. Also prick out 'th' to go after the 18. Outline first in white and then with colour using a medium writing tube. Finally attach the candles in their holders, the flooded 18 and two keys to the top of the cake, and a key into each empty panel on the sides.

**21st birthday cake for a boy (cricket theme)**
Flat ice a square cake in pale green icing on a board 10 cm/4 inches longer than the cake. Mark a strip on top of the cake for the wicket and using a fine writing tube and the same green icing work a very fine squiggly pattern to cover the top of the cake, except for the wicket. Leave to dry.

Draw a plaque on a stiff card about 15 × 5 cm/5 × 2 inches. Cover with non-stick parchment or waxed paper and outline and flood in white (see page 132). When dry, pipe 'Happy Birthday' and the name on the plaque in green or a contrasting colour. Also draw four '21s' and outline and flood in white for the sides of the cake. Using marzipan, mould two bats from a brown colour. Make stumps either by painting matchsticks with brown food colouring or by covering them with marzipan. Mould a ball from deep red marzipan and, if liked, a coloured cap. Leave all to dry.

Pipe a thick shell border round the top and base of the cake using white icing and pipe a twisted line down the corners of the cake using the same tube. Position the plaque and attach to the cake with a small border of green icing. Arrange the stumps, bats, ball and cap in position and attach. Stick a '21' to the centre of each side of the cake. If candles are requested these can be arranged in a double row on the cake board at the corner below the plaque.

followed by two medium coloured ones and two pale ones at the bottom of the curves, continuing on with two medium and two dark roses to complete the curve. Attach two medium roses below each other coming down under the point of the curve.

Using white icing and a medium star tube for the top border of the cake, work a shell edging that comes over the edge of the cake and finishes on the side. Work a straight double star border all round the base using the same tube. To complete the cake, position two dark and two pale roses alternately on top of the lattice at the joins of the curves and a decoration in the centre of the cake of six dark, six medium and six pale roses.

**18th birthday cake for a girl**
Flat ice a 20 cm/8 inch or larger round cake in white. Leave to dry. Make 18 white icing roses or stars and as the icing sets place a candle in each one and leave until hard, making sure from time to time that the candles are still upright. Draw an '18' and eight key shapes on stiff card and outline and flood (see run-outs page 132). They can be white or a contrasting colour to match the candles. Leave to dry.

Divide the top of the cake into 12 sections, marking with a dot of icing on the edge, and do the same round the base to correspond. Using a medium star tube and white icing, work twisted scrolls between the marks, making each one thicker in the middle and tailing off at the end, round the top edge of the cake. Using a fine star tube, pipe a thin line of shells from the joins of each scroll in a straight line down the side of the cake to the base. Using a fine writing tube and white or coloured icing, fill in the alternate panels with fine lace work (see page 138).

*18th Birthday Cake*

# NOVELTY CAKES

All children love to have a surprise birthday cake. This cake usually appears before the party and is then severely scrutinized by the child before the all-important verdict is forthcoming. The problem often is to think of something a little different but which is still fairly simple to design, assemble and decorate, for time is always short when there is a birthday and party to arrange. Some children like to have their mother's version of something they have seen at another party, but often a complete surprise delights even more.

Many children do not like fruit cakes or marzipan so all these novelty ideas are made with a Victoria sandwich (layer) cake mixture (using any flavour you wish) and can have a layer of marzipan added, if you like. The icing will be much easier if there is a layer of marzipan. If the cake has a lot of loose crumbs brush it all over with Apricot Glaze (see page 107) before adding the marzipan or butter cream. If you prefer a fruit cake, try a Light Fruit Cake (see page 99), using a deep cake tin in place of two sandwich tins (layer cake pans). When baked and cold proceed as for the sponge cake. With fruit cakes it is advisable to use marzipan before icing unless the cake is to be consumed within two or three days.

## Mark's castle

Make up three times the recipe quantity of Victoria Sandwich (Layer) Cake (see page 6), in chocolate or vanilla flavour for preference, i.e. using 300 g/12 oz (1½ cups) butter, sugar, etc. Grease and bottom line (or flour) two 20 cm/8 inch and one 15 cm/6 inch round sandwich tins (layer cake pans) and a rectangular tin about 28 × 18 × 4 cm/11 × 7 × 1½ inches. Divide the cake batter between the tins, level the tops and bake in a moderately hot oven (190°C/375°F, Gas Mark 5). Allow 15 to 25 minutes for the sandwich (layer) cake tins and about 35 to 45 minutes for the rectangular tin, or until well risen and firm to the touch. Turn out onto wire racks and leave to cool.

Make up twice the recipe quantity of chocolate Butter Cream (see page 104). Transfer 6 tablespoons of the butter cream to a small bowl and make it a very dark brown by adding extra sifted cocoa powder (unsweetened cocoa) and a little brown food colouring or gravy browning. Sandwich the two larger cakes together with a little butter cream and place on a 30 cm/12 inch square cake board. Spread the base of the small round cake with butter cream and place on top of the layered cake. Completely mask the whole cake in butter cream. Cut the rectangular cake into five pieces, crossways, and stand one pillar at each corner, sticking it to the cake. Cut the remaining piece in half, then sandwich the two pieces together to form a square block and stand on top of the cake. Cover all these pieces with butter cream and leave to set for a little while.

At one side of the cake make a drawbridge using about six chocolate finger biscuits (cookies), and place one biscuit (cookie) around the sides of the cake at each corner where the pillars join. Then with a piping bag fitted with a thick writing tube and filled with the dark brown butter cream write the child's name on top of the cake above the drawbridge, and pipe 'doorways' and 'windows' on each tower. Change to a medium

*Little Bear Maypole Cake*

star tube and pipe a 'wall' around the top of each tower, around the edge of each cake and a border around the base of the castle. To complete the cake put the required number of candles on top of the central tower, stand a soldier on top of each tower and stick a paper flag outwards from each tower over the window.

## Little bear maypole cake

For this delightful cake, make two or three (if you want a deep cake) round 23 cm/9 inch sandwich cakes (layers) using the basic Victoria Sandwich (Layer) Cake mixture for each tin, and in any flavour. Make up 1½ recipe quantities of Butter Cream (see page 104) and spread a little over one (or two) cakes. Cover these with a thin layer of raspberry jam or lemon curd and sandwich the cakes together. Place on a board and spread a thin layer of butter cream all round the sides of the cake. Stick chocolate finger biscuits (cookies) all round the sides of the cake so the tops show just over the edge of the cake to represent a fence. Cut the biscuits (cookies) to the required length if necessary. Colour 75 to 100 g/3 to 4 oz (1 cup) desiccated (shredded) coconut a pale green by soaking in water to which green food colouring has been added. Drain well and leave to dry.

Brush the top of the cake with Apricot Glaze (see page 107) and spoon the green coconut in an even layer over it. Make a maypole from a long thin stick covered first in foil and then with ribbons wound around it. Position in the centre of the cake pushing it right down to the board. Stand five or six model bears around the edge of the cake (or use other animals or models, if preferred). Attach several narrow ribbons in different colours to the top of the maypole with a pin and arrange these over the cake taking them out to the bears. The maypole and edge of the cake can also be decorated with artificial or sugar flowers. Use the remaining butter cream to decorate the top and base of the chocolate biscuit (cookie) fence.

## Numeral and clock cakes

The age of a child can be shown on the face of a clock made on a cake, with the hands set at the age of the child. The cake can be round or square for a simple 'clock cake' or for some ages (e.g. 6, 8, 9 and 10) the clock face can be worked onto a numeral-shaped cake. If you want to make a number but cannot buy the required tin, then simply bake a large slab cake (or two in some cases) and, when cold, cut out the required shape.

Place the cake on a board and cover completely with a layer of coloured butter cream to match the flavour of the cake. For the clock face, first cut out a small circle of coloured marzipan and place it in the centre of the cake. Then using a contrasting or darker-coloured marzipan, cut out the 'hands' and numbers for the face and position on the cake with the time set at the age of the child. With a star tube, pipe a border round the circle in the centre of the cake, the top edge and the base of the cake. The sides of the cake can be decorated with stars or scrolls of icing, or the child's name can be written around it. If it is a numeral-shaped cake, write 'Happy Birthday' and the child's name on top of the plain part of the cake and position the required number of candles.

The numerals and hands for the clock can also be worked in piped butter cream, if preferred, using a contrasting or darker colour. Alternatively, the cake can be iced in royal icing if a layer of marzipan is added first.

## Fudge cottage

For this cake, make up a One-Stage Sponge (see page 7), using 150 g/6 oz ($\frac{3}{4}$ cup) soft 'luxury' margarine, 150 g/6 oz (1 cup) light soft brown sugar, 150 g/6 oz ($1\frac{1}{2}$ cups) plain (all-purpose) flour, $1\frac{1}{2}$ teaspoons baking powder, 3 eggs and 1 tablespoon coffee essence (strong black coffee). Turn into a greased and lined (or floured) 18 cm/7 inch square deep cake tin. Bake in a moderate oven (180°C/350°F, Gas Mark 4) for about 50 minutes or until well risen and just firm to the touch. Turn out onto a wire rack and leave until cold.

Make up one recipe quantity of coffee Butter Cream (see page 104). Cut two 3 cm/$1\frac{1}{4}$ inch slices off one side of the cake (see diagram 1) and then a slanting slice off one side of both the slices (diagram 2). Place these two pieces on top of the cake for the first part of the roof and one of the triangular pieces on top to complete the slanting roof (diagram 3), sticking to the cake with a little butter cream. Stand the cottage cake on a board and completely mask with butter cream.

'Tile' the roof with chocolate buttons, beginning at the edge of the roof and working up to the point of the roof. Make a chimney from some of the remaining sponge, attach to one end of the roof and mask in butter cream. Colour a little butter cream a much darker brown using gravy browning and use to outline a door on one side of the cottage and windows on each side of the door and all around the house. Use chocolate finger biscuits (cookies) cut to size to fill in the door and for beams across the ends of the house below the tiles (see diagram). Using liquorice allsorts (candies) position two plain tubes of liquorice for chimney pots and cut pink liquorice sandwiches in half to make shutters. Place these on each side of the windows all round the house.

Using the dark brown butter cream, mark a path from the door to the edge of the cake board. For grass, colour a little desiccated (shredded) coconut pale green, brush the board with Apricot Glaze (see page 107) and sprinkle on top. Make flower borders using little gem biscuits (cookies) or sugar flowers. If candles are required, these can be attached to one end of the cake board as part of the garden.

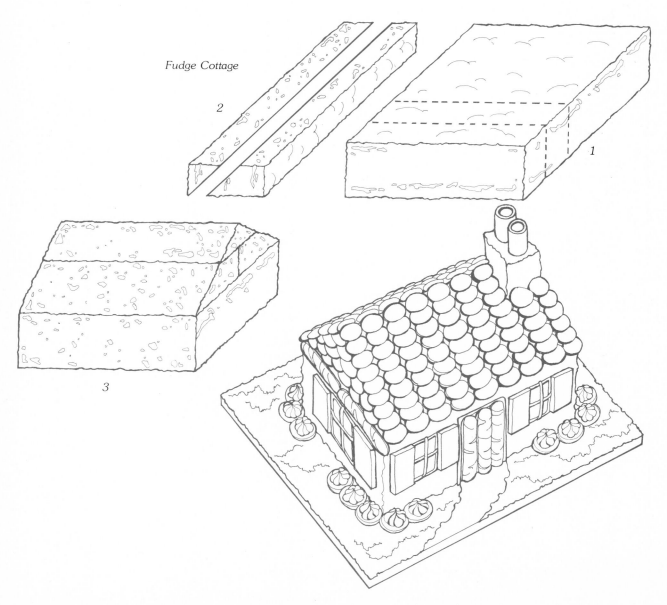

Fudge Cottage

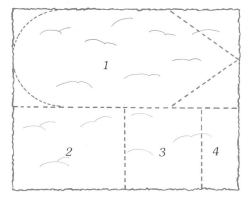

*Jolly Roger*

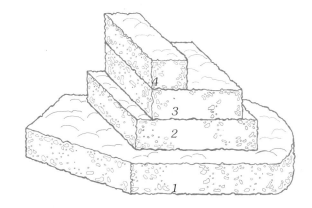

## Horseshoe cake

For a child who enjoys horses and ponies this cake might fit the bill. Use a horseshoe-shaped cake tin (or a large round cake tin, cutting the cooked cake to shape) and half fill with a Victoria Sandwich (Layer) Cake mixture (see page 6). When baked and cooled, place the cake on a cake board and mask completely in green Butter Cream (see page 104). Then either using a contrasting coloured butter cream or a deeper shade of green, write 'Happy Birthday' and the child's name on the top along one side. With a star tube outline a shell edging all round the top and base of the cake. Position the required number of candles at one end of the cake and four or five model show jumps, gates or hedges around the curve. One jump should have the horse and rider attached to it as if in action.

## Jolly Roger

Make up $2\frac{1}{2}$ recipe quantities of the Victoria Sandwich (Layer) Cake mixture (see page 6), i.e. 250 g/10 oz ($1\frac{1}{4}$ cups) butter, sugar, etc. Grease and line a rectangular baking tin, about $30 \times 25 \times 5$ cm/$12 \times 10 \times 2$ inches. Add the cake batter, spreading it slightly thicker in the corners and around the edges of the tin. Bake in a moderately hot oven (190°C/375°F, Gas Mark 5) for about 45 minutes or until well risen and firm to the touch. Turn out onto a wire rack and leave to cool.

Cut the cake into four pieces following the diagram and assemble, sticking together with apricot jam. The whole cake can be brushed with Apricot Glaze (see page 107) to prevent crumbs getting into the butter cream. Make up 1 to $1\frac{1}{2}$ recipe quantities of Butter Cream (see page 104) and use some of it to coat all round the sides of the ship.

Colour about 2 tablespoons of the butter cream a light brown and use to cover all the lower deck and front of the upper deck to represent the wooden boards. Colour most of the remaining butter cream pale blue (or any other colour) and use to cover all the remainder of the ship. Before it sets, place two chocolate finger biscuits (cookies) on the forward upper deck for masts and arrange peppermint or coloured polos (lifesavers) for portholes all over the lower and upper decks. To make a railing to go all round the edge of the ship, cut chocolate matchsticks (candies) into three pieces and stick into the butter cream fairly close to each other right on the edge of the cake. Candles can be fixed to the tops of the upper decks, if required. Colour a little butter cream in a dark colour, and write JOLLY ROGER on the bows, and also pipe a few coils of rope on the forward deck. Finally add a paper flag flying from the stern.

## Father Christmas cake

For a Christmas celebration make a fat Swiss (Jelly) Roll (see page 15) or buy a ready-made one. Cut a 4 cm/$1\frac{1}{2}$ inch slice off one end for the head. Brush the front with Apricot Glaze (see page 107). Colour about 50 g/2 oz marzipan pink. Roll out and use to cover the front of the small piece of cake, for the face. Mould a nose with a little more pink marzipan and attach to the face. Place the head on top of the body and push a skewer right through head and body into the cake board to secure it.

Colour 225 g/8 oz ($\frac{1}{2}$ lb) marzipan red and roll out three-quarters of it to make a cloak for Father Christmas. Brush the cake with apricot glaze and wrap the cloak round it, allowing the bottom to flow over the board about 2 cm/$\frac{3}{4}$ inch. Mould half the remaining red marzipan into a pointed hat and position on the back of the head. Use the remainder to make two arms. Make up a little fairly stiff royal icing and put into a piping bag fitted with a medium star tube. Pipe a border all round the edge of the cloak, round the neck and hat and to give a long beard, hair and eyebrows. Position the arms across the body to hold the sack of goodies over his shoulder; then make a sack from a little brown-coloured marzipan and fix onto his back. Fill the sack with assorted sweets (candies). Finish off the eyes with small pieces of chocolate and finally add a pom-pom of icing to the tip of his hat. Leave to dry.

# SUCCESSFUL CAKE-MAKING

The most important thing to remember when making a cake is to read the recipe carefully before you begin; then follow it, using the ingredients, utensils, method and oven temperature stated. Making cakes and decorating them is enjoyable and need give you no worries about failure if you know the basic rules and a little about the ingredients you are working with.

## KNOW YOUR INGREDIENTS

The basic ingredients in cake making include flour, sugar, fat, eggs, raising (leavening) agents and liquids, plus all the extras such as nuts, dried fruit, cherries, etc. This sounds simple enough, but do you know which flour to use and why? Whether caster, granulated or brown sugar will give the best result? And why or how much raising (leavening) agent is required for guaranteed success? All the recipes in this book have been carefully tested and give the correct quantities, but when you come to experiment yourself, you need to know why a particular flour or fat will give you the result you want.

### Flour

All flours must be kept in a cool, dry place preferably in an airtight container and each bag should be used up before starting a new one for if kept too long flour will begin to stale. Always sift flour before adding to any type of mixture; this incorporates extra air and removes any impurities or lumps.

Most people think of flour as either plain (all-purpose) or self-raising (self-rising), and the latter is often used exclusively for all cooking and baking to be sure of getting the correct amount of raising (leavening) agent. However, both these flours should be used for specific purposes.

Gluten is the substance which makes all the difference to the volume and texture in bread when baked. For this reason there is a strong (high-gluten) flour available (often called bread flour) which is produced specially to give the volume required, particularly in yeast cookery. Strong flour can also be used for puff pastry, Yorkshire puddings and some steamed puddings but must not be used for cakes.

*Plain (all-purpose) flour:* unless otherwise specified in a recipe it is wise to use plain (all-purpose) flour and particularly in recipes where little or no rise is required, e.g. pastry. However, should plain (all-purpose) flour need to be converted to self-raising (self-rising), add $2\frac{1}{2}$ teaspoons baking powder to each 225 g/ 8 oz (2 cups) flour. Cake flour, available in the US, is made from soft wheat and gives a lighter crumblier texture to cakes. It may be used interchangeably with all-purpose flour in these recipes, remembering that 1 cup of cake flour equals 1 cup less 2 tablespoons all-purpose flour.

*Self-raising (self-rising) flour:* this is so popular because the correct amount of raising (leavening) agent has already been added to the flour. However, in some recipes only a certain amount of rise is required and standard self-raising (self-rising) flour will have too much raising (leavening) agent. In this case the recipe may call for part self-raising (self-rising) and part plain (all-purpose) flour.

*Other flours:* various types of brown flours – wholemeal, wholewheat or graham, stoneground, etc. – can be used to give flavour and texture, particularly to breads and scones. They can also be used to replace a small proportion of white flour in some cakes to give variety. Try replacing 50 g/2 oz ($\frac{1}{2}$ cup) from 225 to 350 g/8 to 12 oz (2 to 3 cups) white flour with brown flour in a rubbed-in cake, tea bread or scone recipe.

### Raising (leavening) agents

Any way of introducing air or gas into bread, cakes, puddings, etc., to make them rise during cooking is termed a raising (leavening) agent. This can be achieved by beating air into the eggs and sugar for sponge cakes, but the most usual raising (leavening) agent is carbon dioxide produced by the action of yeast or chemicals.

*Baking powder:* this is the most often used agent and is a combination of an acid ingredient (bicarbonate of soda/baking soda) and an alkaline ingredient (cream of tartar) which when moistened react together to give off carbon dioxide. This forms tiny bubbles in the dough or batter which expand during cooking and are set by the heat to give the required light texture. However, if too much baking powder is added the cake will rise well at first during baking but then collapse giving a heavy soggy texture.

*Bicarbonate of soda (baking soda):* this is used particularly in recipes with sour milk, honey, treacle (molasses) or a lot of spice.

*Sour milk:* this is used in scones and gingerbreads as an additional raising (leavening) agent with either self-raising (self-rising) flour, or with or in place of cream of tartar.

*Yeast:* this is used for bread doughs and is activated by the addition of liquid, sugar and warmth. Dried (active dry) yeast comes in granulated form complete with full reconstituting instructions and will store in an airtight container for several months. Fresh (compressed) yeast will keep for about 1 week in the refrigerator, or in the freezer (in suitable amounts for use) for up to 6 months.

## Sugar

A very important factor in cake making, sugar gives the flavour and all-important sweetness to the finished result. Caster sugar is widely used especially for creamed mixtures because of its fine texture, but other sugars can be used with care to give colour, flavour and texture.

*Caster sugar:* most commonly used for all cake making in Britain, especially for creamed mixtures. It is all important in whisked sponges where the sugar must have a fine texture.

*Granulated sugar:* when used in creamed mixtures British granulated sugar usually produces slightly less volume because of the coarser texture, and can have a slightly gritty taste. However, for rubbed-in mixtures it works well. American granulated sugar is finer than British granulated and can be used in all recipes calling for either caster or granulated sugar.

*Icing (confectioners') sugar:* this is the finest of all sugars, used widely in cake decorating, icings and fillings. It is used for some biscuit (cookie) recipes and meringues, but in cakes it gives a poor volume and hard crust to the baked cake.

*Demerara (raw) sugar:* the coarsest of all grained sugars, demerara (raw) can replace granulated sugar in rubbed-in mixtures and in some tea breads, and it is excellent for sprinkling on top of cakes before baking to give a crunchy topping. It does not cream, but is good when used in a melted mixture, such as a gingerbread, when it is partly dissolved before the actual cooking. (If raw sugar is not available in your area, light brown may be substituted.)

*Soft brown sugar:* this is available in dark and light varieties and gives a 'caramel' taste. It will cream well and is widely used in rich fruit cakes for colour and flavour. It can replace white sugar in creamed mixtures as it gives the same volume. It is also used widely in melted mixtures.

*Golden syrup (light corn syrup):* can be used to replace part of the sugar content in a recipe and is blander, lighter and sweeter than treacle (molasses). It is often used in melted mixtures.

*Black treacle (molasses):* a dark syrup with a strong flavour and colour, treacle (molasses) is used in melted mixtures, especially gingerbreads, where its special flavour is required. A little is often added to rich fruit cakes to give a good dark colour.

*Honey:* gives a delicious flavour, but do not use more than one-third to one-half quantity of sugar as it causes over-browning.

## Fat

The fats most often used are butter and margarine. Of these butter gives the best flavour, but in most recipes the two are interchangeable. For rich cakes and cakes which need to mature or are to be stored for some time it is best to use butter. One-stage cake mixes require a special soft or 'luxury' margarine for the recipe to work satisfactorily. Other fats such as lard, blended white vegetable fat (shortening), dripping and oil can all be used in cake-making but when using oil, specially proportioned recipes must be used to achieve good results. Blended vegetable fats (shortening) give light spongy cakes with a good volume but lack flavour – they also need specially proportioned recipes (although they are fine in pastry). Lard rubs easily into flour giving the best texture for pastry and some biscuits (cookies). Use fat at room temperature; if taken straight from the refrigerator it will not rub-in or cream satisfactorily.

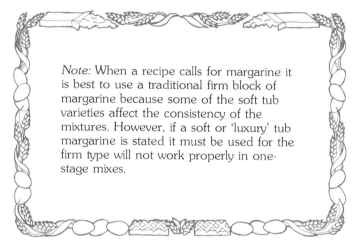

*Note:* When a recipe calls for margarine it is best to use a traditional firm block of margarine because some of the soft tub varieties affect the consistency of the mixtures. However, if a soft or 'luxury' tub margarine is stated it must be used for the firm type will not work properly in one-stage mixes.

## Eggs

Eggs vary in size and this will affect the recipe you are going to make. Large eggs (sizes 1 and 2) and standard eggs (3 and 4) give more or less the same results but anything smaller will definitely affect the mixture. For every 3 medium or small eggs (sizes 5 and 6), add an extra one when following a recipe.

Never use eggs straight from the refrigerator or the mixture is likely to curdle – they should be kept at room temperature for cake-making. Take care when separating eggs for meringue; if any yolk is mixed with the white to be beaten, the fatty content of the yolk will lessen the volume of the beaten whites and change the texture slightly. A little egg yolk has the same effect as using a greasy bowl.

# GLOSSARY

### Beating
To turn ingredients over and over quickly in order to incorporate as much air as possible using a spoon, fork, whisk, rotary beater or electric mixer.

### Caramelize
To cook white sugar very slowly, on its own or with a little water, until it turns a pale to golden or darker brown.

### Cream
To beat fat and sugar together to give a soft, very pale and fluffy mixture. This can be done with a wooden spoon or electric mixer. If the fat is hard it should be creamed alone until soft before adding the sugar; if oily it will prevent proper incorporation of air during creaming thus giving less volume – the ideal is to start with fat at room temperature.

### Dredge
To coat the surface of a food heavily with a dry substance, such as flour or sugar.

### Dropping consistency
The term used to describe the texture of the uncooked cake mixture. A well-filled spoonful of mixture held on its side should drop in a count of 5 without shaking the spoon. A soft dropping consistency means the mixture is too stiff to pour but it will drop off a spoon easily, while a stiff dropping consistency will need a shake to dislodge the mixture from the spoon but it is too soft and sticky to handle easily.

### Dust
To sprinkle the surface of something lightly with flour or sugar, e.g. the top of a cake with sugar either before or after cooking.

### Fold-in
The method used to combine a beaten or light mixture with other ingredients without losing volume. Use a spoon or spatula and, making a sharp clean movement, cut through the mixture. Then with a lifting movement bring the heavier mixture up from the bottom and turn it over. Repeat the slicing and lifting movement, turning the bowl round as the folding continues. Always fold a lighter mixture into a heavier one, e.g. sifted flour into creamed or whisked mixtures, so the air is not pressed out.

### Glaze
To brush the surface of a food before or after cooking with a transparent substance, e.g. jelly, jam, syrup, milk or beaten egg so that the food is just coated but is still visible through the glaze. If glazed before cooking it usually gives a gloss or shine to the finished food. A glaze improves both the appearance and the flavour of a dish.

### Knead
To push together and mould dough between your fingers and with the palms of your hands to give the required consistency ready for rolling or shaping. With yeast dough the process takes about 10 minutes by hand or 3 to 4 minutes with an electric mixer fitted with a dough hook. Kneading is necessary to develop the gluten and to distribute the yeast and gas evenly throughout the mixture to give the required rise during proving and cooking. For pastry and scone doughs the kneading should be lighter, just bringing the outside of the dough to the centre with the fingertips, repeating the process until the dough is smooth.

### Whip
To incorporate air into a substance such as cream to give a lighter consistency and much greater volume.

# CAKE-MAKING EQUIPMENT

In grandmother's day all she possessed for cake making and baking were the bare essentials – mixing bowls, jug, wooden spoons, forks, knives, sieve (strainer), flat whisk, rotary whisk and perhaps a few other bits and pieces, as well as a selection of tins – and she managed to produce wonderful results. We are much luckier and our task has been greatly simplified by the introduction of electrical aids. A hand-held or larger electric mixer takes a lot of the hard work out of beating and creaming and cuts the time down considerably when making cakes and bread. An electric blender is a boon for chopping or grinding nuts, making breadcrumbs, etc. These aids are not necessities, but they do greatly reduce the preparation time and labour involved in cake making today, and this is an important factor for those people who live busy working lives.

### Cake tins
As with most kitchenware there is an enormous choice when it comes to cake tins. For bare essentials buy a pair of sandwich tins (layer cake pans), one or two larger deep cake tins, a baking sheet or two, a shallow Swiss (jelly) roll tin, a flan ring (tart pan) and patty (shallow muffin) tins and gradually build up your collection from there. But whatever you buy choose good, strong, easily-cleaned tins because they will last forever if properly treated. Special easy-clean and non-stick surfaces are favoured by some; they do help difficult cakes and buns slide out easily, but some tins still require a little greasing, and give a very different appearance to the side of the baked cake when compared with a cake baked in a paper-lined tin – usually somewhat heavy looking and rather shiny.

Kitchen foil baking cases can be used several times for cakes if they are well looked after, and you can mould your own shapes to bake in if you use three or four thicknesses of foil. This is particularly useful for making unusual shapes for children's parties, etc.

*Sandwich tins (layer cake pans):* these are widely used and should always be bought in pairs. The most popular sizes are 18 and 20 cm/7 and 8 inch, and 23 cm/9 inch are good for gâteaux. Square sandwich tins (layer cake pans) are also useful, not only for cakes but for many other purposes including bar cookies, shortbread, etc. Again 18 and 20 cm/7 and 8 inch are the best sizes to have.

*Deep cake tins (springform pans):* the most useful sizes for round deep cakes are 18, 20 and 25 cm/7, 8 and 10 inch, and for square cakes (mostly used for gingerbreads, fruit cakes, etc., which need to be cut into cubes or slices) 15, 18 and 20 cm/6, 7 and 8 inch. Loose-bottomed round cake tins help greatly with the removal of the cake. Spring-release tins are also good (especially for gâteaux and soft-textured cakes which can fall apart so easily) for the sides split open or into two parts leaving the cake standing on the base. Some of these also have a tubular fitting.

*Tube tins or ring moulds:* these are useful for making party cakes, savarins, gâteaux, etc. They can be plain or fluted and a 23 cm/9 inch size is probably the most versatile, although they are available in many other shapes and sizes.

*Flan (tart) rings:* it is worthwhile having at least one or two loose-bottomed fluted flan tins (tart pans) or the plain and fluted flan rings which stand on a baking sheet. These come in almost any size you could wish for.

*Swiss (jelly) roll tins, etc.:* a selection of shallow square and oblong tins are useful for making slab cakes, bar cakes, biscuits (cookies), etc., as well as for Swiss (jelly) rolls.

*Loaf tins:* it is essential to have at least a 450 g/1 lb ($7\frac{1}{2} \times 3\frac{3}{4} \times 2$ inch) and a 900 g/2 lb ($9 \times 5 \times 3$ inch) loaf tin for use both in yeast cooking and cake making. For people who make their own bread a larger selection is necessary. There are also extra long bread tins and fluted loaf tins available to make unusual shapes.

*Small tins and moulds:* small patty (shallow muffin) tins, both plain and fluted, are needed for small tarts and cakes. There is an enormous variety of small tins available to suit all types of cake making – deep, shallow, fluted, sloping-sided, etc. – and they are the sort of equipment that can be gradually collected, when required.

### The right tin for the job
Always use the size of cake tin stated in the recipe: if the tin used is too large, the cake may be pale and flat looking instead of a good shape with a nicely rounded top. If the tin is too small or too shallow the mixture will rise over the edges resulting in a most uneven and unhappy looking cake. When making layered cakes always use straight-sided tins; it makes it so much easier to give a good shape to the finished cake.

# PREPARATION OF TINS

If using special non-stick tins, follow the manufacturer's instructions, although on the whole they do not need lining and only rarely greasing. With all other tins it is necessary to either grease and flour or line with greaseproof (waxed) paper and grease again before adding the raw ingredients to prevent cakes sticking and over browning.

### Greasing

It is best to use melted lard or oil for greasing cake tins to guard against sticking although some people use butter, margarine or dripping. A pastry brush dipped into the warm or cold fat or oil is the easiest way of covering the whole surface of the tin evenly. Otherwise use soft kitchen paper. It is not necessary to grease a tin if lining it with pastry dough.

### Dredging

After greasing the tin, dredge it liberally with flour, shaking out the excess. (This is an alternative to lining the tin with paper for cakes that are not baked for a long time.) To give a crisper crust to cakes such as fatless sponges, dredge with an equal mixture of flour and caster sugar.

### Bottom lining

Cut out a single piece of greaseproof (waxed) paper or non-stick parchment to fit the bottom of the tin to be used. Grease the inside of the tin completely first, then position the paper on the bottom and grease the paper. (If you use non-stick parchment it is not necessary to grease the paper and it can be used several times if wiped clean after use.) Bottom lining prevents the cake bottom falling out or getting stuck and is used for sponge and sandwich (layer cake) mixtures and lightly fruited cakes, but not for rich cakes.

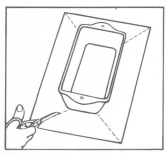
Make a cut to the corner

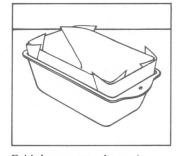
Fold the paper to fit neatly

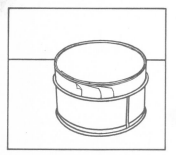
Make a shallow tin deeper

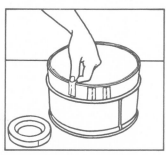
Secure the edges with tape

### To line a deep tin

For rich fruit mixtures which require long cooking, it is necessary to use a double thickness of greaseproof (waxed) paper or non-stick parchment to prevent over browning and drying out. Tie a treble thickness band of brown paper or newspaper around the outside of the tin as an added protection against over-cooking the outside of the cake.

Cut one or two double strips of greaseproof (waxed) paper long enough to go round the whole tin with a little extra for overlapping and wide enough to come 2.5 cm/1 inch above the rim of the tin. Fold up the bottom edge of the strip about 2 cm/$\frac{3}{4}$ inch and crease it. Open out and cut into this strip at 1.5 cm/$\frac{1}{2}$ inch intervals – this enables the paper to mould round the inside of any shaped tin.

Place the tin on a double thickness of greaseproof (waxed) paper and draw around the base of it, then cut out just a little inside the line. Grease the inside of the tin, position one bottom paper and grease just around the edge. Put the long strips in, pressing to the sides with the cut edges spread out over the bottom (fold into corners with square or rectangular tins) and grease all over. Finally position the second bottom paper (which keeps the snipped edges of the band in place) and grease again.

For lining with a single thickness of paper put the sides in first and then the bottom paper and grease all over.

### To line a shallow rectangular tin

For Swiss (jelly) rolls and similar cakes, it is always wise to line and grease for easy removal. Cut a piece of greaseproof (waxed) paper or non-stick parchment at least 5 cm/2 inches larger than the tin (larger still if the sides of the tin are more than 2.5 cm/1 inch deep). Place the tin on the paper and from each corner of the paper make a cut from the angle to the corner of the tin. Grease the inside of the tin and put the paper in so that it fits neatly, overlapping the paper at the corners to give sharp angles. Brush the paper with fat or oil. (Non-stick parchment does not need greasing.)

### To line a loaf tin

Use the same method as for lining shallow rectangular cake tins (see above) but cut the paper about 15 cm/6 inches larger than the tin. Grease the tin, position the paper, folding it neatly so that it fits the corners, then grease again. In some cases it is only necessary to line the bottom of a loaf tin, in which case cut an oblong the same size as the bottom, put in position and grease the paper and the tin.

### To make a shallow tin deeper

Use the same method as for lining a deep cake tin but use two or three thicknesses of paper and cut it so that it stands 2.5 cm/1 inch or so above the top of the tin. Secure the overlapping edges with sticky tape (scotch tape), staples or paper clips.

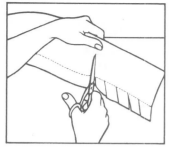

*Cut into the strip*

*Draw round the base of the tin*

*Position the long strip*

*Put in the bottom paper*

# BAKING THE CAKE

It is essential that all cakes are put into a preheated oven that has reached the temperature stated in the recipe; if this rule is not followed there are sure to be disasters. So turn on the oven at least 15 minutes before required.

Unfortunately, ovens vary in temperature; and you are probably able to gauge whether your own is hotter or cooler than it states. From this you can adjust the temperatures given in the recipes if you feel it necessary. However if your oven gives an uneven rise to cakes, or the cooking times vary a great deal, have it checked for it may need a little adjustment. Or invest in an oven thermometer and test the heat from time to time.

### The following points should be noted:

1. Remember that oven shelves should be arranged before heating the oven.
2. Keep the oven clean. Gas ovens, in particular, need careful attention – if the burners become clogged up the heat distribution will be uneven.
3. Use tins that fit in the oven – baking tins, Swiss (jelly) roll tins, etc., must have at least 2.5 cm/1 inch to spare all round to ensure even circulation of the heat.
4. Position cakes correctly when first put in the oven – they will probably sink if moved halfway through cooking. Small plain cakes, scones and Swiss (jelly) rolls should be placed towards the top; pastry just above the centre; sponge and sandwich (layer) cakes, tea breads, small rich cakes, farmhouse-type cakes and biscuits (cookies) in the centre or just above; and rich fruit cakes, large cakes and shortbreads below the centre.
5. If opening the oven door during cooking first make sure there are no draughts in the kitchen. Open the door carefully and gently, and shut it carefully, for a bang will make most cakes fall. (Avoid looking into the oven until the cake is at least three-quarters cooked.)
6. Put loaf tins or awkward-shaped tins on a baking sheet before placing in the oven, especially if they are rather full. This will prevent overflowing in the oven or the loaf tins slipping sideways between the rungs of the shelves.

### Testing if a cake is cooked

With small cakes it is fairly easy to test if they are cooked for they should be well risen, golden brown and firm to the touch, and just beginning to shrink away from the sides of the tins when taken from the oven. Cool for a few seconds then turn onto a wire rack and leave to cool completely.

With larger cakes it is more difficult for often they will look cooked but when turned out either have a soggy patch at the bottom or sink in the middle, both indicating a little longer in the oven was required. The cooking time stated in the recipe should be correct, but if your oven is not quite accurate or you use a different sized tin you will have to decide when it is ready. With a sponge or sandwich (layer) type cake, press the top very lightly with the fingers – it should be spongy and only give a very little, and if ready it should rise again immediately, leaving no impression in the top.

With a fruit cake insert a warmed skewer into the centre of the cake; if it comes out clean all is well. If any mixture is sticking to the skewer, continue baking for a further 15 minutes and test again. The cake should also be firm to the touch, but it does not 'give' like a sponge cake. Also try 'listening' to the cake closely; if there is any slight sizzling it requires further cooking. Large rich fruit cakes must be cooled for a while in the tin before turning out or they can be cooled completely in the tin.

### Oven temperature guide

| Oven description | Electricity | | Gas Mark |
|---|---|---|---|
| | °C | °F | |
| Very cool | 110 | 225 | $\frac{1}{4}$ |
| | 120 | 250 | $\frac{1}{2}$ |
| Cool | 140 | 275 | 1 |
| | 150 | 300 | 2 |
| Moderate | 160 | 325 | 3 |
| | 180 | 350 | 4 |
| Moderately hot | 190 | 375 | 5 |
| | 200 | 400 | 6 |
| Hot | 220 | 425 | 7 |
| Very hot | 230 | 450 | 8 |
| | 240 | 475 | 9 |

### High altitude baking (US)

If you live at 3,000 feet above sea level, or above, use the following chart to adjust the proportions of ingredients when baking cakes. This will prevent the cakes falling or giving unpredictable results.

| INGREDIENT | 3,000 ft | 5,000 ft | 7,000 ft |
|---|---|---|---|
| **Liquid:** add for each cup | 1 to 2 tablespoons | 2 to 3 tablespoons | 3 to 4 tablespoons |
| **Baking powder:** decrease for each teaspoon | $\frac{1}{8}$ teaspoon | $\frac{1}{8}$ to $\frac{1}{4}$ teaspoon | $\frac{1}{4}$ teaspoon |
| **Sugar:** decrease for each cup | 0 to 1 tablespoon | 1 to 2 tablespoons | 1 to 3 tablespoons |

# STORAGE HINTS

Always leave any baked cake on a wire rack until completely cold before storing it. Then use a container that is completely airtight whether it be a tin, polythene (plastic) container or anything else. Most cakes are best eaten fresh and some (especially certain whisked sponges, scones and griddle cooked cakes) are best eaten the day made. However, gingerbreads and some tea breads are better stored for a few days before cutting, while rich fruit cakes should be left for several weeks to mature before adding marzipan and icing. When storing a cake for any length of time it should be wrapped first in greaseproof (waxed) paper and then put into a tin with a tight fitting lid or wrapped tightly in foil. However the cake is wrapped, it must be stored in a cool place; too much warmth will make fruit cakes begin to go rancid after a time.

Iced cakes are best stored in a tin or airtight container which does not actually touch the cake's surface. If the cake is an awkward shape make a 'hat' from foil and place it carefully over the cake.

Wedding and celebration cakes which have been royal iced and decorated need to be covered lightly to prevent dust or any 'bits' settling on the cake, for it is very difficult to remove a dirty mark from a white cake. Lay sheets of tissue paper gently over the cake, securing where necessary to keep out dust. Do not cover completely in foil or cling film or the cake will sweat. To prevent the icing hardening too much and to avoid the risk of damage or dust settling, it is wise to ice and decorate the cake as near as possible to the celebration.

All biscuits (cookies) must be stored in something airtight; but never store cakes and biscuits (cookies) in the same container, for the crisp biscuits (cookies) take up moisture from the cake and become soggy and spoiled.

## Freezing cakes and biscuits (cookies)

Most types of cakes, gâteaux and biscuits (cookies) freeze well and are still in excellent condition after thawing. Creamed mixtures, whisked sponges, fruit cakes, small buns, etc., are all suitable. If undecorated the recommended storage time is 6 months. However, if the cake is very highly spiced it is better not to freeze it because in some cases the spice will intensify and in others turn slightly musty flavoured. With icings and fillings it is safe to freeze butter creams, fudge fillings and frostings (but not the boiled variety) for up to 6 to 8 weeks, but avoid filling cakes with jam which will make them soggy or custard fillings which tend to separate. In these cases it is wiser to freeze the layers of cakes separately and assemble and decorate when thawed. If the cake is decorated, 'open freeze' (flash freeze) – put in the freezer without wrapping and when solid over-wrap with freezer film or foil or put into an airtight container. Carefully mark 'fragile' and don't put anything on top of it.

Undecorated cakes can be wrapped in freezer foil or heavy gauge polythene (plastic), with as much air excluded as possible, and sealed with freezer tape.

To thaw cakes, remove from the wrapping and place on a plate at room temperature. The time it takes will vary according to the size, shape and density of the cake but the following times are a rough guide:

30 to 60 minutes for small buns and cakes
1 to 2 hours for sponge or other layers of cakes
3 to 4 hours for larger cakes

## Special hints

All cakes, biscuits (cookies), tea breads, gâteaux, etc., must be cold before wrapping and freezing. Tea breads freeze very well for 3 to 4 months, but if fairly spicy freeze for only 2 to 3 weeks. Scones should be slightly undercooked or they may be a bit drier than usual when thawed. They can also be thawed out in a moderate oven (160°C/325°F, Gas Mark 3) for 15 to 20 minutes and served straight from the oven.

Uncooked cake mixture does not freeze. However pastry freezes well, particularly choux paste which can be piped into the required shape.

Iced cakes must be completely unwrapped before thawing. If a cake has been frozen with a fresh cream filling and decoration it is best thawed in the refrigerator, for 8 hours or overnight.

Biscuits (cookies) can be frozen, preferably without fillings, but as they will generally keep for 2 weeks in an airtight container without freezing it is often a waste of freezer space to freeze too many. However if you want to make a large batch of biscuits (cookies) from time to time, bake some for immediate use and freeze quantities of the uncooked dough to thaw and make when required.

Both cooked and uncooked biscuits (cookies) should freeze for up to 6 months. If they are a little soft after thawing, pop them into a hot oven for a few minutes to crisp up. Finish off the filling and decorating when cold.

Rich fruit cakes keep perfectly well for months if wrapped first in greaseproof (waxed) paper and then put into an airtight container or wrapped in foil.

# WHAT WENT WRONG

All the recipes in this book have been carefully tested to give perfect results. If the directions for each recipe are followed exactly there should be no reason for failure.

However, sometimes a cake is a flop and it is not always obvious what went wrong. It may be that the metric and imperial or American measures have been mixed up. Each set of measures has been carefully planned to give a perfectly balanced recipe. If more than one set of measures are used the proportions will be upset – usually with disastrous results. Another reason for failure is often that the wrong sized tin has been used or the cake has been put into the oven before it has reached the required temperature. Always remember to switch on well in advance, to be sure that the oven has reached the temperature stated in the recipe.

If none of these reasons applies to your problem, then here are some further hints which might put you right again.

## Sandwich and sponge cakes
Domed top – insufficient beating or oven too hot.
Hollow top – too much raising (leavening) agent or oven too cool.
Over-cooked outside with a soft doughy centre – oven too hot and put too high in oven.
Close doughy texture or damp patch at the base – too much sugar or liquid; insufficient creaming or too little flour or raising (leavening) agent.

## Swiss (jelly) rolls
Pale and flabby – undercooked, oven too cool and placed too low in the oven.
Too thin or uneven – not enough air beaten into the mixture.

## Sponges
Shallow and uneven – insufficient beating and oven too cool; may need more raising (leavening) agent.
Sticking to tin and sticky and doughy texture – needs a few more minutes cooking.
Very wrinkled surface – slightly undercooked in a tin too small.

## Fruit cakes
Sinking centre – insufficient creaming; too much raising (leavening) agent in rich cakes; incorrect oven temperature.
Sinking fruit – insufficient creaming; too much fruit or fruit too heavy; too much liquid or raising (leavening) agent.

Large holes – too much raising (leavening) agent.
Close texture and bad rise – insufficient raising (leavening) agent or creaming; oven too cool.
Too dry – not enough liquid, fat or sugar or over-cooked; too much raising (leavening) agent.
Hard outside crust and soggy centre – oven too hot and cake cooked too quickly; too much liquid. Too much melted mixture including syrup in gingerbreads, etc.
Cracked top – usually tin too small and oven too hot. Too little liquid and too much raising (leavening) agent.

## Yeasted fare
Small volume – either insufficient or far too much rising (causing a collapse).
Pale and rather soggy – oven too cool, too low in the oven and not cooked long enough.
Thin and spreading – too much liquid or far too much rising.
Coarse texture – yeast insufficiently dissolved or far too much rising causing a very open texture due to part collapse.

## Scones
Uneven or poor rise – too little raising (leavening) agent or oven too cool.
Tough and chewy – over-kneading.
Rough and badly shaped – not enough kneading and poor shaping.
Hard with a close texture – not enough liquid.
Pale with a doughy centre – undercooked, oven too cool or too low in the oven.

## Rubbed-in mixtures
Close texture – too much liquid or baking powder.
Uneven and full of holes – air trapped in cake caused by putting small spoonfuls of mixture into the tin.
Dry cakes – mixture too stiff or oven too hot. Inadequate lining of large cake tin (particularly important for fruit cakes).

## Shortcrust pastry
Hard and brittle – too much water or liquid added to the rubbed-in ingredients.
Too short or crumbly – fat proportion too high (half fat to flour should be used except for rich pastries).
Dry and tasteless – lack of salt, insufficient liquid or too much extra flour kneaded in during rolling out.

# INDEX

## A

All-purpose flour 148
Almond:
  To use almonds as cake
    decorations 118
  Almond butter cream 104
  Almond butter wafers 86
  Almond cookies 84
  Almond paste *see* Marzipan
  Almond sponge fancies 24
  Almond squares 29
  Crunchy topped almond cake
    37
French almond cake 36
American (boiled) frosting 106
American wedding cake 102
Animals made with marzipan
  123
Anniversary cake 100
Apple:
  Apple cake 43
  Apple crunch 35
  Apple and raisin tea bread
    61
Apples (marzipan) 123
Apricot:
  Apricot butter cream 104
  Apricot glaze 107
  Apricot swiss (jelly) roll 13
  Apricot tea bread 58

## B

Bakewell tarts 22
Baking the cake 153
Baking powder 148
Baking soda 148
Banana tea loaf 60
Bananas (marzipan) 123
Bara brith 62
Barm brack 63
Bath buns 68
Battenburg cake 14
Beating 150
Bicarbonate of soda 148
Birds (run-out) 133

Biscuits and cookies:
  To freeze biscuits 154
  Almond butter wafers 86
  Almond cookies 84
  Bourbon biscuits 77
  Brandy snaps 84
  Chocolate biscuits 76
  Chocolate caramels 87
  Chocolate quickies 87
  Coconut rings 78
  Easter biscuits 79
  Flapjacks 81
  Florentines 85
  Grantham gingerbreads 83
  Hazel nutties 84
  Hazelnut cinnamon shorties 78
  Jumbles 82
  Lemon biscuits 76
  Macaroons 86
  Melting moments 82
  Oat crisps 81
  1-2-3 biscuits 78
  Orange biscuits 76
  Orange creams 76
  Peanut butter cookies 80
  Pinwheels 82
  Shortbread 78
  Sugar biscuits 76
  Sweetmeal biscuits 83
  Viennese biscuits 79
  Walnut bars 86
Black Forest gâteau 89
Black treacle (molasses) 149
Boiled fruit cake 46
Borders (piped
  decorations) 128
Bourbon biscuits 77
Brandy snaps 84
Brown soda loaf 59
Brownies 31
Bun loaf 62
Buns. *See also* Little cakes
  Bath buns 68
  Chelsea buns 65
  Chocolate cherry buns 26
  Chocolate dot buns 26
  Coconut buns 22
  Devonshire splits 68
  Doughnuts 64
  Ginger rockies 21
  Honey buns 25
  Hot cross buns 67
  Mixed fruit buns 26
  Rocky buns 21
  Swiss buns 69

Butter cream (butter icing) 104
Butter cream, rich 107
Butterflies (run-out) 133
Butterfly and rose cake 139
Butterscotch caramel gâteau 88
Butterscotch frosting 107
Butterscotch sponge cake 10

## C

Cake boards 137
Cake flour 148
Cake marker 124
Cake tins 151; to prepare 152
Caramelize, to 150
Caraway fruit ring 50
Carnations (piped icing) 131
Caster sugar 149
Cats (marzipan) 122, 123
Celebration cakes:
  To decorate 137–43
  American wedding cake 102
  Anniversary cake 100
  Christening cakes 142
  Christmas cake 96
  Eighteenth birthday cake
    for a girl 143
  General celebration cake 142
  Glacé fruit cake 99
  Golden wedding cake 101
  Light fruit cake 99
  Simnel cake 98
  Twenty-first birthday cake for
    a boy (cricket theme) 143
  Wedding cake 102–3
  Yule log 98
Cheese and onion scones 52
Cheese scones 52, 54
Cheesecakes:
  Crumb cheesecake 95
  Fresh fruit cheesecake 94
  No-cook orange cheesecake 94
  Orange-flavoured crumb
    cheesecake 95
Chelsea buns 65
Cherry:
  Black Forest gâteau 89
  Cherry and walnut loaf 49
  Chocolate cherry buns 26
  Farmhouse cherry cake 41
  Rich cherry cake 48

Chestnut:
  Chestnut gâteau 92
  Chestnuts in syrup 119
Chocolate:
  Chocolate American frosting
    106
  Chocolate biscuits 76
  Chocolate butter cream 104
  Chocolate butterflies 23
  Chocolate caramels 87
  Chocolate cherry buns 26
  Chocolate coated rolls 19
  Chocolate cream gâteau 90
  Chocolate decorations for
    cakes and gâteaux 118
  Chocolate dot buns 26
  Chocolate éclairs 30
  Chocolate glacé icing 105
  Chocolate icing (frosting) 106
  Chocolate meringue gâteau 91
  Chocolate meringues 30
  Chocolate orange cake 10
  Chocolate quickies 87
  Chocolate raisin sponge cake
    12
  Chocolate sponge cakes 26
  Chocolate truffle cakes 23
  Chocolate Victoria sandwich
    (layer) cake 6
  Dark chocolate cake 42
  Devil's food cake 45
  No-cook chocolate cake 48
Choux paste 111
Christening cakes 142
Christmas bells cake 140
Christmas cake 96; decorations
  for 140–1
Christmas roses (piped icing) 130
Christmas trees (marzipan) 122
Cider loaf cake 61
Clock cakes 145
Coburg cakes 25
Coconut:
  To use as a cake decoration
    118
  Coconut buns 22
  Coconut feather sponge cake 12
  Coconut pyramids 32
  Coconut rings 78
  Coconut streusel cake 50
  Farmhouse coconut cake 41
Coffee:
  Coffee American frosting 106
  Coffee butter cream 104
  Coffee cup cakes 26

Coffee éclairs 30
Coffee fudge cake 11
Coffee glacé icing 105
Coffee loaf cake 40
Coffee meringue nests 27
Coffee meringues 30
Coffee sponge cake 12
Coffee Victoria sandwich
   (layer) cake 6
Coffee walnut sponge cake 8
Cold fondant 107
Confectioners' custard 105
Cookies see Biscuits and cookies
Cranberry tea bread 58
Cream, to 150
Cream horns 34
Cream puffs 35
Cream slices 28
Crème pâtissière 105
Cricket theme twenty-first
   birthday cake 143
Croissants 75
Crumb cheesecake 95
Crunchy topped almond cake 37
Crystallized flowers 119
Crystallized ginger cake 51
Cupcakes 26

## D

Daisies (piped icing) 131
Danish pastries 72–3
Dark chocolate cake 42
Date:
   Date tea bread 59
   Date and walnut cake 47
   Farmhouse date cake 41
   Lemon and date scone bar 63
Decorating cakes:
   Basic equipment 112
   Christening cakes 142
   Christmas cakes 140–1
   Decorating the sides of a cake
      114
   Decorations for cakes and
      gâteaux 118–19
   Designs for royal iced cakes
      134–5
   Eighteenth birthday cake 143
   Filling the cake 114
   General celebration cake 142
   Marzipan modelled decorations
      122–3
   Novelty cakes 145–7
   Piped decorations 127–31
   Run-outs 132–3
   Simple toppings 115
   Sugar decorations for sponge
      and sandwich cakes 114
   Twenty-first birthday cake 143
   Wedding cakes 137–9
   With butter icing 115
   With feather icing 115

With fondant icing 116
With glacé icing 114
With marzipan (almond paste)
   120–1
With royal icing 124–6, 134–5
Deep cake tins 151
Demerara sugar 149
Designs for royal iced
   cakes 134–5
Devil's food cake 45
Devonshire splits 68
Dough cake 74
Dredge, to 150
Doughnuts 64
Drop scones (Scotch pancakes)
   55
Dropping consistency 150
Dundee cake 46
Dust, to 150

## E

Easter biscuits 79
Easy-clean tins 151
Eccles cakes 32
Éclairs 30
Eggs 149
Eighteenth birthday cake 142
Equipment for cake
   decorating 112
Equipment for cake making
   151–2
Everyday fruit loaf 41

## F

Fairy cakes 26
Family cakes:
   Apple cake 43
   Boiled fruit cake 46
   Caraway fruit ring 50
   Cherry and walnut loaf 49
   Coconut streusel cake 50
   Coffee loaf cake 40
   Crunchy topped almond cake
      37
   Crystallized ginger cake 51
   Dark chocolate cake 42
   Date and walnut cake 47
   Devil's food cake 45
   Dundee cake 46
   Everyday fruit loaf 41
   Farmhouse cherry cake 41
   Farmhouse coconut cake 41
   Farmhouse date cake 41
   French almond cake 36
   Fruited gingerbread 38
   Golden gingerbread 39
   Granny's tea cake 40

Honey orange cake 51
Madeira cake 45
No-cook chocolate cake 48
Old-fashioned ginger cake 39
Old-fashioned plum cake 42
One-stage mixed fruit cake 49
Orange marmalade cake 51
Parkin 38
Rich cherry cake 48
Rose cake 43
White chiffon cake 45
Wholemeal fruit cake 47
Farmhouse cherry cake 41
Farmhouse coconut cake 41
Farmhouse date cake 41
Fat 149
Father Christmas (marzipan) 122
Father Christmas cake 140, 147
Feather icing 115
Filling the cake 114
Fillings see Icings and fillings
Flaky pastry 110
Flan (tart) pastry, rich 111
Flan (tart) rings 151
Flapjacks 81
Florentines 85
Flour 148
Floury sultana (raisin) scones 52
Flowers made with marzipan 122
Flowers piped in icing 130–1
Fold-in, to 150
Fondant icing 106; to use 116
Freezing cakes and biscuits 154
French almond cake 36
Frosted fruit cake decorations
   119
Frostings 106, 107
Fruit. See also Apple etc.
   Boiled fruit cake 46
   Caraway fruit ring 50
   Everyday fruit loaf 41
   Fresh fruit cheesecake 94
   Frosted fruit cake decorations
      119
   Fruit scones 52
   Glacé fruit cake 99
   Iced fruit plait (braid) 70
   Light fruit cake 99
   Marzipan fruits 123
   Mixed fruit buns 26
   Old-fashioned plum cake 42
   One-stage mixed fruit cake 49
   Wholemeal fruit cake 47
Fruited gingerbread 38
Fruited girdle scones 55
Fruited tea ring 71
Fudge cottage 146

## G

Gâteaux:
   Black Forest gâteau 89
   Butterscotch caramel gâteau 88

Chestnut gâteau 92
Chocolate cream gâteau 90
Chocolate meringue gâteau 91
Decorations for gâteaux
   118–19
Gâteau St Honoré 95
Hazelnut gâteau 90
High peak gâteau 93
Peach shortbread gâteau 93
Pineapple cream gâteau 88
Strawberry shortcake 91
Genoese sponge cake 9
Ginger:
   Crystallized ginger cake 51
   Fruited gingerbread 38
   Ginger cream sandwich cake 8
   Ginger rockies 21
   Golden gingerbread 39
   Grantham gingerbreads 83
   Old-fashioned ginger cake 39
Girdle scones, fruited 55
Glacé fruit cake 99
Glacé icing 105; to use 114
Glaze, to 150
Glossary 150
Gluten 148
Golden gingerbread 39
Golden syrup 149
Golden wedding cake 101
Graham flour 148
Granny's tea cake 40
Grantham gingerbreads 83
Granulated sugar 149

## H

Halloween decorations
   (marzipan) 122
Hazelnut:
   To use hazelnuts as cake
      decorations 118
   Hazel nutties 84
   Hazelnut cinnamon shorties 78
   Hazelnut gâteau 90
   Hazelnut meringues 27
Herb scones 52
High peak gâteau 93
Holly and Christmas rose cake
   140
Holly leaves (marzipan) 122
Honey 149
Honey buns 25
Honey orange cake 51
Honey walnut scones 55
Horseshoe cake 147
Hot cross buns 67

## I

Iced fruit plait (braid) 70
Icing bags 124; to make
   paper 126

Icing comb or scraper 124
Icing nail 124
Icing ruler 124
Icing (confectioners') sugar 149
Icing sugar, approximate
  quantities for round and
  square cakes 136
Icing turntable 124
Icings and fillings. *See also*
  Decorating cakes
  Almond butter cream 104
  American (boiled) frosting 106
  Apricot butter cream 104
  Butter cream (butter icing)
  104
  Butterscotch frosting 107
  Chocolate American frosting
  106
  Chocolate butter cream 104
  Chocolate glacé icing 105
  Chocolate icing (frosting) 106
  Coffee American frosting 106
  Coffee butter cream 104
  Coffee glacé icing 105
  Confectioners' custard (crème
    pâtissière or pastry cream)
    105
  Fondant icing 106
  Glacé icing 105
  Lemon butter cream 104
  Lemon or orange glacé icing
    105
  Liqueur butter cream 104
  Marzipan (almond paste) 104
  Minted butter cream 104
  Mocha butter cream 104
  Mocha glacé icing 105
  Orange butter cream 104
  Rich butter cream 107
  Royal icing 107
  Seven minute frosting 107
  Sugar paste (cold fondant)
    107
  Walnut butter cream 104
Ingredients for cake making
  148–9
Ivy leaves (marzipan) 122

**J**

Jelly roll *see* Swiss roll
Jolly Roger 147
Jumbles 82

**K**

Kitchen foil baking cases 151
Knead, to 150

**L**

Lace and daisy wedding cake
  138
Lady fingers 20
Lard 149
Lardy cake 71
Lattice rose wedding cake 138
Layer cake pans 151
Layer cakes *see* Sponge and
  sandwich cakes
Leaves (marzipan) 122
Leaves (piped icing) 131
Lemon:
  Lemon biscuits 76
  Lemon butter cream 104
  Lemon and date scone bar
    63
  Lemon glacé icing 105
  Lemon praline sandwich cake
    16
  Lemon scones 52
  Lemon sponge cake 12, 13
  Lemon Victoria sandwich
    (layer) cake 6
Lemons (marzipan) 123
Light corn syrup 149
Light fruit cake 99
Lilies (piped icing) 131
Lining cake tins 152
Liqueur butter cream 104
Little bear maypole cake 145
Little cakes. *See also* Buns
  Almond sponge fancies 24
  Almond squares 29
  Apple crunch 35
  Bakewell tarts 22
  Brownies 31
  Chocolate butterflies 23
  Chocolate éclairs 30
  Chocolate meringues 30
  Chocolate sponge cakes 26
  Chocolate truffle cakes 23
  Coburg cakes 25
  Coconut pyramids 32
  Coffee cup cakes 26
  Coffee éclairs 30
  Coffee meringue nests 27
  Coffee meringues 30
  Cream horns 34
  Cream puffs 35
  Cream slices 28
  Cup cakes 26
  Eccles cakes 32
  Fairy cakes 26
  Hazelnut meringues 27
  Madeleines 22
  Maids of honour 34
  Matrimonial cakes 32
  Meringues 30
  Mincemeat slices 34
  Orange meringue bars 29
  Palmiers 31
  Profiteroles 30
  Sacristans 31
  Shell cakes 23
  Sponge (lady) fingers 20
Loaf tins 151
Loose-bottomed cake tins
  151

**M**

Macaroons 86
Madeira cake 45
Madeleines 22
Maids of honour 34
Malted tea loaf 57
Marble cake 19
Margarine 149
Mark's castle 145
Marmalade tea bread 58
Marrons glacés 119
Marzipan:
  To cover a cake 120–1
  To make marzipan 104
  Approximate quantities for
    round and square cakes 136
  Marzipan animals and fruit 123
  Seasonal decorations in
    marzipan 122
Matrimonial cakes 32
Melting moments 82
Meringues:
  To make meringues 30
  Chocolate meringue gâteau 91
  Chocolate meringues 30
  Coffee meringue nests 27
  Coffee meringues 30
  Coloured meringues 30
  Hazelnut meringues 27
  Orange meringue bars 29
Mincemeat slices 34
Minted butter cream 104
Mocha butter cream 104
Mocha glacé icing 105
Mocha sandwich cake 9
Molasses 149
Molasses scones 53

**N**

Narcissi (piped icing) 130
Narcissus cake 139
No-cook chocolate cake 48
No-cook orange cheesecake 94
Noel cake 140
Non-stick tins 151
Novelty cakes 145–7
Numeral and clock cakes 145
Nuts as cake decoration 118.
  *See also* Almond etc.

**O**

Oat crisps 81
Oat and treacle drop scones 56
Old-fashioned ginger cake 39
Old-fashioned plum cake 42
One-stage mixed fruit cake 49
One-stage short pastry 110
One-stage sponge cake 7
1-2-3 biscuits 78
Orange:
  Chocolate orange cake 10
  Honey orange cake 51
  No-cook orange cheesecake 94
  Orange biscuits 76
  Orange butter cream 104
  Orange caraway ring 18
  Orange creams 76
  Orange-flavoured crumb
    cheesecake 95
  Orange glacé icing 105
  Orange marmalade cake 51
  Orange meringue bars 29
  Orange sandwich cake 16
  Orange sponge cake 12
  Orange tea loaf 57
  Orange Victoria sandwich
    (layer) cake 6
Orange blossom (piped
  icing) 130
Oranges (marzipan) 123

**P**

Palmiers 31
Pansies (piped icing) 130
Paper icing bags, to make 126
Parkin 38
Pastries, pastry-based cakes:
  Almond squares 29
  Apple crunch 35
  Cream horns 34
  Cream puffs 35
  Cream slices 28
  Danish pastries 72–3
  Eccles cakes 32
  Maids of honour 34
  Mincemeat slices 34
  Palmiers 31
  Sacristans 31
  Spicy palmiers 31
Pastry:
  Choux paste 111
  Flaky pastry 110
  One-stage short pastry 110
  Puff pastry 110
  Rich flan (tart) pastry 111
  Shortcrust (pie) pastry 109
Pastry cream 105
Patty tins 151

Peach shortbread gâteau 93
Peanut butter cookies 80
Pears (marzipan) 123
Pie pastry 109
Pillars 137
Pineapple cream gâteau 88
Pinwheels 82
Piped decorations 127–31
Pistachio nuts as decorations 118
Plain (all-purpose) flour 148
Plain scones 52
Poinsettias (marzipan) 122
Primroses (marzipan) 122
Primroses (piped icing) 130
Profiteroles 30
Puff pastry 110

## R

Rabbits (marzipan) 123
Raised trellis (piped) 128
Raising (leavening) agents 148
Raspberry:
  Walnut raspberry roll 15
Red and white trellis cake 140
Ring moulds 151
Rocky buns 21
Rolls:
  White bread rolls 66
Rose cake 43
Rose and scroll wedding cake 138
Roses (marzipan) 122
Roses (piped icing) 130
Rosettes (piped decorations) 127
Rough icing 126
Royal icing 107; to use 124–6, 127, 134–5
Ruby wedding cake 100
Rum babas 74
Run-outs 132–3

## S

Sacristans 31
Salty scones 52
Sandwich cakes see Sponge and sandwich cakes
Sandwich tins 151
Savoury tea loaf 62
Scones:
  Cheese and onion scones 52
  Cheese scones 52, 54
  Drop scones (Scotch pancakes) 55
  Floury sultana (raisin) scones 52
  Fruit scones 52
  Fruited girdle scones 55
  Herb scones 52
  Honey walnut scones 55
  Lemon scones 52
  Oat and treacle drop scones 56
  Plain scones 52
  Rich scones 52
  Salty scones 52
  Scone round 54
  Spiced treacle (molasses) scones 53
  Spicy scones 52
  Sultana (raisin) scones 54
  Walnut scones 54
  Wholewheat scones 54
Scotch pancakes 55
Scrolls (piped decorations) 127
Self-raising flour 148
Seven minute frosting 107
Shallow muffin tins 151
Shell cakes 23
Shells (piped decorations) 128
Sherried spice cake 18
Shortbread 78
Shortcrust (pie) pastry 109
Shortening 149
Simnel cake 98
Soda bread 59
Soft brown sugar 149
Sour milk 148
Spiced treacle (molasses) scones 53
Spicy palmiers 31
Spicy scones 52
Sponge (lady) fingers 20
Sponge and sandwich (layer) cakes. See also Little cakes
  Apricot Swiss (jelly) roll 13
  Battenburg cake 14
  Butterscotch sponge cake 10
  Chocolate coated rolls 19
  Chocolate orange cake 10
  Chocolate raisin sponge cake 12
  Chocolate Victoria sandwich (layer) cake 6
  Coconut feather sponge cake 12
  Coffee fudge cake 11
  Coffee sponge cake 12
  Coffee Victoria sandwich (layer) cake 6
  Coffee walnut sponge cake 8
  Genoese sponge cake 9
  Ginger cream sandwich (layer) cake 8
  Lemon praline sandwich (layer) cake 16
  Lemon sponge cake 12, 13
  Lemon Victoria sandwich (layer) cake 6
  Marble cake 19
  Mocha sandwich (layer) cake 9
  One-stage sponge cake 7
  Orange caraway ring 18
  Orange sandwich (layer) cake 16
  Orange sponge cake 12
  Orange Victoria sandwich (layer) cake 6
  Sherried spice cake 18
  Sugar decorations for sponge and sandwich (layer) cakes 114
  Victoria sandwich (layer) cake 6
  Walnut raspberry roll 15
Springform pans 151
Star cake 140
Stars (marzipan) 122
Stars (piped decoration) 127
Stoneground flour 148
Storage hints 154
Strawberry shortcake 91
Strawberries (marzipan) 123
Strong (bread) flour 148
Sugar 149
Sugar biscuits 76
Sugar decorations for sponge and sandwich (layer) cakes 114
Sugar paste (cold fondant) 107; to use 127
Sugar syrup 115
Sultana (raisin) scones 54
Swans (run-out) 133
Sweetmeal biscuits 83
Swiss buns 69
Swiss (jelly) roll tins 151
Swiss (jelly) rolls:
  Apricot Swiss roll 13
  Chocolate coated rolls 19
  Walnut raspberry roll 15

## T

Tea breads:
  Apple and raisin tea bread 61
  Apricot tea bread 58
  Banana tea loaf 60
  Bara brith 62
  Barm brack 63
  Brown soda loaf 59
  Bun loaf 62
  Cider loaf cake 61
  Cranberry tea bread 58
  Date tea bread 59
  Fruited tea ring 71
  Iced fruit plait (braid) 70
  Lemon and date scone bar 63
  Malted tea loaf 57
  Marmalade tea bread 58
  Orange tea loaf 57
  Savoury tea loaf 62
  Soda bread 59
Templates 134, 135
Trellis (piped decoration) 127
Tube tins or ring moulds 151
Twenty-first birthday cake 143

## V

Vegetable fats (shortening) 149
Victoria sandwich (layer) cake 6
Viennese biscuits 79
Violets (piped icing) 131

## W

Walnut:
  Cherry and walnut loaf 49
  Coffee walnut sponge cake 8
  Date and walnut cake 47
  Honey walnut scones 55
  Walnut bars 86
  Walnut butter cream 104
  Walnut raspberry roll 15
  Walnut scones 54
Wedding cakes 102–3; to decorate 137–9
Whip, to 150
White bread rolls 66
White chiffon cake 45
Wholemeal flour 148
Wholemeal fruit cake 47
Wholewheat or graham flour 148
Wholewheat scones 54
Witches and broomsticks (marzipan) 122
Writing (piped) 128

## Y

Yeast 148
Yeast baking:
  Bath buns 68
  Chelsea buns 65
  Croissants 75
  Danish pastries 72–3
  Devonshire splits 68
  Dough cake 74
  Doughnuts 64
  Fruited tea ring 71
  Hot cross buns 67
  Iced fruit plait (braid) 70
  Lardy cake 71
  Rum babas 74
  Swiss buns 69
  White bread rolls 66
  Yorkshire teacakes 66
Yule log 98

## NOTES FOR AUSTRALIAN USERS

All measures in this book are given in metric, imperial and American. In Australia, the 250 ml (8 fl oz) measuring cup is used in conjunction with the imperial pint of 20 fl oz. If Australian users follow the American column they should remember that the American pint is 16 fl oz. It is also important to note that the Australian tablespoon has been converted to 20 ml, which is larger than the tablespoon used in all columns in this book and, therefore, 3 level teaspoons should be used where instructed to use 1 tablespoon. Kitchen scales may be used to follow either the metric or imperial columns but only one set of measures should be followed as they are not interchangeable.

## ACKNOWLEDGMENTS

The author and publishers would like to thank The Baker Smith School of Cake Decorating, Tongham, Farnham, Surrey, for their kind help and co-operation during the preparation of this book.

Photography by Bryce Attwell
Cakes prepared and iced by Rosemary Wadey
Photographic styling by Roisin Nield
Illustrations by Isobel Balakrishnan